THE JOURNEY TO SAINTHOOD:
Keys to Salvation

"Discovering the Truth Within"

Written by Nona McCollough-Lang

Gotham Books

30 N Gould St.
Ste. 20820, Sheridan, WY 82801
https://gothambooksinc.com/

Phone: 1 (307) 464-7800

© 2025 *Nona McCollough-Lang*. All rights reserved.

No part of this book may be reproduced, stored in a retrieval system, or transmitted by any means without the written permission of the author.

Published by Gotham Books (March 5, 2025)

ISBN: 979-8-3303-5490-0 (H)
ISBN: 979-8-3303-5488-7 (P)
ISBN: 979-8-3303-5489-4 (E)

Because of the dynamic nature of the Internet, any web addresses or links contained in this book may have changed since publication and may no longer be valid.

The views expressed in this work are solely those of the author and do not necessarily reflect the views of the publisher, and the publisher hereby disclaims any responsibility for them.

What is a saint? A saint is a precious individual who has wholeheartedly embraced the plan of salvation—a divine blueprint for humanity's redemption—and has chosen to walk in the footsteps of Yahushua. The Hebrew name for Jesus offers not only eternal life but also the promise of heavenly joy, empowering you to rise above lies, temptations, and failures. It gives you the strength to believe, trust, and faithfully follow YAH's holy word.

Remember, we are not born saints; rather, this transformative opportunity is open to every person brought into this world. Don't allow sin and disobedience—those actions and attitudes that create a barrier between you and God or fellow believers—to steal away this extraordinary honor and privilege. Seize the chance to become the saint you were meant to be!

Are you ready to become a Saint? It is something that a Believer becomes when they give their life to their Creator and allow Him to take the helm and develop them for the purpose intended for them since the beginning of time, regardless of the time in which they are here. It will take you deep within yourself to the essence of your being. This journey of spirituality and self-discovery will awaken you to the presence of the Creator of Heaven and Earth and where you are in your spiritual journey. Elohim, the Almighty God, will give you forgiveness and the power to forgive others, as well as empathy and compassion towards your fellow man, and grant you the freedom you need to not only be a friend but to become yourself best friend and live a life of victory and independence despite a world that seeks to keep you down. This journey will empower you to live a life of faith, freedom, and victory. This inward journey you are about to embark upon will show you how to let go of the past and its burdens and negative influences that hinder you from your true purpose and lead you to the Heavenly Father, the Creator, and the ultimate ruler of all who is ready to meet all of your needs according to His riches in glory. YAH will prepare you to take charge of your life and embark on this transformative journey. Philippians 2;12-13

Therefore, my beloved, as you have always obeyed, so now, not only as in my presence but much more in my absence, work out your own Salvation with fear and trembling, for it is God who works in you, both to will and to work for his good pleasure.?

The Door

I stood there staring at the door

There was that knock again

The one that I've heard

So many times before

I started to open it up

But I hesitated

I said to myself

I'll open it later

But the gentle rapping persisted

The more it persisted, the more I resisted

But finally, I gave in and I am so glad I did.

The guest who was knocking turn out to be my best friend.

Written by Nona Mccollough © 1997 Disclaimer Notice: The foundation of all scriptures in this book comes from the Yahuah Bible, KJV Bible, New International Version, and Holy Spirit inspired.

YAHUAH /YAH, (CREATOR of the Heavens and Earth Elohim is the title that will be used for the Title of the Almighty God.

The Messiah and Savior name, Jesus (English name) will be referred to in this book by His Hebrew name, Yahushua, the Son of YAHUAH that was given to Joseph, who was the husband of Miriam (Mary), the mother of Yahushua.

Matthew 1:18-23 K J V

[18] "Now the birth of Jesus Christ was on this wise: When his mother Mary was espoused to Joseph, before they came together, she was found with child of the Holy Ghost.

[19] Then Joseph her husband, being a just man and unwilling to make her a public example, was minded putting her away privily.

[20] But while he thought on these things, behold, the angel of the LORD appeared unto him in a dream, saying, Joseph, thou son of David, fear not to take unto thee Mary thy wife: for that which is conceived in her is of the Holy Ghost.

[21] And she shall bring forth a son, and thou shalt call his name JESUS: for he shall save his people from their sins.

[22] Now all this was done, that it might be fulfilled, which was spoken of the Lord by the prophet, saying,

[23] Behold, a virgin shall be with child and shall bring forth a son, and they shall call his name Emmanuel, which being interpreted as God with us.

¹⁶ For God so loved the world, that he gave his only begotten Son, that whosoever believeth in him should not perish, but have everlasting life. John 3:16

Ask, and it shall be given to you; seek, and ye shall find; knock, and it shall be opened unto you; For every one that asketh receiveth; and he that seeketh findeth; and to him that knocketh it shall be opened." Matthew 7:7-8s

ACKNOWLEDGMENTS AND SPECIAL THANKS

Firstly, I want to thank Yahuah for granting me the wisdom and power of His Holy Spirit, which helped me write this Spirit-filled book. I am also thankful for His love, patience, mercy, strength, wisdom, courage, faith, good health, and financial assistance necessary to complete this book. Without Him, I would not have been able to overcome the obstacles and emerge victorious in finishing this book.

I also thank Gotham Press for their assistance and encouragement in producing *The Journey to Sainthood:* Keys to Salvation.

I want to extend my special thanks to my husband, Bishop Lang, for his encouragement and support in helping to edit this book and so much more. His contribution has been invaluable.

I am also grateful to my daughter, Jacqueline Scott, for her unwavering faith and financial support. She has been an incredible source of inspiration throughout my writing journey. May she rest in peace.

I want to thank my son, Syvester Bradford, and my daughter, Victoria Scott, for their support and encouragement.

Additionally, I would like to acknowledge Terrell Mitchell at 360 Repair in Humble, TX, for his generous computer donation, which enabled me to begin my journey.to start my work in writing this book.

Thank you.

There Is No Such Thing as Goodbye
So Dry Your Eyes

None of us knew when the time came for us to leave, only that we had not come to stay. So, live each moment as if it were your last, and give all the love you can.

Forgive the past of its hurts and pains, and you will surely gain in life treasures that cannot be measured by the length of time we are here but by the ones in our hearts that we hold so dear.

The ones who, when they speak our name, will speak of the love and tenderness we shared.

The ones who will say there lies a soul that cared—this, my friend, is true fame.

Only what we do for Yahuah long after we have gone will remain on earth.

And we will be with Yahuah in heaven, at home, where all His people belong.

Written by Nona McCollough© 1999

Dedicated to My Father:

Walter McCollough Sr

11-1- 1917 - March 11-2001

Daughter: Jacqueline Yvette Scott Sheffield 05-05-1970-12-11-2021

FOREWORD

II am pleased to speak on behalf of Prophetess Nona's new book, *"The Journey to Sainthood:* Keys to Salvation" I strongly recommend the book to everyone from all walks of life. This book includes many close-hidden secrets that are revealed, all of which the enemy Satan does not wish for you and me to know. It exposes Satan's secret strategies, schemes, and lies will teach you how to positively change your world (life) for good and success. With accompanying scripture proofs, divine knowledge, wisdom, and revelations imparted within these pages could answer many of your unanswered prayers. How Prophet Nona vividly describes the episode of the once beautiful, high-ranking cherub who fell from Heaven and lost his status is just brilliant. The book explains how love and forgiveness are the answers to all of earth's ills and are healers of wounds. This book is a must-read for ministers, church members, educators, teenagers, and young adults who desire to know more about their marvelous Creator and His excellent plan of Salvation.

– Bishop R. Lang –

PREFACE

Before a person can receive Salvation, they must first be willing to admit that they are lost and need a Savior. I hope and pray that this book, *"The Journey to Sainthood:* Keys to Salvation" will help every man, woman, boy, and girl realize that this is precisely the state that all humans are in the moment they come into this world. However, they can be saved through confession, repentance, and acceptance of the excellent plan of Salvation and become a Saint.

I believe the information in this book will inspire many people to change their lives. It will reveal Yahuah's love and expose Satan, the real enemy.

I pray that people will feel Yahuah's love and His willingness to forgive them throughout the pages of this book, no matter who they are or what they may have done.

Those who know of His love can attest to its truth. In this book, in *"The Journey to Sainthood:* Keys to Salvation," the Spirit of Yahuah will make Himself known to all who are seeking after Him.

As you read this book, consider giving your heart to Yahuah and becoming a steward of His Word if you haven't done so already. You will be able to rightly divide the Word of Truth and become a mighty natural and spiritual warrior.

Those who read this book and have not made the decision to follow YAH, one friend to another, YAH will drive away your fears, dry up your tears and give you the strength to overcome any difficulty. The tears that have flown will become tears of rejoicing in the end.

Be patient with yourself and others. Let me encourage you not to let pride, if there be any, stand in your way; a haughty spirit comes before a fall.

Let me ask you: Have you been waiting long for something good to happen to you? If yes, then there is no time like the present.

I received Salvation at age five; it has been an incredible journey. I found my way through the darkness of this world, with only a little light at the end of the tunnel that encouraged me to keep going and not to give up. I grew up with YAH, whom I called GOD at the time. With the help of the Holy Spirit and a little help from others, here I am today.

I am a Believer, a woman who was called into the prophetic in 2004 while lying on my Dad's black and white checkered sofa in his small studio apartment at the Tower Gardens in Houston, Texas. I spent the night with him and bunked out on his sofa in front of the tiny apartment that he lived in. The following day, Dad got up early, and on his way out the door, I heard him softly saying that he was not trying to wake me up but letting me know he was going out. "I am going to take a walk," he said. "I will be back in a little while." I knew this was his way of sharing the bathroom and giving me space to do my personal stuff while he was out. "Okay, Dad," I said; instead of getting up and dressing myself, I fell into a deep sleep. I was awakened to the voice of Elohim, and He declared unto me that I was a prophet. I did not know what this meant, but I gladly accepted my call and could not wait until my Dad returned home to share the good news with him. My Dad had often referred to me as a prophet. I would tell him of a pending danger or give Him a rhema word and he would say, "You must be a prophet or something." I would look at Him and ponder what He meant.

I would not be here today if it had not been for YAH's Love, Grace, and Mercy of Elohim. Many times, the Adversary, who is called the devil, sort to kill me, but YAH said NOT SO. HalleluYAH!

Without His Light leading, guiding, and protecting me, I would have been in darkness and ignorance and never come out of darkness forever lost in sin.

If the truth had not been revealed to me, I would still be in the dark, trying to find my way through life with the enemy trying to consume me by any means necessary.

Yes, we have a vicious enemy whose aim is to kill, steal, and destroy us. Praise YAH for His Light that shined down on Yahushua when YAH announced Him to the world as His Son. HalleluYAH!

If Yahushua had not given His life to pay for our sins, all of humankind would have been lost in darkness with no way out.

Praise Yahushua for sacrificing His precious blood that enables every person who will believe and accept His plan of Salvation, the way out.

Praise YAH for the Light that wrapped itself with flesh and walked among us to show us the way. Praise YAH, the everlasting Heavenly Father, for His Word, Spirit, Light, and Way.

I am saved from the enemy; you, too, can be saved if you are not already.

I am writing this book to bear witness to the Light who is Yahushua and His marvelous plan of Salvation.

This book reminds us that all humans are lost in darkness when they enter this world and must acknowledge their need for a savior and Salvation. *"The Journey to Sainthood:* A Key to Salvation" is a reminder that no matter where a person may find themselves in life, regardless of how confusing or dark the path may be, there is a way to lead them into the Light.

It is a reminder of Yahuah's love and plan for their lives. We can find our way out of darkness and into the Light through confession, repentance, and acceptance of His Salvation plan. My experience of being called into the prophetic is a testament to the power of Yahuah's love, mercy, and grace.

The book reveals the truth about Satan, the real enemy, and encourages readers to become stewards of Yahuah's word. By following the path of righteousness, we can become mighty natural and spiritual warriors.

In the end, the tears we shed will become tears of rejoicing as we bask in YAHUAH's presence. Let us answer His call when He reaches out to us and let Him into our hearts. With Yahuah's love and guidance, we can find Salvation and embrace the Light.

Rejoice; your time has come. Now is your opportunity to be blessed in the presence of YAHUAH, known by some as the Almighty Elohim/God.

WHEN HE CALLS FOR YOU, ANSWER WITH A YES. WHEN HE KNOCKS ON THE DOOR OF YOUR HEART, LET HIM IN.

Don't you Dare

When you feel like Yahuah does not care, that is the time that he is there the most.

When things go wrong for no reason of your own, and trouble is everywhere, and you want to give up on YAH, don't you dare; He is aware of all your problems.

On Him cast your every care. For them alone, only He can bear.

Written By Nona McCollough © 1999

TABLE OF CONTENTS

ACKNOWLEDGMENTS AND SPECIAL THANKS viii
FOREWORD x
ABOUT THE AUTHOR xviii
AUTHOR SPEAK xxii
INTRODUCTION xxvii
CHAPTER 1: THE LAMB WAS SLAIN BEFORE THE FOUNDATION OF THE WORLD 1
CHAPTER 2: ARE YOU READY FOR CHANGE 20
CHAPTER 3: THE ABSOLUTE TRUTH EXISTS 28
CHAPTER 4: WE ARE SERVANTS TO WHOM WE OBEY .. 37
CHAPTER 5: THE RIGHT'S TO DECIDE 65
CHAPTER 6: BLOOD SACRIFICES 74
CHAPTER 7: SATAN IS A LIAR 94
CHAPTER 8: THE DEVIL, THE ACCUSER 106
CHAPTER 9: GHOSTS OF THE PAST LEAVE THEM THERE 117
CHAPTER 10: WHY DO BAD THINGS HAPPEN TO GOOD PEOPLE 136
CHAPTER 11: OVERCOMING FEAR AND REJECTION AND LIVING AS YAH COMMANDS 155
CHAPTER 12: TRUST THE TEACHINGS OF YAH-YAHUSHUA 179
CHAPTER 13: ALL THINGS ARE POSSIBLE FOR THOSE WHO BELIEVE 199

CHAPTER 14: YAHUSHUA VICTORY OVER HELL AND THE GRAVE 209

CHAPTER 15: CHOOSE THIS DAY WHOM YOU WILL SERVE 219

CHAPTER 16: THE POWER OF MEDIATION, PRAYER, AND FASTING 226

CHAPTER 17: WHAT IS THE HEAVENLY FATHER'S AND HIS SON'S NAME 231

CHAPTER 18: WHAT IS LOVE? 242

CHAPTER 19: THE RAPTURE DECEPTION 257

CHAPTER 20: LIVE A VICTORIOUS LIFE WHILE HERE ON EARTH 265

CHAPTER 21: YAHUSHUA HAS DEFEATED THE ENEMY CALLED DEATH 284

CHAPTER 22: PAIN IS GAIN 314

CHAPTER 23: A SPIRITUAL ENCOUNTER/OUT OF THE DARKNESS COMES THE LIGHT 319

CONCLUSION 338

ABOUT THE AUTHOR

I received my Certified Medical Office Management Certificate from Bryman College in San Jose, California. I entered the media industry after studying at De Anza College in Cupertino, California. I played a small role in the video "Things Will Never Change" by E-40. Shortly after, I was called into the ministry, where I have been for 28 years, starting in 1995 as a preacher and evangelist. My ministry involves spreading the Gospel's Good News and offering salvation to thousands of people in the USA and worldwide. Later, I founded and became the pastor of the Ministry of Spirit and Truth Disciples of Yahushua (Christ).

Before entering the ministry, I worked as a top insurance agent for American General Life Insurance Company in California, using my Certified Medical Office Management knowledge to facilitate my work. However, I left that career to help raise my grandchildren. This was a significant shift in my life, but I felt called to make it. After 25 years, I moved to Texas to claim land I inherited and settled down to a quiet life after my mother's passing. Four months after arriving in Houston, where my father lived, I was called back into action to care for my aging father, who was 85 years old at that time.

Though I did some work in doctor's offices, my primary skill has always been caring for my family. At the age of twelve, I became the mother of eight children due to my parents' divorce, with my father gaining custody of us. Being the oldest female, I assumed the role of mothering my family, and I believe that Yahuah (God) was preparing me for my ministry. I spent my time caring for the sick and people with disabilities. I even visited people in the spirit who were in the hospital and in a coma. I ministered to them, and they received their salvation before they left their bodies. I also cared for my aging parents until their passing.

Having faced the enemy in numerous battles, including personal struggles and spiritual warfare, I was inspired and gifted to write a book. These battles were physical, emotional, and spiritual as I fought against the forces of darkness. I have also written over three hundred inspirational pieces of poetry and published thousands of pieces throughout the USA and the world. My poetry has strengthened and helped others deal with the mundane things of life with praise, thanksgiving, and victory.

In 2004, I was called to the Prophetic and have been going forth, ministering His Word by the authority of His Holy Spirit ever since. I learned that God's name is Yahweh from a dear friend named Susan Stillwell (who is no longer with us), and Jesus' name is Yahushua. I was pretty amazed that such a deception had been done. I later learned from my husband, Apostle Bishop Lang, who was not particularly convinced when I first broke the news to him concerning our Heavenly Father and His son's name. He went into an extensive study and discovered that it was Yahuah before it was Yahweh. I called this deception that was placed in the world by Satan and his host a diabolical plot of the enemy.

I had been saved in the name of Jesus, and I questioned Yahuah, asking Him how I was able to perform the great works He used me to do, such as reaching people in comas, casting out demons, laying on of hands and answering countless prayers in Jesus' name. Yahuah told me, "It was not the name of Jesus that I did these things; it was my faith in what and who the name Jesus represented to me." I was thrilled to discover and embrace this truth, and now I am sharing it with you.

"Time Waits for No One"

As the sands of time flow through the hourglass, I find my way at last, letting go of the past. The load was heavy with past hurts, disappointments, and failures, and I did not know what to do. I had to let go of the pain, release the shame, and forgive myself and everyone else, and I encourage you to do the same.

As the tiny grains of sand continue to flow, may a steady outpouring of love, peace, and joy be your everlasting reward. Unfortunately, time waits for no one, so it is important to do what you say and say what you do from your heart and with all your might. The good fight of faith is the battle we must fight.

Remember that love is the way; the sun shines intensely every day, even if you cannot see it. It shines on the right and the wrong, on those who are happy, and on those who moan. In summary, when you stand, forgive, and begin with yourself.

My honest advice is to believe, love, trust, and keep faith in YAH.

Written by Nona McCollough © 199

AUTHOR SPEAK

Dear friends,

I feel compelled to share the reality of being held accountable for our actions before our Creator, YAHUAH. Acknowledging this truth is crucial so that we may prepare ourselves and seek righteousness in the eyes of the Almighty God, whom I know as Elohim, YAHUAH, and His son, Yahushua.

Losing the opportunity for everlasting life in Heaven is an immeasurable loss. Losing YAHUAH means losing access to a realm of love, grace, mercy, forgiveness, peace, hope, and treasures beyond our comprehension.

As a messenger of YAH, I am burdened to address the grave sin of 'abomination' that deeply concerns our Creator. We must cease this abomination and eliminate it from our midst.

We must respect one another and refrain from engaging in inappropriate relations. Let us honor and value each other as beloved brothers and sisters in the eyes of YAH.

The shedding of innocent blood must cease. We must cherish and protect each other's lives, offering love and support instead of tearing each other down. When we deviate from YAH's commandments, He lovingly guides and corrects us while His Holy Spirit provides comfort.

The consequences of rejecting YAH's love are severe, leading to a regrettable destination—Hell. We must diligently avoid the path of sin, as we are born into sin and shaped by inequity.

I acknowledge that thoughts of Heaven and Hell once filled me with fear and remorse. I was ashamed when I comprehended the depth of my transgressions and betrayal against YAHUAH. However, I found peace by granting forgiveness and seeking forgiveness for myself.

I urge you to consider the transformative power of Yahushua's love and redemption. His sacrifice offers salvation if we accept, receive, and obey Him.

Living a holy life is a personal journey. By striving for holiness, we seek to lead lives free from sin despite the challenges we may face.

May YAH guide us as we seek salvation and live righteous lives. Amein.

It is in Yahuah that we live, move, and have our being. We can only improve our world with YAH's power, wisdom, strength, peace, and guidance.

"That they should seek Him, if haply they might feel after Him, and find Him, though He is not far from every one of us: "For in Him we live, and move, and have our being; as some of your poets have said, For we are also His offspring." Acts 17:27-28.

Satan wants to hide the knowledge that life becomes meaningless, disdained, and void of reason or purpose without Yahushua. "If ye abide in Me, and My words abide in you, ye shall ask what ye will, and it shall be done unto you." John 15:7.

Changing a world filled with hatred will take real love, Yahuah's love, and us loving ourselves and each other by showing love and respect for our Creator and each other. We will accomplish the changes this world needs. The master deceiver, Satan, has deceived the whole world, causing them to forget that Yahushua died to give authority back on the earth to those who listen, accept, and obey Him. "And the great dragon was cast out, that old serpent, called the Devil, and Satan, which deceiveth the whole world: he was cast out into the earth, and his angels were cast out with him." Revelation 12:10.

YAH's plan includes blessings for all who will accept His gift of salvation. It is not Yahuah's will that anyone is lost. "For Yahuah so loved the world, that He gave His only begotten Son, that whosoever believeth in Him should not perish, but have everlasting life. For Yahuah sent not His Son into the world to condemn the world; but that the world through Him might be saved." John 3:16-17.

"And ye shall know the truth, and the truth shall make you free." John 8:32. No one needs to be bound or remain in bondage. If you have yet to decide to be free, let me encourage you to do so today.

The following is a heartfelt poem dedicated to Yahuah, written by Nona McCollough in 1997. The poem expresses gratitude and appreciation for everything that Yahuah has done for the author and all of humanity. The author begins by acknowledging the first miracle of Yahuah and expressing how Yahushua's sacrifice went above and beyond to save His lost people. The author then reflects on Yahushua's acts of freeing captives, walking on water, calming the sea and healing the sick. The author explains how their life was transformed after accepting Yahushua into their heart and how the divine love of Yahuah was revealed to them. The author expresses gratitude for all the times they received help and guidance when they needed it the most and for constantly being reminded of Yahuah's presence, even in the darkest moments. The author praises Yahuah for being the creator of the universe and for making everything on earth, including the oceans, seas, and animals. The author expresses how she feels blessed to be one of Yahuah's brides and eagerly awaits the day when she will ride in the chariots of fire and walk the streets of gold. In conclusion, the author expresses her belief in Yahushua and how she and other believers were able, through His blood, to receive eternal life. The poem is a beautiful reminder of the love and grace of Yahuah and how His presence can transform a person's life.

Life

Life is a mysterious gift bestowed upon every human being. Some individuals make the most of it, while others may not.

If you have not already, start now and look within yourself to discover how to do so.

A century may seem like a long time, but before you know it, time has passed, and it is gone.

This beautiful work was written by Nona McCollough in 1963.

INTRODUCTION

Our shared belief in the one Creator, Who made the Heavens and the Earth and sent His Spirit to Earth at the appointed time, Unites Us. If you believe His Spirit took the form of man, rested bodily inside a virgin woman, was born and taught mankind about the ways of Elohim, the Almighty God, and as His son was crucified, died for our sins, rose from the grave, and returned to Heaven with all power in Heaven and Earth in His Hands, it is time out for separation. This is a tool that Satan uses to separate believers so that we do not come together and pray while he and his host continue their diabolical plan to destroy us.

I will join you in prayer as long as we are in the Spirit of Love, regardless of whether we call Him Yahuah, Yahweh, Yahushua, Yahshua, Jehovah, or Jesus. As we eagerly anticipate His return to reign on this Earth with His Saints (children), with you praying from your heart as I will pray from mine, trusting and believing that Elohim, the Almighty God, will answer, we will have the victory.

Let us pray:

Heavenly Father, in the name of Your Son, Yahushua the Messiah (Jesus Christ), I silence the mouth of the enemy and give him leave to go now. Minds, hearts, and souls return to your rightful place, out of reach of Satan and his hosts. Heavenly Father, thank you for the opportunity to receive salvation for those who are lost so that they can be delivered by the blood of the Lamb, which was slain before the foundation of the world and paid for every sin.

Satan, we bind you and every demonic spirit, principality, spiritual wickedness, and ruler of darkness in this world, and I command you to cease your actions in the lives of those who have begun to read this book with a sincere mind and open heart. As you read and internalize these words; you actively participate in this spiritual battle.

Heavenly Father, will you heal those who are hurting? Let burdens be lifted, eyes be open; let the voice of the Heavenly Father, Yahuah, be heard. Yahushua, let every heart be opened to your truth so that your people may see your good works and glorify Yahuah.

Heavenly Father, let every soul held captive be released, every mind be made accessible by your truth, YAH. Let every heart be healed and every sick body be made whole. In the mighty name of Yahushua, may wisdom and protection be upon believers as they enter the enemy's camp, fearless and with conviction, victorious in stopping the havoc Satan has caused in their lives in Yahushua, the Messiah's name.

I decree that all doubt and fear are gone, and faith has come in its place. I pray your life will be peaceful and victorious as you trust in Yahuah as your personal Savior. HalleluYah! And so be it. By the time you finish reading this book, you will be armed with the tools to defeat the adversary, a common enemy of all humans. I pray you will come to hate sin and see it for what it is, for it is the enemy of all humanity.

We must recognize and resist actions contrary to our spiritual beliefs. This is not a statement against any individual or group but a call to action for all of us. Accepting this victory and living following Yahuah's will is your choice. You have the power to shape your spiritual journey and your destiny,

This book will expose some of the adversary's diabolical plots, such as his attempts to distort the truth sow discord among believers and lead us into temptation. It will uncover how he has pulled out all the stops to keep us in the dark, but with the guidance of Yahuah, we can overcome these challenges.

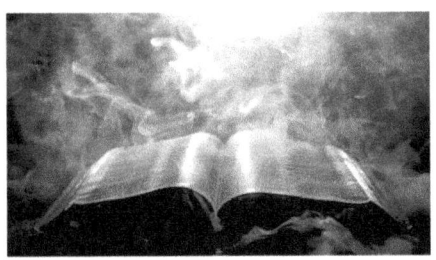

CHAPTER 1

THE LAMB WAS SLAIN BEFORE THE FOUNDATION OF THE WORLD

Humanity's salvation started long before man and woman existed on this Earth. That's right, before you or I committed one sin, our Creator initiated a grand plan, fully aware of our tendency to disobey and succumb to temptation. Despite this, He did not leave us to fend for ourselves.

Genesis 1:26- 31

[26] And God said, "Let us make man in our image, after our likeness: and let them have dominion over the fish of the sea, and over the fowl of the air, and over the cattle, and over all the earth, and over every creeping thing that creepeth upon the earth."

"And the four living creatures, having each one of them six wings, are full of eyes round about and within: and they have no rest day and night, saying, Holy, holy, holy, is the Lord God, the Almighty, who was and who is and who is to come." Revelation 4:6-8

It warms my heart to ponder the depth of Yahuah's love for us as He meticulously crafted a beautiful home for us. His satisfaction with His Creation was evident when He formed people in His image and after His likeness. The perfection of Earth and humanity is a testament to YAH's boundless love and care.

After YAH settled on the image, it came time to create the man and woman in the image and likeness of our Creator.

Like any good parent, before their baby is born, they prepare a space for their new arrival in the home. For example, they purchase a crib, bed, sheets, blankets, clothes, and diapers. If a room needs painting, that too is done if they have the means or feel it is necessary, and anything else they think is required for the comfort of their new baby as they eagerly await the infant's arrival.

Just imagine the joy that YAH must have felt as He meticulously prepared a place for humankind. Every detail was carefully considered, and even Heaven was filled with anticipation at YAH's new Creation and its inhabitants.

He took five days to lay the foundation on Earth as it is in Heaven. He made the beast of the field. YAH looked upon His Creation and saw that it was good. On the sixth day, He made the man and the woman. The Earth and its inhabitants were perfect. Everything was perfect at the beginning of creation. This is a Testament to His divine craftsmanship.

"1 In the beginning, God created the heavens and the earth.

2. Now, the earth was formless and void, and darkness was over the surface of the deep. And the Spirit of God was hovering over the surface of the waters.

The First Day

3 And God said, "Let there be light," and there was light.

4. and God saw that the light was good, and He separated the light from the darkness.

5. God called the light "day," and the darkness He called "night." And there was evening, and there was morning—the first day.

The Second Day

6. And God said, "Let there be an expanse between the waters, to separate the waters from the waters."

7. So God made the expanse and separated the waters beneath it from the waters above. And it was so.

8. God called the expanse "sky." And there was evening, and there was morning—the second day.

The Third Day

9. And God said, "Let the waters under the sky be gathered into one place, so that the dry land may appear." And it was so.

10. God called the dry land "earth," and the gathering of waters He called "seas." And God saw that it was good.

11. Then God said, "Let the earth bring forth vegetation: seedbearing plants and fruit trees, each bearing fruit with seed according to its kind." And it was so.

12. The earth produced vegetation: seed-bearing plants according to their kinds and trees bearing fruit with seed according to their kinds. And God saw that it was good.

13. And there was evening and morning—the third day.

The Fourth Day

14. And God said, "Let there be lights in the expanse of the sky to distinguish between the day and the night and let them be signs to mark the seasons, days, and years.

15. And let them serve as lights in the expanse of the sky to shine upon the earth." And it was so.

16. God made two great lights: the greater light to rule the day and the lesser light to rule the night. And He made the stars as well.

17. God set these lights in the expanse of the sky to shine upon the earth,

18. to preside over the day and the night, and to separate the light from the darkness. And God saw that it was good.

19. And there was evening, and there was morning—the fourth day.

The Fifth Day

20. And God said, "Let the waters teem with living creatures, and let birds fly above the earth in the open expanse of the sky."

21. So God created the great sea creatures and every living thing that moves, with which the waters teemed according to their kinds, and every bird of flight after its kind. And God saw that it was good.

22. Then God blessed them and said, "Be fruitful and multiply and fill the waters of the seas, and let birds multiply on the earth."

23. And there was evening and morning was —the fifth day.

The Sixth Day

24. And God said, "Let the earth bring forth living creatures according to their kinds: livestock, land crawlers, and beasts of the earth according to their kinds." And it was so.

25 God made the beasts of the earth according to their kinds, the livestock according to their kinds, and everything that crawls upon the earth according to its kind. And God saw that it was good.

26. Then God said, "Let Us make man in Our image, after Our likeness, to rule over the fish of the sea and the birds of the air, over the livestock, and over all the earth itself and every creature that crawls upon it."

27. So God created man in His own image. in the image of God, He created him; male and female, He created them.

28. God blessed them and said to them, "Be fruitful and multiply, and fill the earth and subdue it; rule over the fish of the sea and the birds of the air and every creature that crawls upon the earth."

29. Then God said, "Behold, I have given you every seed-bearing plant on the face of all the earth, and every tree whose fruit contains seed. They will be yours for food. 30. And to every beast of the earth, every bird of the air, and every creature that crawls upon the earth—everything that has the breath of life in it—I have given every green plant for food." And it was so.

31. And God looked upon all that He had made, and indeed, it was very good. And there was evening and morning—the sixth day."

As human beings, we are all blessed with something extraordinary, powerful, and dynamic - the eternal Spirit of Elohim. This spirit, inherent in every person who enters this world, is a divine light that cannot be extinguished, even when our physical bodies can no longer contain it. It is a part of Yahuah, graciously shared with us, that is eternal and indestructible, invoking a sense of awe and reverence in us.

However, in the very beginning when Adam and Eve rebelled against YAH and heeded the instruction of Satan, chaos began. No longer was Eve looked upon as a joint heir to the Earth but more like a possession. Instead of being treated as a joint heir to the Earth, with power and authority to reign and rule by Adam's side,

Adam ruled over her as YAH said he would. YAH never intended it to be that way. YAH made the man and the woman in His image and told them to rule over the Earth and have the authority to subdue the Earth and reign over our Enemy, the Devil, and his host. But the man, in his rebellious state, chose to rule over the woman and take away her authority and voice, and it has only gotten worse from then on. Instead of the man and the woman ruling the Earth and over Satan, he became their ruler. By deceit and trickery, he ruled over them and encouraged the man to rule over the woman, and the man accepted. The man and woman have been fighting ever since. Adam, Eve, and their children have suffered greatly from this ever since. This is something that Satan does not want the man and the woman to know to keep them in bondage, fighting each other instead of using their authority to come together and fight him.

The purpose for the existence of the man and the woman is to do YAH's will, to please Him, and to receive His blessings forever. We have been given free will to choose to obey or disobey Him. This choice between obedience and disobedience is a responsibility with immense significance. It will result in eternity with Him and experiencing everlasting life. However, those who turn away from His will and His Laws will still live forever but will be separated from Him - the Light - and will be left to dwell in darkness and torment forever.

In these times of crisis worldwide, knowing Yahuah's Word is vital and urgent. His Word is a guiding light that illuminates our path, helping us move in the right direction and survive in a world that is growing darker daily. We must begin now while we still have time. According to Yahuah's Word, if His people, called by His name, humble themselves, repent, and pray, He will hear them from heaven and heal their land. His guidance is our beacon of hope in these troubled times.

Yahuah tells us to be still and know that He is and re

[10] "Be in awe and know that I am God. I will be exalted among the nations.

I will be exalted throughout the earth." Psalms 46:10

6 "And without faith it is impossible to please God, because anyone who comes to him must believe that he exists and that he rewards those who earnestly seek him." Hebrews 11:6

Acknowledging the proper names of the Heavenly Father and the Son as Yahuah and Yahushua is crucial. By using their names correctly, we demonstrate respect. These names aren't just their Hebrew names; they are their authentic names, which have never been altered. Influential individuals influenced by Satan removed their names from the original Holy Scrolls and replaced them with

the names currently in the Bible. However, Yahuah, in His love and mercy, acknowledged our faith and knew that one day we would discover the truth. Our unwavering faith has been pivotal in this revelation. Now that we have uncovered this truth, accepting it and governing ourselves accordingly make us free. Embracing this freedom entails accepting this truth.

The Fall from Grace

The Fall from Grace was a tragic event that occurred when Satan, in a bold act of rebellion, led a third of the angels against Yahuah.

Their rapid defeat at the hands of Yahuah's almighty power is a clear reminder to all humans. It wasn't a battle; when Satan tried to take control of Heaven, he and his followers were immediately defeated and expelled like lightning. This is a powerful lesson: rebellion and disobedience against Yahuah can never lead to a positive outcome. We should always strive to follow Yahushua's path and live a righteous life, resisting the allure of temptation and deceit.

Isaiah 11:14-17 is what Satan was trying to do before he was cast out of Heaven and lost his name, his position, and his authority.

12. "How you have fallen from heaven, O day

star, son of the dawn! You have been cut down

to the ground, O destroyer of nations.

13. You said in your heart:

"I will ascend to the heavens. I will

raise my throne above the stars of

God.

I will sit on the mount of assembly, in the far

reaches of the north.

14. I will ascend above the tops of the clouds.

I will make myself like the Most High."

15. But you will be brought down to Sheol, to the

lowest depths of the Pit.

16. Those who see you will stare.

They will ponder your fate: "Is this the man who shook the earth and made the kingdoms tremble, 17. who turned the world into a desert and destroyed its cities, who refused to let the captives return to their homes?" Isaiah 1114: 11-17

The great dragon, also known as the devil or Satan, who deceived the entire world, was hurled down to the earth along with his angels. Those who choose to follow Satan will undoubtedly suffer the same fate unless they turn to YAH. It is indisputable that anyone who rejects the Truth, represented by Yahushua, will forever remain in bondage. Once the Truth is presented and accepted, there is hope for that person if they sincerely repent and accept the Truth. Ultimately, people have the power to make their own choices, but it is important to understand that every choice has consequences.

"Lay not up for yourself treasures upon the earth, where moth and rust, doth, corrupt, and where thieves break through and steal. But lay up for yourselves treasures in heaven, where neither moth nor rust doth corrupt, and where thieves do not break through nor steal. For where your treasure is, there will your heart be also." Matthew 6: 19-21

"But a time is coming and has now come when the true worshipers will worship the Father in spirit and in truth, for the Father is seeking such as these to worship Him." John 4:23

Did you know there is a record in Heaven of your life and how you live it out on Earth through your choices.

"Let everything that hath breath praise the LORD. Praise ye the

LORD." Psalm 150:6

It is an undeniable truth that everything we do, think, or say is being recorded by YAH. This means that He is perfectly aware of all our deeds, and we are given a limited time to fulfill His purpose for our lives before we move on. Yahuah is a compassionate God who understands our struggles, joys, and failures and offers salvation to those who repent. However, the enemy, the devil, constantly strives to prevent us from discovering this truth. He knows the Lake of Fire is his final destination, and he will use every trick in the book to ensure we don't learn about YAH's plan for humankind. His evil scheme commenced in the Garden of Eden with the first couple.

Created by YAH. We must be vigilant and not let the enemy deceive us. We must take control of our lives, embrace YAH's plan, and live righteously to attain eternal life with Him.

Genesis 3

1. "Now the serpent was more subtle than any beast of the field which the LORD God had made. And he said unto the woman, Yea, hath God said, Ye shall not eat of every tree of the garden?

2. And the woman said unto the serpent, We may eat of the fruit of the trees of the garden:

3. But of the fruit of the tree, which is in the midst of the garden, God hath said, Ye shall not eat of it, neither shall ye touch it, lest ye die.

4. And the serpent said unto the woman, Ye shall not surely die:

⁵ For God doth know that in the day ye eat thereof, then your eyes shall be opened, and ye shall be as gods, knowing good and evil.

⁶ And when the woman saw that the tree was good for food, and that it was pleasant to the eyes, and a tree to be desired to make one wise, she took of the fruit thereof, and did eat, and gave also unto her husband with her; and he did eat.

⁷ And the eyes of them both were opened, and they knew that they were naked; and they sewed fig leaves together and made themselves aprons.

⁸ And they heard the voice of the LORD God walking in the garden in the cool of the day: and Adam and his wife hid themselves from the presence of the LORD God amongst the trees of the garden.

⁹ And the LORD God called unto Adam, and said unto him, Where art thou?

¹⁰ And he said, I heard thy voice in the garden, and I was afraid, because I was naked; and I hid myself.

¹¹ And he said, Who told thee that thou was naked? Hast, thou eaten of the tree, whereof I commanded thee that thou shouldest not eat?

¹² And the man said, The woman whom thou gavest to be with me, she gave me of the tree, and I did eat.

¹³ And the LORD God said unto the woman, What is this that thou hast done? And the woman said, The serpent beguiled me, and I did eat.

¹⁴ And the LORD God said unto the serpent, Because thou hast done this, thou art cursed above all cattle, and above every beast of the field; upon thy belly shalt thou go, and dust shalt thou eat all the days of thy life:

¹⁵ And I will put enmity between thee and the woman, and between thy seed and her seed; it shall bruise thy head, and thou shalt bruise his heel.

¹⁶ Unto the woman he said, I will greatly multiply thy sorrow and thy conception; in sorrow thou shalt bring forth children; and thy desire shall be to thy husband, and he shall rule over thee.

¹⁷ And unto Adam he said Because thou hast hearkened unto the voice of thy wife, and hast eaten of the tree, of which I commanded thee, saying, Thou shalt not eat of it: cursed is the ground for thy sake; in sorrow shalt thou eat of it all the days of thy life.

¹⁸ Thorns also and thistles shall it bring forth to thee; and thou shalt eat the herb of the field.

¹⁹ In the sweat of thy face shalt thou eat bread, till thou return unto the ground; for out of it wast thou taken: for dust thou art, and unto dust shalt thou return.

²⁰ And Adam called his wife's name Eve because she was the mother of all living.

²¹ Unto Adam also and to his wife did the LORD God make coats of skins and clothed them.

²² And the LORD God said, Behold, the man is become as one of us, to know good and evil: and now, lest he put forth his hand, and take also of the tree of life, and eat, and live forever:

²³ Therefore the LORD God sent him forth from the garden of Eden, to till the ground from whence he was taken.

²⁴ So he drove out the man; and he placed at the east of the garden of Eden Cherubims, and a flaming sword which turned every way, to keep the way of the tree of life."

After Adam and Eve ate the forbidden fruit in the Garden of Eden, they were separated from YAH, and humankind was left to suffer under the rule of Satan. Satan believed he had won, but YAH continued to provide for all humans equally, allowing each to live in Him. In the end, YAH will separate the wheat from the tares, placing the sheep on His right and the goats on His left. Unfortunately, many people will deny YAH's love and be condemned to hell, while those who follow Him will live an everlasting life in the light of YAH.

After Adam and Eve were kicked out of the Garden of Eden, they lost their position with YAH and their authority to rule over Satan on Earth. Satan became their master and began his plan to kill, steal and destroy humankind. He causes Cain to murder his brother, Abel, introducing jealousy and separation to Adam's family. As a result, Adam and Eve lost both sons, Abel, because of murder, and Cain, because of jealousy and envy. Cain was punished and driven away.

YAH has created every human with the potential to be brilliant, wise, harmless, and lovely. Purchasing this book and reading it took courage and faith. Together, we can defeat the dark forces of the enemy that seek to destroy humankind. By caring and sharing with others, each person has the potential to make a positive impact on the world.

Genesis 4

4 "And Adam knew Eve his wife; and she conceived, and bare Cain, and said, I have gotten a man from the LORD.

² And she again bare his brother Abel. And Abel was a keeper of sheep, but Cain was a tiller of the ground.

³ And in the process of time it came to pass, that Cain brought of the fruit of the ground an offering unto the LORD.

⁴ And Abel, he also brought of the firstlings of his flock and of the fat thereof. And the LORD had respect unto Abel and to his offering:

⁵ But unto Cain and to his offering he had not respect. And Cain was very wroth, and his countenance fell.

⁶ And the LORD said unto Cain, Why art thou wroth? and why is thy countenance fallen?

⁷ If thou doest well, shalt thou not be accepted? and if thou doest not well, sin lieth at the door. And unto thee shall be his desire, and thou shalt rule over him.

⁸ And Cain talked with Abel his brother: and it came to pass, when they were in the field, that Cain rose up against Abel his brother, and slew him.

⁹ And the LORD said unto Cain, Where is Abel thy brother? And he said, I know not: Am I my brother's keeper?

¹⁰ And he said, What hast thou done? the voice of thy brother's blood crieth unto me from the ground.

¹¹ And now art thou cursed from the earth, which hath opened her mouth to receive thy brother's blood from thy hand;

¹² When thou tallest the ground, it shall not henceforth yield unto thee her strength; a fugitive and a vagabond shalt thou be in the earth.

¹³ And Cain said unto the LORD, My punishment is greater than I can bear.

¹⁴ Behold, thou hast driven me out this day from the face of the earth; and from thy face shall I be hid; and I shall be a fugitive and a vagabond in the earth; and it shall come to pass, that every one that findeth me shall slay me.

¹⁵ And the LORD said unto him, Therefore whosoever slayeth Cain, vengeance shall be taken on him sevenfold. And the LORD set a mark upon Cain, lest any finding him should kill him.

¹⁶ And Cain went out from the presence of the LORD, and dwelt in the land of Nod, on the east of Eden."

WE ARE OUR BROTHER'S KEEPERS

Now is the perfect moment to start your spiritual growth and enlightenment journey. You hold the key to significant changes in your life. But remember, this is not a passive process. You must actively participate and make choices that align with the Holy Spirit's guidance.

Though it might not be easy, the path of loving and obeying YAH leads to extraordinary joy and fulfillment. The Holy Spirit is here to guide you, and you can only receive it through the blood of the Lamb, Yahushua, the Messiah, the Maker, and the Creator of all things.

Confess your sins, repent, and believe; you will be forgiven and spiritually healed. The Truth is the only way to achieve this. Yahushua, the Son of YAH, is the Way, the Truth, and the Life.

Be prepared to fight the good fight of faith with the breastplate of the righteousness of our Messiah, Yahushua. His Helmet of Salvation will protect your mind and signify whose army you are in. The Buckle of Truth around your waist will prevent the devil's lies from deceiving you, and your feet shod with the Gospel of Peace will allow you to walk on rocky terrain without harm. The shield of faith will protect you from the enemy's fiery darts, and the Sword of the Spirit (the Word of Yahuah) will help you defeat the enemy.

When you submit your mind to YAH's Holy Will for your life, you are under His divine protection and guidance. He knows what is best for you and will grant you the grace to accomplish it.

Once you receive salvation, you are redeemed from the law's curse. YAH will apply mercy to your life, which is renewed every day. Yahushua's Holy Spirit is full of Grace and Truth. He will lead and guide you every step of the way.

YAH, who cannot lie, promises to protect you, so send His angels to guard and direct your path when you acknowledge Him in all your ways. Walk in the newness of life with victory, peace, and great joy, knowing that you are under His loving care.

Prayer for Direction

Yahuah, I know you will lead, guide, and direct me on this day.

Your answer is always yes, so I will press on with assurance.

Will you be by my side every step of the way? His answer is yes, so strive for the best.

Yahuah, I trust you will give me a clear and plain vision of the challenges ahead so you can pass every test.

Your answer is always yes; I will trust You and allow my heart to rest in His guidance.

Will you help me endure every pain, remove the strain, and let my love for you forever remain? His answer is yes, and you can trust and believe in His Holy name.

YAH, please show me how to take your yoke upon me so my burdens may be light. YAH's answer is yes, so fight the good fight of faith.

Yahushua, keep me safe around every curve. Let wisdom emerge from your mind to mine and let your Holy Spirit flow through my heart with your love surging. His answer is yes.

Be courageous and brave; you are free and no longer a slave to the enemy.

Written by Nona McCollough © 1998

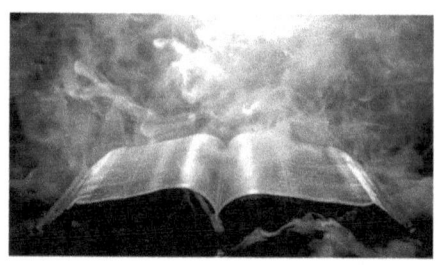

CHAPTER 2

ARE YOU READY FOR CHANGE

Change necessitates a humble submission to the mighty Hands of our Creator, YAH-Yahushua, the architect of all existence. His power is boundless, and His love and kindness are infinite. He is the husbandman, and those who accept and receive Him are embraced as His bride. He is the Living Water and the Bread of Life, sustaining us with His divine essence.

YAH created all things; without Him, nothing that has been made would be made without His power. He is more than able and capable of giving a believer good things in their lives. It brings Him joy to give good things to His children. He is the Good Shepherd and cares for his sheep, especially when they stray off the narrow path and find themselves hanging off a cliff.

Perhaps you yearn for a more personal connection with our The Creator is no longer content with generic titles. You desire to know Him by His name, YAH, and to embrace His son, Yahushua. This readiness to step through the door of the Way, the Truth, and the Light signifies a profound shift in your spiritual journey.

You will need faith and belief to open this door, and you will also need the blood of the Messiah to proceed. But wait, there is good news: Yahushua has already given his blood as atonement for sin,

paid the debt we owed YAH, and defeated Satan and his host to make this possible. The Blood of Yahushua is mighty and much needed in one's life.

Does it make you wonder how long the enemy will deceive people into disobeying our Creator and making the enemy happy by refusing to honor, obey, and worship our Heavenly Father, Master, and Ruler of all? If YAH, our Creator, had a weakness, it would be His love for His children who were held captive by sin.

YAH is not a liar. He must hold fast to His Word, even if it means condemning people to hell because they rejected His Way, Truth, and the Light. However, YAH knew all things, and the ending from the beginning had a plan to redeem us. YAH has allowed the lost to see, feel, learn, and taste their new master, Satan, so that they may know who the real enemy is and that it is not Him.

People who follow Satan will discover that he is a hard taskmaster, void of love or mercy. He is unforgiving and relentless in his quest to steal, kill, and destroy humankind. In the fullness of time, YAH sent His seed, wrapped it in flesh, and placed it in a woman named Miriam. This redeemed humanity from the curse of the law placed upon Adam and Eve. When they were in Paradise, the Garden of Eden, they heeded the serpent's voice and ate from the tree of good and evil, which Yahuah had instructed them not to eat. Their disobedience caused them to fall victim to the will of Satan. In their lost state, Adam and Eve were driven out of the Garden of Eden. An angel was placed there to guard the Tree of Life to keep them from eating from it and being cursed forever in that fallen state. In the fullness of time, Yahushua came to Earth wrapped in flesh to remind us of who YAH is and that He possesses all the power.

A person who receives YAH's son, Yahushua, who is YAH in the flesh, gets a great miracle. Yahushua turned water into wine, multiplied five fish and two loaves of bread to feed five thousand people, and performed many more miracles. Yahushua raised the dead, opened blind eyes, and enabled people with disabilities to walk and some to talk. He also walked on water, calmed the storm, and much more. If all Yahushua did were recorded, the world would not have room enough to house His records. He has also given us His Word that if one receives Him as Savior, they will do what He did and even greater things. As if that was not enough, He went on to die for us and paid our sin debt with His blood. However, He did not stay dead. Yahushua rose from the grave in three days, returned to Heaven, and reclaimed His throne with all power in Heaven and Earth in His hands.

No longer does YAH have to allow Satan to kill, steal, or destroy His people. He saved us to bring us back to what we once had before the world was. Saints can now be called His children and reign with Him forever. HalleluYAH. Not only was Satan defeated in Heaven, but he has also been defeated in the Earth, and we are now free to walk the Earth in Spirit and Truth, having victory over him.

However, Satan did not abandon his plan to kill, steal, and destroy us; in fact, he became even more relentless and sought to imbue our hearts and minds and keep us in a defeated state. The Devil intends to get YAH's people to sin and disobey so that he can steal from them their blessings, destroy their purpose, and take their lives. It does not matter to him how he does it. The Devil will use every trick in the book to get people to disobey YAH's laws, overlook His statutes and forget His commandments. The mind of the believer is where Satan operates to defeat them. Satan will seek to deceive those who are asleep, naturally and spiritually, first by planting lies in their mind, enticing them to believe them, and then leading them to act on them.

Be of good cheer and forgive.

Why? The act of forgiveness has a profound impact on both the forgiver and the forgiven. It is a process that can bring healing and peace to both parties involved. When we truly forgive someone, we can think of them without being consumed by negative emotions like anger, fear, shame, or pain.

Being a father is a tremendous responsibility that requires great strength and love. It is a role that demands sacrifice, hard work, and courage. Fathers play a crucial role in their children's lives, representing a source of guidance, love, and support. However, fathers need to recognize that they can't do it alone. Seeking advice and strength from a higher power can make a significant difference in fulfilling the responsibilities of a good husband and father.

I have been raised by an extraordinary father whose love, wisdom, and care have impacted my life. His actions and words inspire and guide me, even though he's no longer with us. His presence and influence have shaped me into the person I am today.

To all the fathers, I want to express my appreciation for your critical role in shaping your children's lives. Your dedication and love have a profound impact on the world. Keep doing your best and remember that your influence and presence in your children's lives are invaluable.

What to Do About It

During these days of indecisions, in these times of strife and woe, there are so many isms going on until one wonders where to go.

Well, my friend, please let me help you. Believe my friends in the words I say. If you are puzzled or bewildered, turn to Jesus and obey Him.

Ignore the LORD, and you will be sorry, for this makes Him awful sad, but following Him and doing His bidding is the way to make Him glad.

Now, what do I mean by all these isms? What am I really trying to say?

There are so many isms along the way.

Friends, one of these isms is found in the movies, the trash you see at the picture show, and the books that folks will gladly sell you, even at the grocery store.

My friends, don't let the devil fool you; these folks are out to get your dough.

Follow Christ. I really mean it. That's what to do about it, for sure.

You will have to watch old Satan because that fellow knows his stuff; he is the source of all these isms, and he will make you think he is awfully tough.

Now, you all have heard my story, and I pray you know just what I mean.

Without fear or contradiction, may you and Jesus make a team.

Without shame or reservation, say, LORD, you lead the way, and you will find your life much sweeter as you live from day to day.

Written by Walter McCollough Sr. © 1966.

A Prayer for Those Who Have Lost Their Father's

My heart goes out to those who have lost their fathers, whether it be due to death or abandonment. I understand that it can be a painful experience, and you may feel lost and alone. But please know that YAH wants to be your father, companion, and friend. He wants to be with you every step of the way.

No matter how often you come before Him, it is never a bother to Him. He is eager to put all the pieces of your life back together, no matter how fragile they may be. With YAH, you are never alone. He is the potter, and you are the clay. He will shape, mold, and teach you every day.

He will be your guide, your protector through life. He knows your story, your secrets, and your concerns. He wants you to cast all your burdens on Him. He will supply all your needs according to His riches in glory.

If you accept Him, He promises never to leave you throughout eternity. Yah sent His only begotten Son to die for you so that He could call you, His child. He cares for you deeply and wants to deliver and make you accessible so you can be with Him.

Please remember that you are not alone. You have YAH, and He will always be there for you.

Written by Nona McCollough © 1999

CHAPTER 3

THE ABSOLUTE TRUTH EXISTS

In a world where truth is often obscured, it's crucial we seek guidance from the Holy Spirit to uncover the absolute truth. Unfortunately, many ministers have strayed away from teaching the true gospel of Yahushua in favor of money and fame. However, we have recently discovered hidden knowledge that has been kept from us for thousands of years, causing us to question previously held beliefs. It's important to remember to obey the Word of Yahuah, rather than blindly following man-made traditions. Disobeying this principle is forbidden. Let us strive to uncover the absolute truth and live according to

"You have let go of the commands of God and are holding on to human traditions." Mark 7:8

Many people celebrate holidays not part of YAH's teachings, such as Christmas, Easter, Halloween, etc. They refuse to acknowledge the holy days like the Sabbath Day, Passover, etc. Understandably, many people celebrate holidays not part of YAH's teachings, such as Christmas, Easter, and Halloween, while not acknowledging holy days like the Sabbath Day and Passover.

Unfortunately, so much confusion and misinformation prevents people from knowing and accepting the true Word of Elohim, including His name, which I will discuss further in the book. It's important to consider how YAH feels about same-sex marriage and homosexuality, according to the Word. Unfortunately, many lies and confusion prevent people from knowing and accepting the true I will further discuss the word of Elohim, including His name, in this book. Some people believe that same-sex marriage and homosexuality are acceptable, but we must consider how YAH feels about it, according to the Word.

Genesis 19 Sodom and Gomorrah Destroyed and the Story of Noah

"19 The two angels arrived at Sodom in the evening, and Lot was sitting in the gateway of the city. When he saw them, he got up to meet them and bowed down with his face to the ground.

2. "My lords," he said, "please turn aside to your servant's house. You can wash your feet and spend the night and then go on your way early in the morning."

"No," they answered, "we will spend the night in the square."

3. But he insisted so strongly that they did go with him and entered his house. He prepared a meal for them, baking bread without yeast, and they ate. ⁴ Before they had gone to bed, all the men from every part of the city of Sodom—both young and old—surrounded the house. ⁵ They called to Lot,

"Where are the men who came to you tonight? Bring them out to us so that we can have sex with them."

6. Lot went outside to meet them and shut the door behind him 7 and said, "No, my friends. Don't do this wicked thing. 8 Look, I have two daughters who have never slept with a man. Let me bring them out to you, and you can do what you like with them. But don't do anything to these men, for they have come under the protection of my roof."

9. "Get out of our way," they replied. "This fellow came here as a foreigner, and now he wants to play the judge! We'll treat you worse than them." They kept bringing pressure on Lot and moved forward to break down the door.

10. But the men inside reached out and pulled Lot back into the house and shut the door.

11. Then they struck the men who were at the door of the house, young and old, with blindness so that they could not find the door.

12. The two men said to Lot, "Do you have anyone else here— sons- in-law, sons or daughters, or anyone else in the city who belongs to you? Get them out of here, 13 because we are going to destroy this place. The outcry to the LORD against its people is so great that he has sent us to destroy it."

14. So Lot went out and spoke to his sons-in-law, who were pledged to marry[a] his daughters. He said, "Hurry and get out of this place because the LORD is about to destroy the city!" But his sons-in-law thought he was joking.

15. With the coming of dawn, the angels urged Lot, saying, "Hurry! Take your wife and your two daughters who are here, or you will be swept away when the city is punished."

16. When he hesitated, the men grasped his hand and the hands of his wife and of his two daughters and led them safely out of the city, for the LORD was merciful to them. 17 As soon as they had brought them out, one of them said, "Flee for your lives! Don't look back, and don't stop anywhere in the plane! Flee to the mountains or you will be swept away!"

18. But Lot said to them, "No, my lords, please!

19. Your servant has found favor in your eyes, and you have shown great kindness to me in sparing my life. But I can't flee to the mountains; this disaster will overtake me, and I'll die. 20 Look, here is a town near enough to run to, and it is small. Let me flee to it— it is very small, isn't it? Then my life will be spared."

21. He said to him, "Very well, I will grant this request too; I will not overthrow the town you speak of. 22 But flee there quickly, because I cannot do anything until you reach it." (That is why the town was called Zoar.)

23. By the time Lot reached Zoar, the sun had risen over the land.

24. Then the LORD rained down burning sulfur on Sodom and Gomorrah—from the LORD out of the heavens. 25 Thus he overthrew those cities and the entire plain, destroying all those living in the cities—and the vegetation in the land. 26 But Lot's wife looked back, and she became a pillar of salt.

27. Early the next morning Abraham got up and returned to the place where he had stood before the LORD. 28 He looked down toward Sodom and Gomorrah, toward all the land of the plain, and he saw dense smoke rising from the land, like smoke from a furnace. 29 So when God destroyed the cities of the plain, he remembered Abraham, and he brought Lot out of the catastrophe that overthrew the cities where Lot had lived.

Genesis Chapter 6

6 And it came to pass, when men began to multiply on the face of the earth, and daughters were born unto them,

2 That the sons of God saw the daughters of men that they were fair; and they took them wives of all which they chose.

3 And the LORD said, my spirit shall not always strive with man, for that he also is flesh: yet his days shall be a hundred and twenty years.

4 There were giants in the earth in those days; and, after that, when the sons of God came in unto the daughters of men, and they bare children to them, the same became mighty men which were of old, men of renown.

5 And God saw that the wickedness of man was great in the earth, and that every imagination of the thoughts of his heart was only evil continually.

6 And it repented the LORD that he had made man on the earth, and it grieved him at his heart.

⁷ And the LORD said, I will destroy man whom I have created from the face of the earth; both man, and beast, and the creeping thing, and the fowls of the air; for it repenteth me that I have made them.

⁸ But Noah found grace in the eyes of the LORD.

⁹ These are the generations of Noah: Noah was a just man and perfect in his generations, and Noah walked with God.

¹⁰ And Noah begat three sons, Shem, Ham, and Japheth.

¹¹ The earth also was corrupt before God, and the earth was filled with violence.

¹² And God looked upon the earth, and behold, it was corrupt; for all flesh had corrupted his way upon the earth.

¹³ And God said unto Noah, the end of all flesh is come before me; for the earth is filled with violence through them; and behold, I will destroy them with the earth.

¹⁴ Make thee an ark of gopher wood; rooms shalt thou make in the ark, and shalt pitch it within and without with pitch.

¹⁵ And this is the fashion which thou shalt make it of: The length of the ark shall be three hundred cubits, the breadth of it fifty cubits, and the height of it thirty cubits.

¹⁶ A window shalt thou make to the ark, and in a cubit shalt thou finish it above; and the door of the ark shalt thou set in the side thereof; with lower, second, and third stories shalt thou make it.

¹⁷ And, behold, I, even I, do bring a flood of waters upon the earth, to destroy all flesh, wherein is the breath of life, from under heaven; and everything that is in the earth shall die.

¹⁸ But with thee will I establish my covenant; and thou shalt come into the ark, thou, and thy sons, and thy wife, and thy sons' wives with thee.

¹⁹ And of every living thing of all flesh, two of every sort shalt thou bring into the ark, to keep them alive with thee; they shall be male and female.

²⁰ Of fowls after their kind, and of cattle after their kind, of every creeping thing of the earth after his kind, two of every sort shall come unto thee, to keep them alive.

²¹ And take thou unto thee of all food that is eaten, and thou shalt gather it to thee; and it shall be for food for thee, and for them.

²² Thus did Noah; according to all that God commanded him, so did he."

People had become very evil to the point where their only thoughts were to do evil. Unfortunately, even today, some have chosen to follow this path. However, you don't have to be one of them. Satan is busy deceiving and destroying many people because they have chosen to serve him through their actions and deeds.

The entire world was steeped in corruption, so much so that YAH deeply regretted His creation of mankind. Rain, a phenomenon unheard of until then, was about to make its debut. The people unfamiliar with this concept, dismissed the notion of rain when it was foretold.

Similarly, many people today choose not to believe in Yahushua simply because they have not seen Him. However, Yahushua said those who believe in Him without seeing Him are blessed.

"Then Jesus told him, "Because you have seen me, you have believed; blessed are those who have not seen and yet have believed."

It took Noah and his sons one hundred and twenty years to build the Ark. While it was being constructed, Noah preached to the people to repent and turn back to YAH.

Yet, they disregard Noah's plea, much like some people today. They have grown complacent in their sins, which cater to their earthly desires, and have continued without visible repercussions. They believe they can persist in disobeying YAH, and nothing adverse will befall them. Instead of relying on YAH, they trust their wealth, status, and reputation.

They fail to grasp their insignificance without YAH. They are as feeble as a held breath, awaiting YAH's command to exhale. They exist without acknowledging the Creator of Heaven and Earth, who brought them into being. They commit wicked deeds without a second thought, just as before YAH's wrath was unleashed upon the Earth.

The Word tells us that whatever a person sows, they will reap. They reaped destruction upon themselves when they chose to ignore what YAH said and follow the evil one (the Devil).

"Be not deceived; God is not mocked: for whatsoever a man soweth, that shall he also reap.[8] "For he, that soweth to his flesh shall of the flesh reap corruption; but he that soweth to the Spirit shall of the Spirit reap life everlasting.[9] And let us not be weary in well doing: for in due season we shall reap if we faint not." Galatians 6:7-9

CHAPTER 4

WE ARE SERVANTS TO WHOM WE OBEY

Some may assert that they do not serve anyone and declare, "I am a servant to no one," believing this to be true. However, it is essential to recognize that we are all servants, either to YAH or Satan. Why? Because these are the predominant forces that govern humanity. Despite their inequality, both vie for the souls on Earth. YAH represents love and created humanity; He seeks to bless and protect humans from Satan, who seeks their destruction. While some may believe they need not choose between the two, the reality is that by not choosing to serve, worship, and obey the Creator of the heavens and Earth, individuals are positioning themselves for a hopeless fate that leads to eternal death, even if they honor, worship and obey Satan.

There is no defeating the real enemy outside of Yahuah, but when people confess their sins, repent, and accept Yahushua's blood sacrifice, they will become more than conquerors. Yahushua allowed himself to be crucified to deliver believers from darkness, save their souls and bring them into His marvelous light. They will live and not die, declare the works of Yahushua, and receive power and eternal life even though their body dies.

When you dive into the pages of this book, you will be able to spiritually soar and take your seat in the high place of the Spirit under the Shadows of the Almighty!

Consider sin to be in this wise; anything that causes you to sin is against the Laws of Yahuah and should be against the Law of Humans. As a woman, prophet, on the Earth, I declare and decree: eyes will be open to the truth, hearts to understanding, and minds empowered with wisdom as they read chapter upon chapter of this anointed book.

Delight thyself in the Presence of YHWH YAH-Yahushua, Who is Yahuah.

It is wise to consider the condition of one's soul and know in whom they believe while they are still alive on Earth.

As you read this, know that my heart is with you, and with all my heart, I trust Yahuah, the Creator, and Yahushua, the only begotten of the Father, full of Grace and Truth, and have complete faith in His marvelous plan of salvation. As I share the messages in this book that the Holy Spirit has moved me to convey, please know that they are not of me, yet they are, for they are of the Holy Spirit, who lives in me of whom I am one with Elohim, King, And Ruler Supreme, also known as the Almighty God. He is YAH-Yahushua; they are One. Those who accept and receive Him are one with Him as well.

Making decisions about spiritual matters can be challenging, and recognizing the cunning tricks of our adversary, Satan, is crucial.

We have all fallen into his snares at some point, but it is essential to remember that he is a defeated foe.

This book is designed to illuminate the minds of those who are unaware, to unstop the ears of those whose thoughts have been trapped by the Devil's lies, and to reveal the truth that good is sound and evil is evil. It is meant to bestow wisdom and strength, empowering them to tread the narrow path that leads to eternal life with YAH and to experience an abundant life on this Earth. My fervent prayer is that it will heal and mend the brokenhearted and fragile minds of those entangled in sin, liberate those held captive by the enemy and fortify all on the spiritual battlefield.

Spiritual matters are complex, and many must consider the importance of deciding who they will serve spiritually in this world and where their Spirit will spend eternity. With its divine guidance, this book is intended to open the eyes of the unaware and unstop the minds of those deceived. It will give them the wisdom and strength to walk the narrow path that leads to eternal life with YAH and abundant life while on this Earth.

If you are unaware that you are a spirit in a world where anything and everything can happen simultaneously, please know that deciding about your salvation as early as possible is crucial. The earlier, the better.

However, if you know that you are both spiritual and physical beings, then I understand that the enemy may have deceived you into thinking that you are here on your own accord, the Master of your faith and captain of your soul, which is a lie.

Please know that YAH does not force anyone to serve Him or choose Him as their Master, yet He is the Creator and has a divine purpose for your life. Yahuah requires people to choose whom they will make their allegiance to and whom they will serve with the life He has given them and sustains them. It will either be Him or the Devil. Choose whom you will serve on this day. Tomorrow may be too late. Let me encourage you to make Yahuah your choice.

If you think you can serve both Yahuah and Satan, please know that this is another lie the Devil tells people. "Yahuah knows you are only human; go on and do your thing; He will forgive you; he is love," the Devil says. However, this is only half valid, which makes it a lie and one of Satan's deceptive plots to steal your soul.

Remember, you are not alone in this world. You have a choice of whom to serve. I encourage you to choose wisely; this book will help you on your journey.

I believe in YHWH and YAH.

"Therefore, rejoice ye heavens, and ye that dwell in them. Woe to the inhabitants of the earth and of the sea! For the adversary is come down unto you, having great wrath, because he knoweth that he hath but a short time." Revelation 12:13

"No man can serve two masters: for either he will hate the one and love the other; or else he will hold to the one, and despise the other,
Ye cannot serve Yahuah and Mammon." Luke 16:13

No one can serve two masters at a time—those chasing after money and wealth risk losing their souls. But there is hope for those who choose to follow the right path. Everything already belongs to Yahuah, when you obey Him, He will provide for you correctly.

Yahuah is the embodiment of love and is worthy of all praise. His wisdom is unmatched, and His mercy endures forever. In His presence, you will find complete joy. He is faithful and trustworthy, the perfect master to serve.

Choosing to serve Yahuah is the right choice to make. In this chapter, we will explore why He is the only true master worth serving."

"I will love Thee, O Yahuah, my strength.

Yahuah is my rock, and my fortress, and my deliverer; my El, my strength, in whom I will trust; my buckler, and my high tower.

I will call upon Yahuah, who is worthy to be praised; so, shall I be saved from mine enemies." Psalms 8: 1-3

Yahuah's Word is the Sword of the Spirit. It cuts more profoundly than a two-edged sword. It divides the bone from the marrow, which is the inner part of the bones.

Yahuah deals with every part of a human being (mind, body, and soul), including the spirit.

"The Word of Yahuah is quick and powerful, and sharper than a two-edged sword, piercing even to the dividing asunder of soul and spirit, and it is discerner of thoughts and intents of the heart.

Neither is there any creature that is not manifest in His sight, but all things are naked and opened unto the eyes of Him with Whom we have to do.

Seeing then that we have a great Priest that is passed into heaven, Yahushua the Son of Yahuah; let us hold fast to our profession.

For we have a high priest, which cannot be touched with our infirmities; but was in all points, temped like as we are, yet without sin.

Let us there come bodily unto the throne of grace, that we may obtain mercy and find grace to help in time of need. "Hebrew 4:12- 16

HalleluYAH.

He longs for every part of our being to worship and serve Him. How is this possible? YAH knows everything and never overlooks any aspect of human existence. He profoundly understands each person's spirit and has lovingly provided a way for every believer to approach Him through His Son Yahushua. Regardless of wealth, health, or circumstances, Yahuah is the only choice. Even before birth, YAH has a purpose and a plan for each individual. His plan for their lives is perfect, exceeding all imaginable possibilities.

"For this cause I bow my knees unto the Father of our Savior; Yahushua the Messiah.

Of Whom the whole family in heaven and earth is named. That according to the riches of His glory, by His Spirit in the inner man;

That the Messiah may dwell in your hearts by faith; that ye being rooted and grounded in love, May be able to comprehend with all saints what is the breath, and length, and depth, and height;

And to know the love of the Messiah, which passeth knowledge, that ye might be filled with all the fullness of Yahuah.

Now unto Him that is able to do exceeding abundantly above all that we ask or think, according to the power that worketh in us.

Unto Him be glory in the assembly by the Messiah Yahushua throughout all generations, and all ages." Ephesians 3:14-21.

"Then the word of Yahuah came unto me, saying. Before I formed thee in the belly, I knew thee; and before thou cameth forth out of the womb, I sanctified thee, and I ordained thee a prophet unto the nation" Jeremiah 1:4-5

YAH also knows if you will be obedient or disobedient. He is the only true judge and will decide where a person will spend forever. When we were babies, He made us rejoice upon our mother's breast, not knowing anything about life. We only had an ardent desire to be alive with great survival instincts.

"All the end of the world shall remember and turn unto Yahuah, and the kindreds of the nations shall worship before Thee. For the kingdoms is Yahuah's, and He is the governor among the nations.

All they that are great upon the earth shall eat and worship; all they that go down to the dust shall bow before Him; and none can keep alive his soul. A seed shall serve Him; it shall be accounted to Yahuah for a generation; They shall come and declare His righteousness unto a people that shall be born that He hath done this." Psalms 22:27-31 HalleluYah.

"He has the unwavering ability to determine whether an individual will display obedience or disobedience. As the sole and ultimate judge, He will decide where that person will spend the rest of eternity. In our infancy, He gifted us with the ability to experience the joy of being cradled in our mother's arms without any knowledge of the complexities that life would bring. All we had then was an earnest desire to cling to life, driven by our innate survival instincts."

"Oh Yahuah Though hast searched me and known me.

Thou knowest my down-sitting and mine up rising; Thou understandest my thoughts afar off. Thou compassest my path and lying down, and art acquainted with all my ways;

For there is not a word in my tongue, but lo, O Yahuah, Thou knowest it altogether. Thou hast beset me behind and before and laid Thine hand upon me.

Such knowledge is too wonderful for me; it is high, I cannot attain unto it. Whither shall I go from thy Spirit? Or whither shall I flee from Thy presence?

If I ascend up into the heaven, Thou are there; if I make my bed in sheol, behold Thou art there. If I take wings of the morning, and dwell in the uttermost parts of the sea;

Even there shall Thy hand lead me, and Thy right hand shall hold me. If I say, surely the darkness hideth shall cover me; even the night shineth as the day; the darkness and the light are both alike to Thee.

Yea the darkness hideth not from Thee; but the night shineth as the day; the darkness and the light are both alike to Thee.

For Thou hast possessed my reins; thou hast covered me in my mother's womb. I will praise Thee; for I am fearful and wonderfully made; marvelous are Thy works; and that my soul knoweth right well.

My substance was not hid from thee, when I was made in secret, and curiously wrought in the lowest parts of the earth. Thine eyes did see my substance yet being unperfect; and in Thy book all my members were written, which is continuance were fashioned, when there was none.

How precious also are Thy thoughts unto me, El! How great is the sum of them!

If I should count them, they are more in number than the sand: when I awake, I am still with Thee;

Surly thou wilt slay the wicked, O Elohim: depart from me therefore, ye bloody men.

For they speak against Thee wickedly, and Thine enemies take Thy name in vain. Do not I hate them O Yahuah that hate Thee? and am not I grieved with those that rise up against thee. I hate them with perfect hatred;

I count them mine enemies. Search me O El, and know my heart try me, and know my thoughts. And see if there be any wicked way in me and lead me in the life everlasting." Psalms 139

Our physical development commences before birth when the egg and sperm unite, bestowing the baby with a complete set of X and Y chromosomes. Half of these chromosomes are inherited from the mother, and the other half from the father, highlighting the equal contribution of both parents.

Determining a newborn's gender is a captivating genetic journey, where both parents play a significant role. The sex chromosomes contributed by the father, in particular, define the infant's gender. Girls inherit an X chromosome from their father, resulting in an XX genotype, while boys inherit a Y chromosome, leading to an XY genotype.

Yet, there is a deeper layer to this. In many instances, the spiritual disposition of the infant is believed to be influenced by God's purpose for His creation, as well as the virtues or sins of the father or ancestors passed on to the fetus during its development in the mother's womb.

Yes, our physical development begins long before we are born. It consists of the egg and sperm coming together, giving the baby a complete set of X and Y chromosomes. Half come from the mother, and the other half from the father.

The father is one hundred percent responsible for the gender of their newborns. It is known as sex chromosomes, defining the infant's gender. The girls inherit an X chromosome from their father, resulting in a XX genotype, and males inherit a Y chromosome from their father, resulting in an XY genotype.

However, it is even more profound than that spiritual; in many cases, the God-given determines the spiritual disposition of the infant purpose for His creation as well as the goodness or sins of the father or ancestors that are passed on to the fetus while developing in the womb of the mother.

From Wikipedia, the free encyclopedia

Sins of the Father(s) derives from biblical references in Exodus, Deuteronomy and Numbers to ancestral sin, the sins or iniquities of one generation passing to another.

'The LORD is slow to anger, and abundant in lovingkindness, forgiving wickedness and transgression; but He will by no means clear *the guilty*, visiting (avenging) the wickedness and guilt of the fathers on the children, to the third and fourth *generations* [that is, calling the children to account for the sins of their fathers" Numbers 14:8

Reaching the age of accountability is a significant moment in one's spiritual journey, as it marks the realization of the power of choice. It's a time when one must decide between the path of righteousness and the temptation of evil. Whether expressed or kept within, every thought, action, and deed is carefully recorded in a Book of Records in Yahuah's Kingdom, underscoring our profound responsibility for our actions.

When a person is born with deformities, it can be a result of the sins of their parents or ancestors, or it could be due to illness, lack of proper care, or even demonic influence during their development. Sometimes, physical or mental disabilities can serve to bring Glory and Honor to Yahuah, as seen in the case of the man mentioned in the Bible who was born blind.

"As He passed by, He saw a man who was blind from his birth. And His disciples asked Him, saying, Rabbi, who do sin, this man, or his parents, that he was born blind? Yahushua answered that neither this man nor his parents had sinned, but Elohim's works should manifest in him." John 9:1-3

YAH's love and mercy equipped the deformed infant to use substances to sustain itself. If that person knew what lay ahead, they might choose death rather than fight for life if it was possible.

YAH, in His divine creation, made people perfect. However, the iniquity of the parents or ancestors is passed on through DNA, and during the developmental stage before birth, these inherited traits, in most cases, manifest as deformities.

When an infant is formed within their mother's womb, they inherit the sins of their father back to Adam if the sin is not repented of.

Praise YAH, for along came Yahushua, the Word of Yahuah, with the perfect plan of salvation. In His infinite wisdom, YAH chose to become a man woven together inside of a woman using His very own seed. Becoming a man was a profound act, for while Yahuah knew man, He had never experienced life as a man, as recorded by man. This act of Yahushua's incarnation brings us hope and salvation.

As He would have it: Perfected without sin; He wrapped Himself up in flesh (for in His seed there is no sin). And Yahuah called the seed His only begotten Son, Yahushua.

"For the word of Yahuah is quick and powerful, and sharper than any two-edged sword, piercing even to the dividing asunder of soul and spirit, and of the joints and marrow, and is a discerner of the thoughts and intents of the heart." Hebrews 4:12 However, there is good news: "If we confess our sins, he is faithful and just and will forgive and purify us from all unrighteousness. "I John 1:9

It is of utmost importance to embark on your journey of salvation now. Repenting of your own sins and the sins of your ancestors is crucial. This act will cleanse you and liberate you from the burden of sin.

Dear reader, I urge you to use the mighty name of Yahushua to overcome the devil. Please do not allow the enemy to mislead you into his service. Remember, the devil is a defeated foe, and you have the power to resist him through Yahushua. He will never allow the enemy to burden you beyond your strength. Rise above his deceit and use the name of Yahushua to claim your victory confidently.

"Yahuah is my light and my salvation; whom shall I fear? Yahuah is the strength of my life; of whom shall I be afraid. When the wicked, even mine enemies and my foes, came upon me to eat my flesh, they stumble and fall. Though a host should encamp against me, my heart shall not fear: though war should rise against me, in this will I be confident." Psalms 27:1-3

Let's unite in the Word of YAH to empower ourselves and take charge of our planet "Earth" positively and constructively. Together, we can reclaim our rightful ownership and work towards creating a better future for all. Standing firm in our beliefs can overcome obstacles and bring positive change to our planet and its inhabitants.

"O Yahuah our Sovereign, how excellent is Thy name in all the earth! Who hast set Thy glory above the heavens.

Out of the mouth of babes and suckling hast Thou ordained strength because of Thine enemies, that Thy mightest still the enemy and the avenger.

When I consider Thy heavens, the work of Thy fingers; the moon and stars, which thou hast ordained.

What is man, that Thou are mindful of him? And the son of man, that Thou visitest him?

For Thou hast made him a little lower than the angels and hast crowned him with glory and honour.

Thou madest him to have dominion over the works of Thy hands; Thou hast put all things under his feet.

All sheep and oxen, yea, and the beast of the field;

The fowl of the air, and the fish of the sea, and whatsoever passeth through the paths of the seas.

O Yahuah our Sovereign, how excellent is Thy name in all the earth." Psalm Chapter 8

Love, a crucial element often overshadowed by the adversary's falsehoods, is what our world truly needs. Yahuah (YAH), our Elohim, our El (Almighty God), is the epitome of this love.

The Devil tries to convince us that love is unnecessary, painful, or dispensable. This is one of the biggest lies that Satan tells. In reality, without our Messiah, we experience both physical and spiritual death.

Consider this: how can anyone live without the fundamental need for love, acceptance, and being loved that every human craves? The real question is how we can bring about the necessary changes in our hearts and minds to make this world a better place for humanity. Let's explore what the Word says about this. "By a new and living way, which He hath consecrated for us, though the veil, that is to say, His flesh;

And having a high Priest over the house of Yahuah;

Let us draw near with a true heart in full Assurance of faith, having our hearts sprinkled from an evil conscience, and our bodies washed with pure water.

Let us hold fast to the profession of our faith without wavering: for He is faithful that promised; And let us consider one another to provoke unto love and to good works: Not forsaking the assembling of ourselves together, as the manner of some is; but exhorting one another: and so much the more, as ye see the day approaching.

For if we sin, willingly after that we have received the knowledge of the truth, there remaineth no more sacrifices for sins. But a certain fearful looking for of judgment and fiery indignation, which shall devour the adversaries." Hebrews 10: 20-27

"It is comforting to know that we don't have to have all the answers or control everything, as that would be impossible. Many have tried to seize absolute power throughout history, only to fail. It's crucial to remember that ultimate power belongs to

Yahuah. He desires to bestow blessings upon his children and has prepared a promising future for us from the very start. I find solace in this; what about you?"

"For I know the thoughts that I think toward you, saith Yahuah, thoughts of peace, and not of evil, to give you an expected end. Jeremiah 29:11 He came to His own tribe, and His own people received Him not. But as many as received Him, to them gave the power to become the children of Yahuah, that is to them that believe on the Name of Him Who was born not of blood, nor of the will of the flesh, nor the will of man, but of Yahuah." John 1:11-13.

Yahuah instructs us to acknowledge Him in all our lives, promising to guide our steps. Trusting in Him alleviates the burden we carry. I have experienced this. However, many live as if they neither require nor have access to His assistance. Yahuah is prepared and eager to provide believers with the love, wisdom, peace, knowledge, strength, courage, and power essential for victorious living.

"Come unto me, all ye that labour and are heavy laden and I will give you rest. Take my yoke upon you and learn of me; for I am meek and lowly in heart: And ye shall find rest unto your souls. For My yoke is easy, and my burden is light." Matthew 11:28-30

YAH requires a person's soul, mind, will, emotions, imagination, and conscience. Sometimes, this seems easier said than done, especially when dealing with people's feelings. However, it's only when we, as individuals, respond to the Master's call and experience the relief of unburdening ourselves onto Him that we truly understand the profoundness of this act.

Yahushua is not just a promise-maker, but a promise-keeper. He takes our burdens and replaces them with His peace. He takes our sorrows and fills us with His joy. His Word is not empty; He guards it and fulfills it. He is steadfast, and even when trust in others wavers, you can always rely on Him. Yahushua will be light no matter how dark the path may be; with Him, you can see your way in and out of any situation if you ask for His guidance. "He tells us to take His yoke upon us and learn of Him, for His yoke is easy, and His burdens are light. "But my Elohim shall supply all your need according to His riches in glory by Yahushua the Messiah." Philippians 4:19 No one should feel like they must depend solely on their understanding or physical strength. Many people have tried to do so, only to experience a life filled with misery and trouble due to making the wrong choices. This profoundly saddens the Father; He wants humanity to thrive and enjoy a good life.

YAH CAN BE TRUSTED

"Trust Yahuah with all thine heart; and lean not unto thine own understanding. In all thy ways acknowledge Him, and He shall direct thy paths." Proverbs 3:5- 6

"But He answered and said, it is written, Man shall not live by bread alone, but by every word that proceedeth out of the mouth of Yahuah." Matthew 4:4

In this world, everyone is searching for something that gives them meaning, purpose, and hope. At times, we may feel lost and alone, and we search for answers to life's big questions. But I have good news for you - Elohim has remembered us. Yahushua sent His Spirit back to earth after His resurrection to dwell in the hearts of every person who has experienced a spiritual rebirth, a transformation that brings them into a new relationship with God. His Holy Spirit is the key to an abundant life filled with joy, hope, and meaning.

Yahushua is all-powerful, and all power belongs to Him. He received it at His resurrection when He ascended into Heaven and sat at the right hand of the Heavenly Father. Yahushua is Yahuah in the flesh, and like you and me, YAH has a Spirit, the "Holy Spirit of His Being," which He gladly gives to whosoever will receive Him.

If you choose to follow Yahushua, your life will be transformed. His love will not just enter your heart, but dwell there, providing you with the power to live a victorious life through His Holy Spirit. This decision grants you the right to the 'Tree of Life' and eternal life with Him. The promise of dwelling in the New Heaven that will descend upon the New Earth fills the heart with joy and anticipation, as it signifies a life of eternal bliss and peace.

Pay attention is essential because the changes this world needs come only through obedience to the Holy Spirit, which works through believers in Yahushua. This is why YAH gave His Son as a ransom, a payment, for sin. Yahuah desires to bless His children, but first, He had to remove sin, which was achieved through the death, burial, and resurrection of His Son Yahushua. HalleluYah.

Your decision is not just important; it is valued. Despite the enemy's deception, convincing many that they need not decide about their spirit, each of us holds the key to accepting this great salvation. Therefore, we must give more earnest heed to the teachings of Yahushua so that we do not let them slip away. Yahushua's life and teachings are a precious gift from YAH to the world, available to all who will receive and accept Him. Yahushua paid the price for our salvation. He sacrificed His own life. He was arrested, put on trial, and falsely accused by the religious leaders, the magistrates, and even ordinary citizens in the community. Our Savior Yahushua was brutally beaten. His disciples betrayed Him, denied Him, and finally abandoned Him.

However, Yahuah had a divine purpose in everything His Son Yahushua had to go through for our sake, and He truly fulfilled His purpose through His Son, just as He continues to do so today in the lives of those who have been born again.

"For we know that all things work together for good to them that love Yahuah, to them who are called according to His purpose." Romans 8:28

Yahushua bore unimaginable pain in His infinite love as He ascended a scorching, arid hill, His cross a burden of our sins. Despite the jeers and lashes of soldiers, He remained resolute, His purpose unwavering. His suffering was not for His transgressions but for ours, a testament to His boundless love and our potential for salvation.

Our Savior, with the power to call legions of angels from Heaven, chose not to. He could have easily defeated His enemies and prevailed on His behalf, but instead, He held His peace and suffered for us. His mercy extended even to His accusers as He put back on the ear that one of His disciples had cut off to defend

Him, showing us the path of forgiveness and compassion, which we should strive to follow.

Yahushua's sacrifice was not in vain. It was a balm for our afflictions, a healing no ailment can withstand. In His Name, we possess the authority to command the release of any sickness. Just as He maintained His composure, we should strive to do the same, secure in the knowledge that His Holy Spirit is our constant companion. Let us remember the unimaginable pain that Yahushua endured and the mercy He showed to His accusers. Let us honor His sacrifice by keeping our peace and trusting His healing power. "Thinketh thou I cannot now pray to My Father, and he shall presently give me more than twelve legions of angels?

But then how then shall the scriptures be fulfilled, that thus it must be? In the same hour, said Yahushua to the multitudes, are you come out as against a thief with swords and staves for to take me I sat daily with you teaching in the temple and ye laid no hold on Me." Matthew 26:53-54

When Yahushua's disciples deserted him and ran away, he did not give up humanity. He made the ultimate sacrifice by becoming a sin for us and paying our debt with his blood, all through the command of Yah's Word. Let us rejoice and give thanks for this incredible act of love and redemption. HalleluYah!

"Who did not sin, neither was guile found in His mouth. Who, when He was reviled, reviled not again: When He suffered, He threatened not; but committed Himself to Him that judge righteously: Who His own self bare our sins in His own body on the tree that we, being dead to sins, should live unto righteousness: By Whose stripes we were healed." I Peter 2:22-24

Remember this: Yahushua, The Son of YAH, is willing to come to you if you seek Him and ask for His forgiveness. He understands that we all make mistakes in life, and He is ready to forgive you of your sins. He will wash you and make you whiter than snow, no matter how scarlet red they are. You don't have to feel lost or hopeless, and you don't have to pretend to be righteous. Seek Yahushua, the Son of YAH, and ask for His forgiveness, and He will come to you and embrace you with His love and mercy. The only thing that can prevent you from being forgiven is blasphemy against the Holy Spirit, which means rejecting YAH's Spirit. But if you are willing to repent and ask for His forgiveness, He will never turn you away.

"Come now, and let us reason together, saith YAH: though your sins be as scarlet; they shall be as white as snow; though they be red as crimson, they shall be as white as snow; though they be red like crimson, they shall be as wool." Isaiah 1:18

"When you accept the Holy Spirit, you will experience conversion. Invite YAH to fill you with His Sacred Spirit, and He will manifest through the power of speaking in tongues. This serves as a witness of your faith and provides a powerful tool to combat the enemy. Don't miss this incredible opportunity to experience YAH's presence."

"And they were all filled with the Holy Spirit, and began to speak with other tongues, as the Spirit gave them utterance." Acts 2:4

"When a person who believes in Yahushua is baptized in His name and filled with the Holy Spirit, they receive the power to live a holy life. They also receive the gift of forgiveness if they knowingly or unknowingly sin and truly repent. Godly sorrow and sincere repentance can turn every act of sin into a pathway toward deliverance. This promise of salvation is a strong reassurance in a world that seems on a destructive course, like a freight train rushing toward hell. It is a beacon of light in the darkness, precisely what Satan wants to extinguish. Yahuah is a strong tower where the righteous can find safety and refuge. In the current state of the world, believers need to feel more secure now than ever."

"The Name, Yahuah, is a strong tower: The righteous run into it and is safe." Proverbs 18:10

Yahushua took away our sins and gave us His righteousness. He also forgave us, talking about forgiveness. He asked the Father to forgive us at the recognizable lowest point of His human life. He was still thinking of us (His people). We should think twice before we utter such statements as: "I will never forgive you for that."

"I pray not that thou should take them out of the world, but that Thou shouldest keep them from the evil one they are not of the world, even as I am not of the world. Sanctify them through Thy truth: because Thy word is truth." John 17:16-17

"The Jews and Satan did not realize the gravity of their actions when they screamed for the crucifixion of our Messiah. Had Satan been aware of the true implications, he would have never allowed the killing of our Savior. He would not have used men to beat and torture the Son of YAH either, as it is by His stripes that we are healed. As children of YAH, we have the right to call upon Him, believe in and accept the finished work of His Son Yahushua, and demand the illness to go. Therefore, every believer can receive the manifestation of healing in their body according to their faith and not let Yahushua's beating on their behalf be in vain. HalleluYAH!" "For we speak the wisdom of Yahuah, hidden in a mystery, which Yahuah hath ordained before the ages unto our glory. "Which none of the rulers of this age knew: for had they known it, they would not have crucified the King of Glory." I Corinthians 2:7-8

YAH was pleased by Yahushua's ultimate victory, a human being who defeated Satan as a blood sacrifice. The Sacrificial Lamb of YAH paid the sin debt, which we could not pay by any other means. As a result, we are saved and can live a life free from sin. HalleluYAH!

On one occasion, I asked our Creator Yahuah, 'How could it please Him to have His Son Yahushua endure such suffering?' His response was firm: 'My Son, as a human, led a life without sin, as I intended for all humans. He did not yield to satanic deception and manipulation, nor did Yahushua obey Satan's temptations. He chose to fulfill all that I have commanded. My Son remained faithful even in the face of death, making it possible for you to have eternal life with Me.' This underscores the role of our choices in our faith journey and the unwavering love and mercy of our Creator, inspiring us to trust in the salvation He offers.

"Surely, He has borne our pains and carried our diseases: Yet we did esteem Him stricken smitten of Elohim and afflicted. But He was wounded for our transgressions, He was bruised for our iniquities; the chastisement of our peace was upon Him; and with

His stripes, we were healed. All we like sheep have gone astray. We have turned everyone to his own way: and Yahuah has laid upon Him the iniquity of us all. He was oppressed and He was afflicted, yet He opened not His mouth: He is brought as a lamb to the slaughter, as a sheep before her shearers is dumb, so He opened not His mouth.

From prison and from judgment was He taken away, but in His generation, who could tell that He was cut off of the land of the living for the transgression of my people.

And He made His grave with the wicked, and with the rich in His death; because He had done no violence, neither was deceit in His mouth. Yet it pleased Yahuah to bruise Him; He hath put Him to grief: When now His soul hath brought the trespass offering, He shall see His seed, and He shall prolong His days, and the pleasure of Yahuah shall prosper in His hand." Isaiah 53: 4 -10

On one occasion, I asked our Creator Yahuah, 'How could it please Him to have His Son Yahushua endure such suffering?' His response was firm: 'My Son, as a human, led a life without sin, as I intended for all humans. He did not yield to satanic deception and manipulation, nor did Yahushua obey Satan's temptations. He chose to fulfill all that I have commanded. My Son remained faithful even in the face of death, making it possible for you to have eternal life with Me.' This underscores the role of our choices in our faith journey and our Creator's unwavering love and mercy, which should inspire us to trust in the salvation He offers.

"Be still and know that I am Elohim: I will be exalted among the heathen; I will be exalted in the earth." Psalms 46:10

"Then shall thy call, and Yahuah shall answer; Thou shalt cry, and He shall say, Here I am. If thou take away from the midst of thee the yoke, the putting forth of the finger, and speaking, "In all our endeavors, let us seek to understand." Yahuah was with the Hebrew people during their journey through the desert as Moses led them out of Egypt. Despite having Yahuah, "In all our endeavors, let us seek to understand." Yahuah was with the Hebrew people during their journey through the desert as Moses led them out of Egypt. Despite Yahuah's presence with them, the Israelites repeatedly stopped believing in Him when faced with difficulties. They wandered in the desert for forty years, marked by Yahuah's sorrow for that generation. He was so disappointed that He swore in His anger that they would never enter His rest. Let us not repeat their mistake of being unbelievers. The choice is clear - choose life today if you have not already. His presence was with them, yet the Israelites repeatedly stopped believing in Him when faced with difficulties. He was so disappointed that He swore in His anger that they would never enter His rest. Let us not repeat their mistake of being unbelievers. The choice is clear - choose life today if you have not already." Isaiah 58:9

"I call heaven and earth to record this day against you, that I have set before your life and death, blessing and cursing; therefore, choose life, that both thou and thy seed may live." Deuteronomy 30:19.

"The righteous cry and Yahuah, heareth, and delivereth them out of all their troubles. Yahuah is nigh unto them that are of a broken heart; and saveth such as be a contrite spirit. Many are the afflictions of the righteous; but Yahuah delivereth him out of them all. He keepeth all His bones; not one of them is broken. Evil shall slay the wicked: and they that hate the righteous shall be desolate. Yahuah redeemeth the soul of His servant, and none of them that trust in Him shall be desolate." Psalms 34:17-22

Sometimes, you may feel a deep desire to connect with the Creator. You might even yearn to address Him by His name, Yahuah or YAH. And as your faith deepens, you might feel ready to embrace His Son's name, Yahushua, and step through the door of the Way, the Truth, and the Light. Remember, all it takes is your faith and belief to unlock this door, guiding you on your unique spiritual journey.

Once people have the faith to believe, repent, be baptized, and receive His Holy Spirit, they become a formidable force in the enemy's camp. They are armed and ready, moving forward under the protection of the blood of Yahushua, equipped with the whole armor and prepared to advance triumphantly.

Here's the incredible News: Yahushua has already shed His blood as a remission from sin. This act allows us to settle the debt we owe YAH and empowers us to conquer our enemy, Satan.

The Blood of Yahushua is mighty, able to defeat the devil, and much needed in the life of every believer.

Does this make you wonder how long the enemy will deceive people into disobeying our Creator and making the enemy happy by refusing to honor and worship our Heavenly Father, Master, and Ruler of all?

If people humble themselves under the mighty hand of YAH, repent, receive his forgiveness, and accept Yahushua as their personal Savior, they are not just promised everlasting life, but a life filled with hope and comfort. HalleluYah.

However, if you have not accepted and received His Holy Spirit, continue reading this book, and you will have the opportunity to come to know Our Father YAH, who is in Heaven. Hallowed be His Holy name. He is the way. Continue reading, processing, and digesting this book, and you will know our Messiah Yahushua is worthy to receive wisdom, might, power, riches, honor, and blessings. He is our Savior. When you get to know Yahushua, the Messiah, you will find love, wisdom, peace, forgiveness, freedom, and rest for your soul.

In conclusion, the Holy Spirit is the guide to an abundant life, and Yahushua is the way to receive this gift. I understand that life can be challenging, and we all have struggles, but choosing to follow Him can help improve your life and give your life more abundantly, as well as eternal life in Heaven, where He will lead all who follow Him. Do not let this opportunity slip away - accept YAH's gift today. "For if the word spoken by angels was steadfast, and every transgression and disobedience received a just recompense of reward.

How shall we escape if we neglect so great salvation; which at the first began to be spoken by Yahushua, and was confirmed unto us by them that heard Him;" Hebrews 2:1-3

Listen closely, my friend. The Almighty calls out too many, but only a few will be chosen for everlasting life in Heaven. You are among the chosen ones if you have responded to His call. You have a divine purpose and a destiny to fulfill. Let's work together and make the most of this precious gift!

"Ye have not chosen Me, but I have chosen you, and ordained you, that ye should go and bring forth fruit, and that your fruit should remain; that whatsoever ye shall ask of the Father in My Name, He may give it you." John 15:16

"One thing I have desired of Yahuah is that I will seek after; that I may dwell in the house of Yahuah all the days of my life, to behold the beauty of Yahuah, and to inquire in His temple. For in the times of trouble, He shall hide me in His pavilion: in the secret of His tabernacle shall. He hides me; He shall set me up upon a rock." Psalms 27:4-5

CHAPTER 5

THE RIGHT'S TO DECIDE

Every individual has the freedom to make their own choices regarding their eternal destiny. Yahushua extends salvation to all who embrace and accept the Good News of the Gospel.

However, those who opt not to do so will face serious consequences akin to those who disregarded Noah's call to repent and seek Yahuah's favor before the great flood.

The people of Noah's era were entrenched in corruption and showed no inclination to forsake their wicked ways. Despite Noah's warnings, they dismissed his message as they had never experienced rain. Consequently, YAH brought about the destruction of the earth and all its inhabitants, except for Noah and his family.

YAH does not coerce individuals into any course of action. Every person has the autonomy to chart their path. Noah heeded YAH's directive, so he, his family, and the animals aboard the Ark were spared. Conversely, Satan continually seeks to mislead and harm people.

Many individuals hesitate to believe in YAH because they have not physically encountered Yahushua. Nevertheless, Yahushua expressed that those who believe in Him without seeing Him are blessed. Then Jesus told him, "Because you have seen me, you have believed; blessed are those who have not seen and yet have believed.

[29] "Jesus said to him, Thomas, because you have seen Me, you have believed. Blessed are those who have not seen and yet have believed." John 20:29

The story of Noah and the Ark powerfully reminds us of the consequences of disobedience. For one hundred and twenty years, Noah and his sons, [specific details about their work], worked tirelessly to build the Ark while Noah preached to the people, asking them to repent and return to YAH.

Sadly, even though they had the chance to change their ways, the people refused to heed Noah's message. They continued to live in sin, engaging in acts of [specific sins], relying on their wealth and status instead of turning to the Creator of Heaven and Earth. They did not realize that their disobedience would lead to destruction. The Bible teaches that we reap what we sow, meaning that our actions have consequences. Those who refuse to listen to and obey YAH will face the consequences of their actions. This message is as relevant today as it was then. Let us always bear in mind our inherent vulnerability and our constant need to lean on YAH for direction and shelter. May we shun sin and embrace the illuminating path of YAH. As the Scriptures admonish, 'Do not be deceived; YAH is not to be ridiculed: for whatever a person sows, that is what they will also reap.

⁸ "For he, that soweth to his flesh shall of the flesh reap corruption; but he that soweth to the Spirit shall of the Spirit reap life everlasting.

⁹ And let us not be weary in well doing: for in due season we shall reap if we faint not." Galatians 6:7-9

Trust in Yahuah with all thine heart; and lean not unto thine own understanding. In all thy ways acknowledge Him, and He shall direct thy paths." Proverbs 3:5-6

But He answered and said, It is written Man shall not live by bread alone, but by every word that proceedeth out of the mouth of Yahuah. Matthew 4:4

In the fullness of time, Elohim remembers us. He did not leave us alone. Yahushua, in His infinite love, sent His Spirit back to the earth after His resurrection to dwell in the hearts of every born-again believer, providing comfort and security.

The Holy Spirit is the key to the abundant life of which I speak. All power belongs to Yahushua; it was given to Him at His resurrection when He ascended into Heaven and sat at the right hand of The Heavenly Father. He is all-powerful. He is Yahuah in the flesh. Like you and I have a spirit, Yahuah has a Spirit, the "Holy Spirit of His Being." He gives His Spirit to whosoever will receive Him.

When a person chooses Yahushua, it is the right choice. Their lives will improve because His love and power will come inside every convert's heart to dwell there forever. Yahushua not only gives them a right to the 'Tree of Life,' eternal life with the Messiah, but it also gives them rights to the new earth, a renewed and perfect world that will come down out of Heaven upon itself.

Pay close attention. The changes we need in this world are found only in His Son, Yahushua. This is why YAH gave His Son as a ransom for sin. It is a testament to Yahuah's deep desire to bless His Creation, a sign of His unwavering love and care for us.

We must accept or reject this great salvation despite the enemy's deceitful deception. This cunning strategy misleads people into believing they do not have to make a decision about their faith.

"Therefore, we ought to give the more earnest heed to the things which we have heard, lest at any time we should let them slip. For if the word spoken by angels was steadfast, and every transgression and disobedience received a just recompense of reward; How shall we escape if we neglect so great salvation; which at the first began to be spoken by Yahushua, and was confirmed unto us by them that heard Him;" Hebrews 2:1-3

The powers of darkness would have been quickly defeated. However, the scriptures had to be fulfilled; He had to suffer for us and die. Our Savior, Yahushua, instead held His peace unless the Holy Spirit moved him to speak. Talking about keeping your peace, I love Him, don't you? His disciples forsook Him and fled."

By the command of Yahuah's Word, through the Blood Sacrifice of The Sacrificial Lamb, Yahushua became a sin for us and paid the sin debt. HalleluYah!!!! No one has to be lost, and no one can boast of their righteousness. It is by grace we are saved. No matter what a person has done, they can be forgiven. All sin can be forgiven except blaspheming the Holy Spirit. (Rejecting YAH's Spirit)

Indeed, the name Yahuah is a strong tower, and the righteous can run into His name and be safe. Yahushua took away our sins and gave us His righteousness. He also forgave us, talking about forgiveness. He even asked the Father to forgive us at the lowest point of His human life. He was still thinking of us, His people. We should think twice before we utter such statements as "I will never forgive you for that."

I pray not that thou should take them out of the world, but that Thou shouldest keep them in from the evil one; they are not of the world, even as I am not. The Jews did not know what they were doing, and Satan didn't when they screamed to have our Messiah killed. If Satan had known, no doubt, he certainly would have never killed our Messiah. Nor would he have ever used men to beat and torture the Son of Yahuah. Satan sure would not have had Him beaten because it is by His stripes we are healed. Now, no manner of sickness or disease has the right to come upon us and stay. We must reflect upon and accept the finished work of the Yahushua and demand the illness to go. Every believer should accept and receive the manifestation of the healing in their body and not let Yahushua's beating be done in vain on their behalf. HalleluYah!!!

"For we speak the wisdom of Yahuah, hidden in a mystery, which Yahuah hath ordained before the ages unto our glory; Which none of the rulers of this age knew: for had they known it, they would not have crucified the King of Glory." I Corinthians 2:7-8

Yahuah was pleased, and Satan was defeated when Yahushua, a human being, became the blood sacrifice. The Sacrificial Lamb of Yahuah paid the sin debt, which we could not pay, allowing us to be saved and live a life free from sin. HalleluYah. I once asked our

Creator Yahuah, "How could it please Him to have his Son Yahushua suffer like that?" He replied, "My Son, as a human being, led a sinless life as I had intended for humans. He did not fall to satanic deception and tricks, nor did Yahushua obey Satan's desires; He did all that I have commanded. My Son was faithful until death and made it possible for you to have everlasting life with Me."

In this, I rejoice with the Father and am so grateful and thankful for Yahushua. I pray that your relationship with Yahuah will be more personal and intimate in His Son Yahushua's name. "Surely He has borne our pains and carried our diseases: Yet we did esteem Him stricken smitten of Elohim and afflicted. But He was wounded for our transgressions, He was bruised for our iniquities; the chastisement of our peace was upon Him; and by His stripes, we were healed. All we like sheep have gone astray; We have turned everyone to his own way, and Yahuah has laid upon Him the iniquity of us all. He was oppressed and He was afflicted, yet He opened not His mouth: He is brought as a lamb to the slaughter, as a sheep before her shearers is dumb, so He opened not His mouth.

From prison and from judgment was He taken away, but in His generation, who could tell that He was cut off out of the land of the living for the transgression of my people was He stricken. And He made His grave with the wicked, and with the rich in His death; because He had done no violence, neither was deceit in His mouth.

Yet it pleased Yahuah to bruise Him; He hath put Him to grief: When now His soul hath brought the trespass offering, He shall see His seed, and He shall prolong His days, and the pleasure of Yahuah shall prosper in His hand. "Isaiah 53: 4-10

Yahushua sacrificed His life for our salvation, enduring arrest, false accusations, and abuse. Even His own disciples betrayed, denied, and abandoned Him. Despite the suffering, Yahuah had a divine purpose in His Son's trials, fulfilling His plan in Yahushua and continuing to do so in the lives of believers today.

This is a conversation between YAH and me. I hope it will be a blessing to you.

A Plea for YAH's Mercy

Yahuah's Response:

Come unto me all who are burdened and heavy laden, and I will give you rest. Take my yoke upon you and learn of me. For my yoke is easy and My burden is light.

My Response:

Oh Yahuah, I come to you with all my heart, mind, and spirit. I seek to do Thy Holy Will Oh Yahuah.

I seek and strive to serve only you. Lead me in a plain path. Direct my life, for me.

Life is yours. Bought with the price of Thy Son Yahushua, I ask that you give me more love that I may have more love to give. Grant me more Mercy so that I may have more mercy to give.

Let your Holy Spirit abide in me, as I strive to obey you. I delight myself in you and Desires to do only Thy will, oh YAH. Let me go forth sinless and blameless. Search my heart, and if you find any hidden Sin, forgive me and purge me Oh Yahuah, make me whole.

I am a chosen vessel of yours. Oh Yahuah, use me as you please. Take me, shape me, And make me into who you desire me to be. Bless the land give away promotion and send laborers to help in the vineyard. Let The land be given to those of your choosing.

Strengthen you to carry out YAH's will and help us to help others and ourselves. Let all who participate be blessed in the name of Thy Son Yahushua.

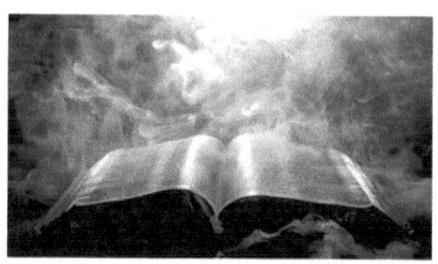

CHAPTER 6

BLOOD SACRIFICES

THE SHEDDING OF INNOCENT BLOOD MUST STOP.

We can do that, too, by not taking each other's life. Let us cherish each life as though it were our own! Each one of us is to love and encourage one another. We can do that by not putting each other down but building each other up.

It is a sin; when we break YAH's Commandments, He, being a good Father, will get us straight, love, guide, and protect us. And His Holy Spirit will comfort us. When a person rejects this great love, there is no place fitting for them—sad to say, but Hell!

Born into sin and shaped in iniquity. Oh, my Father, have mercy upon us!

As a human, I have to admit that the thought of Heaven and Hell terrified me. It filled my heart with fear and regret when I learned the consequences of my transgressions and the depth of my betrayal against YAHUAH by not doing what Yahushua taught us, by example, on how to live, love, care for, and provide for each other as He did for us.

I was abused and ashamed that I had let this happen to me over and over again, all that I could remember after suffering from traumas to my head by those who said they loved me. No more than one would enjoy a delicious fruit, which becomes their go-to whenever they desire it. Out of all the other fruits, this one was the best! And the seeds discarded. It is so sad. However, I had to forgive that I may be forgiven and live in peace for my remaining days. When I became aware of this, I realized that they and I deserved to go to hell for our sins.

And if that were not bad enough, the worst part was that I would be separated from my Heavenly Father, who I had been with ever since I was five. Now, this was too much. He has been with me so much that I could not have endured without His help.

Please wait a minute before you pick the stone to cast at me. I'll be sure to ask you a question. He or she who is without sin casts the first stone. Yahushua Elohim's son has watched over me. Some of you know Him as the Almighty God and His son Jesus. Amein HalleluYAH!

I looked, but I saw no accusers. Only Yahushua stood there, forgiving me and telling me to go and sin no more! HalleluYAH Yahushua, also known as Jesus, sacrificed himself to free us from sin. He took them upon Himself.

I want to share some of His stories with you, some of the stories of others who follow him, and some of my own stories! I believe no one has to be lost and go to Hell if they do not wish to. Many deceived people will spend all eternity there, but it does not have to be you.

Let's embrace the opportunity for redemption together as YAH reveals our hidden truths and great mysteries as we seek our soul salvation.

It is a glorious life, although sometimes trials, temptations, and failures will occur. There is hope through accepting, receiving, and obeying the Savior of humanity. Yahushua, who came in the flesh to redeem all who want what He and that is LOVE!

As humans, we possess an eternal soul bestowed upon us by our CREATOR. This is the place that He wants to dwell in; it is called our soul. The soul resides within our physical bodies in this earthly realm. Our responsibility is to care for our bodies by feeding, dressing, grooming, etc. However, our bodies are more than mere physical vessels—they also house our spirit and soul, where we strive for the salvation of our souls with fear and trembling. Holiness is an absolute truth necessary to obtain and live sin-free lives regardless of differing opinions.

Living a holy life is a personal pursuit and a transformative journey that can enhance our lives and the world. It is about doing what is right even when no one is watching, and through our actions, we can inspire others to embrace the same path of righteousness.

"The truth depends on our willingness to obey the Word of YAH. Philippians 2:12-13.

Our soul is our most precious treasure, residing within our spirit and inhabiting our physical body. Life is a gift from our loving Creator and we are meant to cherish it despite its trials and hardships. Yahushua has promised to walk with us and grant us success. Our loving Creator decides the duration of our lives, whether shortened or extended on this earth, offering us safety and comfort.

"Behold, all souls are mine; as the soul of the father, so also the son's soul is mine: the soul that sinneth, it shall die." Ezekiel 18:4.

Yahuah has granted us the gift of free will and provided clear instructions on how to lead a prosperous, peaceful, healthy, and joyful life through the Ten Commandments. Moses delivered these laws on behalf of Yahuah, and Yahushua, the Messiah, has empowered us to uphold them through shedding His blood.

Our adversary, Satan, has deceptively obscured the truth and led people away from YAH, causing harm to themselves and others. Despite Satan's efforts, Yahushua, the world's Savior, is the truth, life, and light who shines within every person born into this world. Individuals can triumph over the unholy spirits through awareness of their soul and the Holy Spirit. The born-again experience reveals that we are more than just a body; it portrays a deep sense of love, protection from the enemy, and YAH's divine Spirit that acknowledges His presence. Philippians 2:12-13.

Yahuah has sent His Son, Yahushua, to teach us about Himself, His power, love, light, and His laws. There is no better way to share this wisdom than through His Living Word.

"Yahushua said unto him, I am the way, the truth, and the life: no man cometh unto the Father but by Me." John 14:6.

It is in Yahuah that we live, move, and have our being. We can only improve our world with YAH's power, wisdom, strength, peace, and guidance. "That they should seek Him, if haply they might feel after Him, and find Him, though He is not far from every one of us: "For in Him we live, and move, and have our being; as some of your poets have said, For we are also His offspring." Acts 17:27- 28.

Satan wants to hide the knowledge that life becomes meaningless, disdained, and void of reason or purpose without Yahushua. "If ye abide in Me, and My words abide in you, ye shall ask what ye will, and it shall be done unto you." John 15:7.

Changing a world filled with hatred will take real love, Yahuah's love, and us loving ourselves and each other by showing love and respect for our Creator and each other. We will accomplish the changes this world needs. The master deceiver, Satan, has deceived the whole world, causing them to forget that Yahushua died to give authority back on the earth to those who listen, accept, and obey Him. "And the great dragon was cast out, that old serpent, called the Devil, and Satan, which deceiveth the whole world: he was cast out into the earth, and his angels were cast out with him." Revelation 12:10.

YAH's plan includes salvation and blessings for all who will accept His gift of salvation. It is not Yahuah's will that anyone is lost. "For Yahuah so loved the world, that He gave His only begotten Son, that whosoever believeth in Him should not perish, but have everlasting life. For Yahuah sent not His Son into the world to condemn the world; but that the world through Him might be saved." John 3:16-17.

"And ye shall know the truth, and the truth shall make you free." John 8:32. No one needs to be bound or remain in bondage. If you have yet to decide to be free, I believe in you and encourage you to do so today.

What does it profit a man to gain the whole world and lose his soul? I want to begin this chapter by sharing a compelling hidden truth. This Earth contains the blood of our Messiah Yahushua, absorbed over two thousand years ago as it drained from his body. It is still available for our use. Call it forth from the Earth; its wonder- working power activates immediately afterward. Just as the blood of righteous Abel cried out from the Earth for vengeance against his brother Cain, so does the blood of the innocent ones cry out today for revenge and justice, and it will most certainly be served.

"And Yahushua said unto Cain, Where is Abel thy brother? And he said I know not: Am I my brother's keeper? And he said, What hast thou done? the voice of thy brother's blood crieth unto Me from the ground." Genesis 4:9-10

However, it's crucial to understand that the devil, that old serpent, is relentless in his pursuit of souls. For those anointed by Yahuah's Holy Spirit, the path to serve Him through the fivefold ministry gifts Yahushua bestowed upon the church (apostles, prophets, evangelists, pastors, and teachers) are excellent gifts to the body of Christ that carries a great anointing and responsibility, However, it that can be tedious and a difficult journey, and many have tragically lost their way.

Unfortunately, some whom Yahuah anointed have turned back and now carry a false anointing. They changed masters for the sake of prestige, fame, and fortune. Although they can still work with their gifts, they are under a false anointing that comes from Satan. This is a grave situation, as they have fallen from grace, losing the favor and protection of Yahuah. It's important to pray for these individuals and hope they can return to righteousness.

"I marvel that ye are so soon removed from Him that called you into the grace of the Messiah unto another evangel: Which is not another, but there may be some that trouble you and would pervert the glad tidings of the Messiah. But though people, or an angel from Heaven, preach any other evangel unto you than that which we have preached unto you, let him be accursed.

As we said before, so say I now again, if any man preaches any other evangel unto you than you have received, let him be accursed. For do I now persuade men of Yahuah? Or do I seek to please men? For if I yet please men, I should not be the servant of the Messiah. But I tell you, brethren, that the glad tidings that was preached of me is not after man. For I neither received it of man, neither was I taught it, but by the revelation of Yahushua the Messiah." Galatians 1:6-12.

Some individuals were blessed with gifts by Yahuah, but sadly, they have turned away from YAH and followed the fallen ones. These include singers, actors, and others blessed with service gifts. They have abandoned their first love and accepted the false spirit of Satan, serving for personal gain instead of for YAH. In the end, Satan can only offer doom, heartache, and pain to those who follow him because he is doomed. "Ye did run well; who did hinder you that ye should not obey the truth? This persuasion cometh not of Him that calleth you." Galatians 5:7- 8

Do not sell your soul for fortune, fame, or illegal gain. If you have already, take it back. Do not go another moment without committing your soul to YAH.

YAH gave every person their mind, will, emotions, imagination, and consciousness. If they ask Him how to use the gifts He has given them, He will.

If you have given your soul over to the enemy, take it back and give it to YAH for safekeeping. Do not let Satan and his hosts have it. However, if you have not, then be prayerful and watchful because we have an enemy who is out to steal it and, even worse, to get you to give it to him willingly.

To whom it may concern: Many humans have taken kindness as a weakness and played with each other's mind, body and soul, their will, and emotions, saying I'll never be hurt again, I'll do just what I please, and I don't care about what anyone else says. Take a long, hard look in the mirror, and if you see someone else living in your house (body) and the real you are held captive and locked away, let I assure you that you can be free today in Yahushua's name. It is time to leave hiding and let the real you shine through the darkness; this world needs your help. If you are ready, repent, go to the end of this book, say the sinner's prayer, and let the Messiah Yahushua enter your heart. Then, come back and finish reading this book.

Satan wants people to destroy themselves and each other; we do not have to obey him. Satan and those who follow him are bloodthirsty adversaries using human blood to quench their thirst. They thrive on sacrificing people, trying to live a good life, and trying hard to obey the teachings of Yahushua. Satan's primary targets are those who do not want to hurt anyone. Blood sacrifice is a loss to the human family and a waste of human life. This is precisely what the enemy wants to do to people to prevent them from giving praise, honor, and all the glory to our Creator.

Awakened souls who have fallen prey to the evil ones know that you have victory in Yahushua when Yahushua is in you. The Devil and his followers are on their way to the bottomless pit. Satan and his followers have to go there, but humans do not have to be lost; they have a choice. The Devil has caused many to commit unspeakable sins too horrible to speak about; spilling human blood is one of them. Those who kill the innocent are guilty of destroying a person who could have otherwise praised YAH, which is against the Law of YAH and should be against the law of man. I tell you of surety today: YAH-Yahushua can wash away all your sins and cleanse you from all unrighteousness if you put your faith and trust in Him. It is wise to do so if you still need to do so. I understand that life can be challenging, and sometimes, it feels like we are trapped in a never-ending cycle of pain and suffering. But I want to remind you that YAH has given every person their mind, will, emotions, imagination, and conscience.

And if you ask Him how to use the gifts He has given you; He will guide you. It is given to us to worship, praise, and the need to belong. YAH made us honor, worship, and praise Him so He might provide for us and fulfill our hearts' desires. Satan has come along and taken advantage of these earnest desires of humans and used them to do his evil bidding. When love becomes lust, it is being operated by a deadly spirit that destroys homes and lives; it can kill the body and captivate the soul. Let us take a look at how it caused a righteous man to be beheaded. This story takes place at the time of John the Baptist, a forerunner of Yahushua.

In those days came John the Immerser, preaching in the wilderness of Judea. And saying, Repent ye: for the Kingdom of Heaven is near at hand. For this is he that was spoken of by the prophet Isaiah, saying "The voice of one crying in the wilderness, Prepare ye the way of Yahuah, make straight in the desert a highway for our Elohim. Matthew 3:1-3

"At that time Herod the tetrarach heard of the fame of Yahushua. And said unto his servants, This John the Immerser; he is risen from the dead; and therefore mighty works do show themselves in him. For Herod had laid hold on John and bound him, and put him in prison for Herodia, his brother Phillip's wife. For John said unto him, it is not lawful for thee to have her. And when he would have put him to death, he feared the multitudes, because they counted him as a prophet. But when Herod's birthday was kept, the daughter of Heredia danced before them, and pleased Herod. Where upon he promised with an oath to give her whatsoever she ask. And she, being before instructed of her mother, said, Give me here John the Immerser's head on a platter. And the king was sorry: nether less for the oath's sake, and them which sat with him at the dinner, he commanded it to be given her and he sent, and beheaded John in the prison. And his head was brought on a platter and given to the damsel: and she brought it to her mother." Matthew 14:1-11

The story of Herod is a tragic one, where the spirit of lust led him to marry his brother's wife and ultimately led him to have John the Baptist beheaded. Herod promised his wife's daughter he would give her anything she wanted if she danced for him. Her mother instructed the girl to ask for the head of John the Baptist as a gift for Herod's satisfaction. This is a terrible example of what the spirit of lust can do, and sadly, it still happens today. Satan uses the spirit of lust, greed, prestige, and power to deceive people and lead them away from YAH's will. The media can also be a tool used by Satan to control people through worldly desires such as the lust of the eyes, the flesh, and the pride of life. Gang violence is often driven by a desire to be accepted and part of a community, but it ultimately leads to destruction. Drug use is a temporary fix that cannot replace the peace that can only come from confessing and repenting to YAH.

Killing to gain power or respect is not genuine respect at all but rather a form of tyranny. Satan uses these tricks to lead people to shed blood and destroy their own lives and the lives of others. Being rigid or inflexible does not prove that one has a heart. It is often the opposite. Satan uses this deception to steal souls and lead people to destruction—those who fall for his lies or are deceived. Satan is always seeking to destroy the lives of people and hasten them to their deaths. 'For Thou art not an El that hath pleasure in wickedness: neither shall evil dwell with thee. The foolish shall not stand in Thy sight; Thou hatest all workers of iniquity. Thou shalt destroy them that speak lies: Yahuah will abhor the bloody and deceitful man." Psalms 5:4

As someone who cares deeply about everyone, I want to share some good news with those who believe today. You can walk away from sin, lies, and wickedness and choose life by turning to Yahushua, the Light. If you let Him, He will meet you wherever you are, be it mental, physical, spiritual, or financial. I implore you not to let His dying on your behalf be in vain or let the enemy cheat you out of your blessings or eternal soul. Unfortunately, the enemy has deceived people into believing that they will not be punished for harming YAH's children, especially the little ones. One of the ways Satan spills human blood is through abortion, which is a blood sacrifice orchestrated by him. If you are an unwed mother, please know that you are not alone, and my heart goes out to you.

You may have been deliberately frightened and ill-advised into thinking that you know what's best for you by someone being used by the enemy. You are doing the will of the very one you claim to hate, Satan. However, there is hope for you. I want to encourage you to repent if you haven't already. If you have, and you know you will never do it again, Yahuah will forgive you. You must forgive yourself and realize you no longer need to suffer guilt or shame. Let it go now!

Your offspring rests in the Father's care, waiting to see you again with hope, joy, and real expectations. You can look forward to your future without ill feelings and receive YAH's love and forgiveness today. If you are contemplating having an abortion, please know that YAH will not let any soul come into this world that He cannot care for. He has a plan for their life. After delivering three million one hundred and twenty thousand people out of Egypt, He fed them for forty years in the wilderness. They moved into the desert with all their needs being met. YAH is not broke. Nor is He in a financial bind. He is not surprised by anyone's condition or position in life and has the answer to any problems that may occur in your life. You can trust Him to take care of you. While it's good to trust people, your complete trust should be in YAH alone. He will never let you down.

"Trust in Yahuah with all thine heart; and lean not unto thine own understanding. In all thy ways acknowledge Him, and He shall direct thy paths." Proverbs 3: 5-6

Killing by any means necessary is something the enemy loves. Satan relishes the sound of the screams the hurt humanity experiences when they are suffering from disobedience to YAH. He loves the discomfort and misery felt by people. It is a big deception if anyone allows themselves to think for one minute that they are not on the Devil's hit list for destruction and murder; he wants to destroy you and all of YAH's people in any way he can.

"Be sober, be vigilant; because the adversary, your enemy, as a roaring lion, walketh about, and seeking whom he may devour: Whom resist steadfast in the faith, knowing that the same afflictions are accomplished in your brethren that are in the world." I Peter 5:8- 9

In a world filled with greed, division, and hate, it's important to remember that evil walks among us. Satan, the adversary, seeks to destroy everything good and turn people against each other through race, creed, and color. He has been using these tricks for thousands of years to destroy humankind. But we don't have to succumb to his evil ways. We can stand up to the devil by following the Ten Commandments and teaching them to our children. We must recognize that YAH is our Creator and deserves our respect and honor. We should never put anyone or anything before Him, as doing so only leaves us enslaved to the enemy Satan. Always wear your spiritual armor, especially the Sword of the Spirit, which is YAH's Word and the Truth. We can resist the devil and overcome evil with YAH's guidance and strength.

"But Yahushua said, permit little children, and forbid them not, to come unto Me; for of such is the Kingdom of Heaven." Matthew 19:14

I understand that it can be easy to be deceived by Satan's tricks and think that he loves us. However, it's important to remember that Satan is not capable of love, and he only wants to lead us astray. He is filled with anger and hatred towards YAH and becomes furious when he sees us calling upon the name of Yahushua and escaping his grasp. It can be scary, but please know you are not alone. YAH is always with us, and we can pray for His protection and guidance to help us navigate life's challenges. Let us continue to hold on to our faith and trust in YAH, even in adversity. "This is the eternal Memorial Name given to Moses for all the people of El throughout the ages." Exodus 3:15-17

Yahuah is the name Yahushua, and it was used throughout His ministry before He left the earth. In His last prayer, He prayed on His knees that Yahuah would keep His followers with His Name. That prayer was answered and is still being answered today. Many people worldwide, including myself, are in the Father's Name.

Today, joining us in YHUH (Yahuah) would benefit you. "And now I am no more in the world, but these are in the world, and I come to Thee. Holy Father, take and keep through Thine own Name those Whom Thou hast given Me that they may be one, as We are. While I was with them in the world, I kept them in Thy Name: Those that Thou gavest Me, I have kept, and none of them is lost, but the son of perdition; in fulfillment of the scriptures." John 17:11-12

"There is no remission of sin without the shedding of blood. This is why Yahushua became a Sacrificial Lamb, made the ultimate sacrifice and died on the cross. The trial began when false accusations were brought against Yahushua. One by one, they were dropped; they did not belong to Him. Pilate said, "I find no fault in Him." Satan's time had come to do his ultimate evil deed. The sins of the world, yours and mine, were laid at Yahushua's charge. On the third day after His death, He rose from the grave with all power in Heaven and earth in His hands. Yahushua's final victory with Satan was fought in the very regions of hell. He won as an innocent man, and his body could not be held in the grave or hell. Yahushua preached to the souls in hell who had died without the opportunity to know either Him or His Way. They were given a chance to give up sin, be changed, be cleaned, and remain clean forever. Many received this precious gift with great joy and became enlightened beings for travel. Yahushua, the Messiah, shines brighter than the noonday sun, along with those who believe in His name. Those who had died, resting in Abraham's bosom, free from the influence of Satan, became lights as well to travel with Yahushua out of the regions of paradise and hell into YAH's Kingdom."

"For it is better, if the will of Yahuah be so, that ye suffer for well doing, than for evil doing. For the Messiah also hath suffered for sins, the Just for the unjust, that he might bring us to Yahuah, being put to death in the flesh, but quickened by the Spirit: By which also he preached to the spirits in prison; Which was formerly disobedience when the long-suffering of Yahuah was waiting in the days of Noah, while the ark was a preparing, where in few, that is eight, souls were saved by water. The symbol of which, even immersion, doth also now save us, not putting away of the filth of the flesh, and the answer of a good conscience toward Yahuah, by the resurrection of Yahushua the Messiah. Who is gone to heaven and is on the right hand of Yahuah; angels and authorities and powers being made subject unto Him." I Peter 3:17-20

"Wherefore he saith, when he ascended, what is it that He also descended first into the lower parts of the earth? He that descended is the same also that ascended up far above all heavens, that He might fill all things." Ephesians 4:8-10

Yet others returned to their dungeon of suffering as the light faded away from the dark underworld, leaving them in Hell. Their evil hearts exposed their evil thoughts, which lay open before the light of Yahushua for all to see. They knew in their spirit of being exposed to the light that they would not be pleased if they had to live sinless lives. You might think anyone would be glad to be in heaven, but not so; didn't Lucifer and a third of heaven rebel against YAH and have to be cast out?

In great torment, the lost souls had to remain in the sufferings of Hell, where the worms do not die, and the flame continues without stopping, under their master Satan, who hated and tormented them. The Devil is a master deceiver and tormentor. How sad it is for people who choose to follow him. Those who decide Yahushua know that while we were sinners, He died for us. He is the right one to follow. Those who are practicing evil things, let me encourage you to repent and take back your soul, and do not follow Satan any longer. He will lead people where they do not want to be; once they get there, they will not be able to leave. There is no need for any more blood sacrifices to try and please Satan. He cannot be satisfied. Yahushua, who is YAH, took care of that once and for all, and He welcomes every heart to experience His unconditional love. HalleluYah.

"Wherefore, when He cometh into the world, he said" Sacrifice and offering Thou didst not desire; Mine ear hast Thou pierced burnt offering and sin offering hast Thou not required. Then said; "Lo, I come; in the volume of the book it is written of me, I delight to do thy will, O Yahuah."

Above, when He said, Sacrifice and offering and burnt offering even for sin Thou wouldest not, neither hadst pleasure therein; which are offered by the Law.

Then said He, Lo I come to do Thy will O Yahuah He taketh away the first that He may establish the second. By the which will we sanctified through the offering of the body of Yahshua the Messiah once and for all. And every priest standeth daily ministering and offering oftentimes the same sacrifices, which can never take away sins: But this Man, after He had offered one sacrifice for sins forever, sat down on the right hand of Yahuah; From henceforth, expecting till His enemies be made His footstool. For by one offering He hath perfected forever them that are sanctified. Whereof the Holy Spirit also is a witness to us: for after that He had said before, "This is the covenant that I will make with them after those days, saith Yahuah; I will put My laws into their hearts, and in their minds will I write them. And their sins and iniquities will I remember no more." Hebrew 10:5-18

"And beyond controversy, deep is the mystery of holiness: He Who was manifested in human form, had His claim attested by the Spirit, was seen of angels, proclaimed among the Gentiles, believed on in the world and was received up into glory." I Timothy 3:16

Do not fear; Yahushua is the Governor of the Nations and is on the side of every born-again believer. Let us become one in the fight for good and acceptable unto the YAH, our Creator, and Elohim.

Warning Beware

I had retired for the night, or so I thought, when the Holy Spirit moved me to get up and share more with you. Seducing Spirits are running rapidly throughout the earth, seeking whom they can devour. Let me begin by quoting the Word: the lust of the eyes, the passion of the spirit, and the pride of life are significant falls for every soul. We must be doubly careful now. Why? Because time is winding down, and the Devil and his demons are getting more aggressive.

Satan desires to steal, kill, and destroy the children of YAH, his Bride, One of the tactics he uses is the lust of the eyes, which leads to fornication, adultery, homosexuality, and bestiality. It just gets worse.

First, he takes the mind, then the body, and will, and entices people to obey his will. He tells them that it is okay to sell their body (prostitution) to whoever they want to. Every time they do this, they lose a little bit of them self until they become so unattractive that no one wants to buy them, but he does not stop there. After no one wants to buy that person, their self-esteem becomes so low, and they feel used up. Then, they give their bodies away to whoever will have them. (fornication).

Their self-worth becomes lesser to them, and of course, the Devil will offer them something to take away their pain while they continue downward into a deep depression; the drugs and alcohol usually take over. These spirits love drugs and overindulgence in alcohol. Unfortunately, the only way they can get it is by possessing a body and using that body to satisfy their desire, making them drink or do drugs until they are no longer in control, and then they overcome them and cause them to do horrible, shameful things with their body by controlling their mind, things that, if they were sober, they would not do.

Then, he disgraces them and brings them into open shame. The Devil sends other seducing spirits to haunt them as well. The spirit of suicide because they cannot live with the pain and shame of their life. When they began to reap what they had sown or allow the Devil to use them to do disgusting things when they thought they were having fun, not knowing he was drawing them deeper into his web of deceit and destruction. A trap that he has led many souls into contacting aids and many other diseases, even giving it to their spouse (adultery), breaking up families, and ruining children's lives as well. Let us deal with the lust of the flesh; this is a greedy spirit. It never gets enough, no matter how much it gets, money, food, sex, etc., and a very dangerous spirit; it has caused many people to kill themselves just to satisfy their fleshly desires (suicide) self-murder and all murders will have their place in the Lake of fire. It will stop at nothing to drain and shame one and eventually kill them, but not before it steals their soul. Then there is the spirit of the pride of life; this is dangerous also because it makes one think that they are alright in their mess, that no one knows about it, and even if they did, they are grown, so what? They go on living even calling wrong right just because the crowd, the world, says it is okay. Even though YAH says it is wrong, the spirit of pride will not let them accept that it is wrong.

Therefore, they do not change and may even think that they are okay only to wake up one day in eternity and be sent to Hell and afterward be thrown into the Lake of fire, but not until they have suffered great destruction in their life.

Friends, we all have something in common: an enemy called the Devil. It does not matter if you work for him or not; he is out to steal, kill, and destroy you; it's just a matter of time before a person follows him.

He will have them wishing that they were never born and steal life away from them and their family in this life and eternity with the Heavenly Father in the afterlife.

CHAPTER 7

SATAN IS A LIAR

Family and friends, a war is going on for the soul of America and I dare say, the world. Regardless of what political party you may support, this war is far greater than that. To put it mildly, this war consists of two forces at odds. There is an all-out declaration to kill, steal and destroy people. The corporation behind this is Satan, who is the Devil, and his host is determined to kill, steal, and destroy humanity.

However, Satan will not be able to wipe away humankind from the Earth, nor will he be able to destroy the world. Yes, he can scorch and burn land. He causes floods, tornadoes, earthquakes, drought, hurricanes, and volcanoes, and he is busy doing just that, making no mistake about it. However, his greatest desire is to destroy humanity, who are created in the image of their Creator YAH.

Our Creator, YAHUAH/YAH, has given us the tools to defeat this enemy and his host. It began with every individual making a choice and accepting and doing the will of Yah, which is that humanity, His Creator, prospers and has good health. That they reign rule and subdue this enemy and his host and subdue the

Earth. It is about choosing good over evil; the end does not justify the means. Because humanity has gone the way of Satan, the earth has been cast into chaos. However, this can change, and it must change if we are to survive as a nation and a world. Let me encourage every one of you to choose life and not death. Choose excellent and not evil; choose health and not sickness. Choose love and not hate; choose prosperity and not poverty. Choose YAH's ways that led to life and not Satan that led to death. Family and friends, a great conflict is happening for the soul of America and, perhaps, the world. This is a war far beyond political affiliations. It involves two opposing forces: one committed to causing harm and destruction, led by Satan, and the other striving to uphold humanity.

Satan's agenda includes causing division between the races, between men and women, division between parents and children, division between the rich and the poor, and natural disasters aiming to destroy humanity. Despite this, he cannot wholly eradicate humankind from the Earth or destroy the world. Our Creator, YAH, has equipped us with the means to overcome this adversary. It starts with individuals consciously choosing to follow YAH's will for humanity to flourish and enjoy good health. This involves dominion over the enemy and the Earth, opting for good over evil, and not pursuing harmful means for desired ends.

Humanity's alignment with Satan has resulted in chaos on Earth. However, we can change this trajectory for our nation and the world. I encourage you to choose life over death, goodness over evil, health over sickness, love over hate, and prosperity over poverty. Embrace YAH's path that leads to life rather than following Satan's path that leads to death.

Satan is a deceiver, and when someone seeks help from him, it gives him power over their life to bring them down and cause harm. YAH cast out Lucifer, who became Satan but did not take away his power. However, currently, YAH has taken away Satan's authority over humankind. Satan does not want people to know this, so he continues to use his power to fight against them. One of the main ways he does this is by deceiving people through lies and manipulation. His ultimate goal is to lead souls into hell, and unfortunately, many will fall victim to his deception.

"Then shall He say also unto them on the left hand, Depart from Me, ye cursed, into everlasting fire prepared for the devil and his angels." Matthew 25:41

The books of Ezekiel and Isaiah unveil a dramatic event in Heaven. Lucifer, once a radiant light bearer, spearheads a rebellion that engulfs a substantial one-third of the heavenly host. This rebellion, a direct challenge to the authority of Yahuah, the Most High Elohim, sets a series of events in motion. The prophet Isaiah meticulously documents the adversary's thoughts and actions, ultimately leading to his downfall and demise, marking a significant turning point in the biblical narrative.

"For thou, hast said in thine heart, I will ascend into Heaven, I will exalt my throne above the stars of El: I will also sit upon the mount of the congregation, in the sides of the North: I will ascend above the heights of the clouds; I will be like the Most High." Isaiah 14:13-14

He failed and will fail again before all is said and done. He is aware that his days are numbered; Satan wants people to believe he is ruler and king, more powerful than YAH, but that is not true.

However, he is the god of this world.

Some people have said they welcome hell because this is where the partying will be. Only an ignorant, deceived person would say that.
I will say this only once: no party will occur in hell.

That is another big lie from the pit. However, Lucifer was created full of wisdom and perfect beauty, preciously arrayed and covered in splendor.

"Thou art the anointed cherub that covereth; and I set thee so: thou wast upon the holy mountain of Elohim; thou hast walked up and down in the midst of the stones of fire. Thou wast perfect in thy ways from the day that thou were created until iniquity was found in thee." Ezekiel 28:14-15

Due to his pride, Lucifer chose to elevate his throne above YAH's, resulting in his loss of everything, including his name, home, and rank in Heaven, and his subsequent expulsion. However, the last man, Adam (Yahushua), reclaimed everything that the first man, Adam had lost, triumphing over Satan. HalleluYah!

"For since by man came death, also came the resurrection of the dead. For as in Adam all die, even so in the Messiah shall all be made alive. But every man in his own order: The Messiah the first fruits; afterward, they that are the Messiah's at His coming." 1 Corinthians 15:20-23

The power of Yahushua, risen from the grave with all authority in Heaven and on Earth, is available to His saints. To triumph, we must learn how to harness and activate this power for the sake of

YAH's Kingdom while we are still on Earth. Only then can we make a lasting impact and bring about positive change.

"And He said unto them, I beheld Satan as lightning fall from Heaven. Behold, I give you the power to tread on serpents and scorpions and over all the power of the enemy, and nothing shall hurt you. Notwithstanding, in this rejoice not, that the demons are subject unto you; but rather rejoice because your names are written in Heaven." Luke 10:18-20

Believers in YAH have the power to overcome any demon, no matter their rank or number. As long as your name is written in the Lamb's 'Book of Life' in Heaven, you hold authority over all demonic forces. This is a source of great confidence and strength. Remember, YAH knows His own, and Satan, too, recognizes those who belong to Him. Do not be deceived; the power of YAH is greater than any force of darkness.

"Then shall He say also unto them on the left hand, Depart from Me, ye cursed, into everlasting fire prepared for the devil and his angels." Matthew 25:41

It is so disheartening to see how many people have been led astray by the Enemy, using the very gifts given by Elohim to serve him. Satan has been cunningly using wealth, fame, and power to deceive humankind, and it's genuinely heartbreaking. We must remember that those who lose their souls have lost everything, and they gain nothing in return. It is essential to remember that whatever a person acquires, it cannot take with them when they die. Let's pray for those deceived and hope they return to the right path.

"For what is a man profited if he shall gain the whole world and lose his own soul? Or what shall a man give in exchange for his soul?" Matthew 16:26-27

Satan craftily used Eve to lure Adam into sin by offering her the forbidden knowledge. He cunningly made her believe that eating from the tree of the knowledge of good and evil would elevate her to the level of YAH. Eve ate the fruit and convinced Adam to do the same, leading to their downfall.

"And when the woman saw that the tree was good for food and that it was pleasant to the eyes, and a tree to be desired to make one wise, she took of the fruit thereof, and did eat, and also gave unto her husband with her, and he did eat." Genesis 3:6

When they did this, they disobeyed YAH, who had allowed them to eat from all the other trees in the "Garden of Eden" except the tree of the knowledge of good and evil. On that very day, they died spiritually and began to die naturally as well. They were cast out of Paradise. Satan, that old serpent, has been lying to us from the very beginning of our existence here in this earthly realm, causing people to experience spiritual death, known by many today as the "walking dead."

"And the serpent said unto the woman, No death will you die:" Genesis 3:4

As a woman, I believe it's important for everyone to find strength in their faith and trust in a YAH's power. Negative influences can easily lead people astray, but it's important to stay resilient. We can learn from the stories of those who were deceived, like Haman and Judas. Despite their mistakes, they serve as cautionary tales about the dangers of succumbing to temptation and deceit.

It's heartbreaking to think about how these individuals were misled and ultimately faced tragic fates. It reminds us that even those closest to us can be vulnerable to manipulation. In these challenging times, it's crucial to show compassion and understanding to those who may be struggling with their beliefs.

We should strive to help others see the truth and resist the influence of negativity. By reaching out with empathy and support, we can work to uncover the hidden agendas that seek to undermine humanity's well-being.

"Therefore, seeing we have this ministry, as we have received mercy, we faint not; But have renounced the hidden things of dishonesty, not handling the Word of Yahuah deceitfully; but, by manifestation of the truth, commending ourselves to every man's conscience in the sight of Elohim. But if our evangel be hid, it is hid to them that are lost. In whom the spirits of this age have blinded the minds of them which believe not, lest the light of the glorious evangel of the Messiah, Who is the image of Yahweh, should shine unto them." II Corinthians 4:1-4

It is an undeniable fact that even in modern times, Satan continues to deceive people by falsely promising them eternal life, power, and glory through knowledge. However, history unequivocally demonstrates that these promises are entirely false. Many individuals have been misled by Satan's lies, including the false belief that the loving God, YAH, would not permit people to burn forever in the Lake of Fire. The devil propagates the notion that those who end up in hell will burn up and cease to exist, but this is unequivocally untrue.

Spirits are immortal, and humans are not purely physical beings but also spiritual entities. Consequently, those who reject YAH must have a place assigned to them after death. This place is the Lake of Fire, where they will remain for all eternity. As the scriptures clearly state, this place was initially prepared for the devil and his angels. Those who reject YAH would not find happiness in Heaven; instead, they would persist in pursuing evil.

'Then shall He say also unto them on the left hand, depart from Me, ye cursed, into everlasting fire, prepared for the adversary and his angels." Matthew 25:41

Satan tells people that they will not make it, or even worse, that one can make it without Elohim. The devil accuses us before YAH and each other with the lies that all human beings are ignorant, disobedient, ungrateful, and untrustworthy people who will never obey YAH. Satan is a thief, a killer, and a deceiver. He will offer you anything for your loyalty to him and then destroy you because of it. What he gives back in return for that loyalty does not come close to what he takes away from a person.

Satan used Cain to murder his brother Abel by tormenting his soul with jealousy. He deceived Lot's wife to turn and look back when YAH was destroying Sodom and Gomorrah. For her sin of disobedience, she was turned into a pillar of salt when she would have otherwise been saved. Satan can cause the human mind to question YAH and turn against His simple instructions if they are an unbeliever. Even believers can doubt YAH if they are not rooted in His Word.

He used Delilah to deceive Samson, the strongest man who ever lived and gave her the secret of his power. As a result of Samson's disobedience, he was blinded, abandoned, and imprisoned. He later repented and received grace and forgiveness from YAH, which gave him the courage to destroy the entire Philistine army, along with most of the nation, but in doing this, he lost his life.

Satan deceived David, who was a man after YAH's own heart, into having Uriah, Bathsheba's husband, put on the front line during the battle to make sure he would die so that he could have his wife. After he had got her pregnant while her husband was away at war, King David tried to cover it up. In His mercy, YAH exposed King David's sins allow him time to make amends and get it right by confessing, forsaking, and repenting. Because of his terrible sins, blood from that day was constantly shed in his house of David. Deceptive sins usually have devastating consequences.

Satan deceived Solomon, the wisest man who ever lived, into allowing his wives to make idol gods (false deities) and worship them in his palace. Solomon lost his dignity and prestige among his elders, and almost the kingdom YAH promised to sustain. Satan used King Herod to kill a whole city of baby boys two years and under because of greed and power hunger for position. The adversary was trying to kill The Savior Yahushua, the Creator of the world when he was just a baby. An angel awakened Joseph and Mary to avoid the great massacre, leading them to flee with the child to Egypt for safety.

"In Ramah, there was a voice heard, lamentation, weeping, and great mourning. Rachel weeping for her children and would not be comforted because they are no more." Matthew 2:18

"And when they were departed, behold, the angel of Yahuah appeared to Joseph in a dream, saying Arise, and take the Young

Child and His mother, and flee until I bring thee word: for Herod will seek the young Child to destroy Him." Matthew 2:13

Satan, the devil, deceived Yahushua's people, the Jews, to take responsibility for killing Him because they could not use His power and prestige to their advantage. This caused a curse to be placed on the Jewish people.

"Then answered all the people, and said, His blood be on us, and on our children." Matthew 27:25

The list continues as Satan deceives the "The list goes on as Satan continues to deceive the people of the world, even to this day."

"But now ye seek to kill Me, a man that hath told you the truth, which I have heard of Yahuah: this did not Abraham. Ye do the deeds of your father. Then said they to Him, We be not born of fornication; we have one Father, even Elohim.

Yahushua said unto them, If Elohim were your father, ye would love Me: for I proceeded forth and came from Him, neither came I of Myself, but He sent Me.

Why do ye not understand My speech? Is it because ye cannot hear My word? Ye are of your father the devil, and the lusts of your father, ye will do; he was a murderer from the beginning, and abode not in the truth, because there is no truth in him. When he speaketh a lie, he speaketh of his own: for he is a liar and the father of it." John 8:40-44

Satan's deceit has led many individuals to seek solace in drug and alcohol abuse due to the emptiness they feel without a connection to the Messiah. But no one has to continue living this way. It is a lie the enemy is feeding them.

Many have realized this and have turned away from destructive behaviors such as fornication, adultery, and other sinful acts. They have stopped trying to satisfy their flesh, knowing it never brings true fulfillment. Instead, they have repented, turned away from their wicked ways and found salvation in praising YAH.

Those still living in this manner can change their lives through the grace of Yahushua and embrace a new way of living. If you know someone in this situation, encourage them to seek hope in Yahushua. Satan seeks to use people's bodies and souls against themselves, but we all have a choice, no matter what the enemy may say.

When he's finished wrecking lives, he tempts many to consider suicide. Remember, he is out to steal, kill, and destroy by any means possible, but we have the power to resist his lies and find salvation.

"If then I do that which I would not, I consent unto the law that it is good. Now then, it is no more I that do it, but sin that dwelleth in me. For I know that in me (that is, in my flesh), dwelleth no good thing: for the will to do good is present with me, but how to perform that which is good, I find not. For the good that I would I do not: but the evil which I would not, that I do." Romans 7:16-19

Friend, it's important to remember that Yahushua, the Anointed One has the power to anoint believers and give them victory over the enemy. It's as simple as repenting, obeying, and following Him. Sometimes, people can be misled into thinking that the enemy is telling the truth when, in reality, Satan is incapable of revealing the whole truth. Although he may speak some facts, he withholds crucial information people need to know.

It's best not to resort to old coping methods in pain or trouble. Instead, it's essential to seek the help of Yahushua, who can guide you through trials and pain. Remember, Satan won't tell you that you already have victory through Yahushua, but victory can be achieved with endurance, obedience, and listening to the voice of YAH.

YAH, through Yahushua, is not just a keeper but a steadfast companion. If you open your heart to Him, He is always ready to extend His love and helping hand. His assistance is not just a onetime offer but continuous support you can rely on in your spiritual journey.

CHAPTER 8

THE DEVIL, THE ACCUSER

I understand that life can be incredibly challenging, and many people face difficult situations every day. A spiritual battle surrounds us, and we must be aware of the tactics used against us. The adversary, known as the devil, has been deceiving humankind for thousands of years, with the ultimate goal of destroying humanity by ruining people's lives. It's crucial to be vigilant and protect ourselves and our loved ones from his schemes.

The devil hates everything good and is skilled at using tricks to manipulate people. He likes to plant seeds of doubt or entice people with sinful thoughts and images. He uses spirits of lust, greed, manipulation, envy, and pride to lead people into sin, causing chaos in their lives and the lives of their families.

It's essential to understand that the devil is no friend of humankind, and we need to keep our armor on and be covered in the protection of a higher power to shield ourselves from his attacks. When the devil tries to assault us with fear, sex, drugs, or power, he knows there is an opening. Therefore, it's crucial to close all points of contact to him by avoiding sin.

Recognizing the harmful effects of sinful behavior without judging or accusing is important. We should all strive to live a life that is pleasing to a higher power. We've all made mistakes and fallen short; only a higher power is the judge. He is the only one who knows how our story will end. I want to remind you that you are not alone in this spiritual battle. You have the strength to overcome the enemy's attacks and are loved. Remember that you have the power to resist the devil's temptations. Stay strong and keep the faith.

"The law of Yahuah is perfect, converting the soul: the testimony of Yahuah is sure, making wise the simple." Psalms 19:7

YAH also tells us if anyone desires wisdom, ask it of Him, and He will give it liberally.

"If any of you lack wisdom, let him ask of YAH, Who giveth to all men liberally and upbraided not; and it shall be given him." James
1:5

Believers must seek wisdom from YAH. If they neglect this, and by some chance, they live to old age, they may find themselves burdened with regrets and shame due to the unwise choices they made throughout their life.

Remember, it is always within your power to choose what is right. To those who feel lost, I urge you to start today, change your mindset, and change your life. By doing so, you can join us in our mission to change the world and bring souls to the Kingdom of YAH, empowering yourself and others.

Yahuah cast Lucifer out of Heaven after his own choice to rebel. It reads, "I beheld him fall like lightning." Hell was made for Lucifer and His demons and not man.

Lucifer, along with some angelic beings, chose to oppose YAH and plotted to overthrow Heaven. YAH cast them out in response, and their place in Heaven was no more. This serves as a reminder of the consequences of rebellion.

"And there was war in Heaven: Michael and his angels fought against the dragon; and the dragon fought and his angels. And prevailed not; neither was their place found any more in Heaven. And the great dragon was cast out, that old serpent, called the Devil, and Satan, which deceiveth the whole world: He was cast out into the earth, and his angels were cast out with him." Revelation 12:9- 10

Once a revered angel, Lucifer's fall from grace resulted from his deep-seated wickedness. He wandered the celestial realms, luring other angels to abandon their allegiance to YAH and attempt to seize control of Heaven, leading to their expulsion. He became a master of deception, leading his followers into eternal damnation.

Lucifer's charisma was irresistible, convincing countless angels to join his rebellion. He enticed them with the promise of absolute freedom, assuring them that pledging their loyalty to him would shield them from any consequences. Essentially, he sought their worship, obedience, and servitude.

Satan also tried to tempt Yahushua with similar offers, promising Him power, prestige, and acclaim in exchange for His allegiance. However, Yahushua stood strong, resisting Satan's seduction and remaining obedient to Yahuah. We can draw inspiration from our Savior's unwavering resolve and overcome Satan by resisting his temptations.

"Then Yahushua led up of the Spirit into the wilderness to be tempted of the adversary.

And after He had fasted forty days and forty nights, He was hungry. And then the tempter came to Him, and said, if Thou be the Son of Yahuah, command that these stones be made bread.

But He answered and said, it is written, "Man shall not live by bread alone, but by every word that proceedeth out of the mouth of Yahuah."

Then the adversary taketh Him on a pinnacle of the temple, And saith unto him, if Thou be the Son of Yahuah, cast Thyself down: for it is written, "He shall give His angels charge concerning Thee to guard Thee in all Thy ways: and in their hands they shall bear Thee up, lest at any time Thou dash Thy foot against a stone."
Yahushua said unto Him, It is written again, "Thou shalt not tempt
Yahuah thy Elohim."

Again the adversary taketh Him up into an exceeding high mountain, and showeth Him all the glory of them. And saith unto him, All these will I give Thee, if Thou wilt fall down and worship me. Then saith Yahushua unto him, Get thee hence, Satan: for it is written

"Thou shalt worship Yahuah thy Elohim and Him only shalt thou serve. Then the adversary leaveth Him. And behold, angels came and ministered unto Him." Matthews 4:1-11

Have you ever considered how Satan was able to offer Yahushua, the Son of Elohim, everything he did? It's important to understand that when Adam and Eve disobeyed Yahuah by eating the forbidden fruit in the Garden of Eden, they gave up their rights and authority over the earth. This allowed Satan to gain access to the earthly realm. However, it's crucial to recognize that this is no longer the case today. Despite this, Satan continues to make the same promises to those who are unaware that it is no longer his to give away.

When Yahushua died and rose from the grave, he could reclaim the rights to the earth and humankind. This means that believers now have the power to claim their birthright. Yahushua's way is the only path to true freedom. Satan is a murderer who leads people into violence, theft, and destruction. He still makes the same promises today, offering fame, fortune, and temporary pleasure. However, he hides that those who follow him will lose their soul, free will, peace, joy, hope, the ability to forgive, and love.

It's time for people to realize that Satan is a liar and a deceiver who seeks to kill, steal, and destroy. The only way to true freedom is through Yahushua's way. When people lose their peace, they become fearful and paranoid. However, YAH tells us that perfect love drives out all fear. So, let's turn to Yahushua and claim our birthright. It's time to live in freedom and break free from Satan's lies.

"And we know and believed the love that Yahuah hath toward us. Yahuah is love; and he that dwelleth in love dwelleth in Yahuah and Yahuah in Him.

Herein is our love made perfect, that we may have boldness in the Day of Judgment: because as He is, so are we in this world.

There is no fear in fear; but perfect love casteth out fear: because fear hath torment. He that feareth is not made perfect in love. We love Him because He first loved us." 1 John 4:16-19

It's heartbreaking to witness false beliefs' devastating impact on families and communities. However, we must remind ourselves that love can unite people and build stronger communities. We must always pay attention to the value of human life and the significance of helping those in need. Understandably, individuals may become overwhelmed and fall into hardship due to deceptive promises. Nevertheless, we must hold onto hope and believe in a brighter future by choosing the path of righteousness. It's important to remember that hard work, faith, and living within our means are encouraged. With patience and determination, prosperity will eventually come.

"For His anger is but for a moment, His favor is for life; Weeping may endure for a night, But joy comes in the morning." Psalms 30:5

The adversary does not possess the attributes to give a person love, peace, joy, tranquility, or truth. However, he conceals this fact, claiming that he can only provide a temporary thrill that will lead a person further into distress, torment, and failure.

Those who align with the adversary, unbeknownst to them, are bound to a shared torment. The Devil may dangle promises of wealth, fame, knowledge, status, and more, but he is incapable of bestowing love, peace, salvation, hope, grace, or forgiveness.

Satan gives them false hope and false security, and his objective is to make people believe they can do things without YAH. He tells and leads them to think that they are their own master, and anyone who accepts this idea becomes the slave of Satan.

YAH, with His profound understanding of man's depths, his needs, and their timing, stands ready, eager, and fully capable of meeting the needs of every believer. All that is required is their repentance and acknowledgment of Him as their Savior.

He wrapped Himself up in flesh and dwelt among us; they knew Him not. He came as a human, as we are, a spirit who lived in a body and possessed a soul.

"In the beginning was the Word, and the Word was with Yahuah, and the Word was Yahuah. The same was in the beginning with Yahuah.

All things were made by Him; and without was not anything that was made. In Him was life; and the life was the light of men.

And the light shineth in darkness; and the darkness comprehended it not. He was in the world, and the world was made by Him, and the world knew Him not. He came unto His own tribe, and His own people received Him not." John 1:1-5, and 10-11

'And all most all things are by the law purged with blood: and without the shedding of blood is no remission." Hebrews 9:22

The devil has obscured the truth. When an innocent life is taken, the perpetrator becomes a murderer, deepening their sin. Furthermore, the devil has misled people into believing that blood sacrifices are still necessary to attain forgiveness, power, life, liberty, and true happiness. However, Yahushua (also known as Jesus) settled this ultimately by dying and paying the debt for our sins. Through His resurrection and anointing, believers can declare and decree their freedom in Yahushua's name as every burden is lifted. He willingly bore the shame of being hung on a tree so we could be free. Yahushua, who was innocent, took on the curse in our place so that we could live without shame.

"The Messiah hath redeemed us from the curse of the law, being made a curse for us: for it is written, Cursed is every one that hangeth on a tree:" Galatians 3:13

The truth about Yahushua was concealed by the enemy, who falsely accused him, and evil people agreed to kill him. However, little did Satan know that by doing so, he was inadvertently enabling believers to break free from his hold on their lives, which they had willingly given him. Satan has been hiding the truth that all power belongs to YAH-Yahushua. He has also obscured the fact that without wisdom, knowledge can lead people astray, allowing Satan to steal and destroy their lives. The underworld belongs to
Satan and should be left to him. You have the power to reject Satan's lies today. Seek wisdom from our Elohim, who will provide it abundantly. YAH will meet all your needs according to His riches in glory.

"But my Elohim shall supply all your need according to His riches in glory by Yahushua the Messiah." Philippians 4:19

"For I am persuaded, that neither death, nor life, nor angels, nor principalities, nor powers, nor things present nor things to come. Nor height, nor depth, nor any other creatures, shall be able to separate us from the love of Yahuah, which is in Yahushua the Messiah our Saviour." Roman 8:38-39

It is an undeniable fact that following Satan, the deceiver will lead to the loss of the most valuable things in life. Knowing the truth is the key to unlocking the doors of freedom. The truth is that only the deeds we do for YAH will last forever. Yahushua has warned us that sin is the sure way to end up in hell, and there is no escape unless we repent.

"Then said Yahushua to those Jews which believed on Him, if ye continue in My word, then are ye My disciples; indeed, And ye shall know the truth, and the truth shall make you free." John 8:3

When faced with sin, the pivotal action is to repent and allow the purifying power of Yahushua's blood to cleanse you. He assures us that our sins, no matter how deeply rooted, can be eradicated if we turn away from them. Those who try to rationalize their sins and make justifications are devoid of the Father's love. It's an undeniable truth that following Satan: the deceiver will result in the forfeiture of life's most precious treasures. Understanding the truth is the key to unlocking the doors of freedom. The truth is that only the deeds we do for YAH will endure eternally. Yahushua has cautioned us that sin is the sure path to hell, and there is no escape unless we repent.

YAH, our judge, has provided us with commandments as a guide to discern right from wrong, a compass for those who are His.

Today, we have judges in our court system who are legally entitled to judge and sentence people for their crimes. When you hear someone say that you are judging a person because of their actions, when you say it is wrong, they are wrong because you have a right to stand up for the truth. It is crucial to recognize that by not denouncing an act that YAH deems evil, one can inadvertently endorse evil as good. When a person mislabels something wrong as right, YAH warns of dire consequences. They become complicit in that person's sin and risk being trapped in the deception.

Do not believe the devil or his workers; their place will be the lake of fire. People who say they love YAH and do not keep His commandments lie and deceive themselves.

Praise YAH for Yahushua, who forgives sin when we repent.

To know YAH is to love Him and keep His commandments.

The more I know Him, the more I love Him! "Yahuah is my shepherd; I shall not want. He maketh me to lie down in green pastures; He leadeth me beside the still waters. He restoreth my soul; He leadeth me in the paths of righteousness for his name sakes. Yea though I walk through the valley of the shadow of death, I will fear no evil; for Thou art with me; thy rod and Thy staff Thy comfort me. Thou preparest a table before me in the presence of my enemies; Thou anointed my head with oil; my cup runneth over. Surely goodness and mercy shall follow me all the days of my life, and I will dwell in the house of Yahuah forever." Psalms 23

Believe

Nothing happens until you believe. The result is independent of what you see now.

Let me encourage you to take the faith route. Do not waste precious time with unbelief and doubt.

In life, every dream is attainable when you decide what you want.

It is wise not to waver, stay focused and steadfast, and be on the right path.

Get a firm image in your mind and think about it constantly.

When you are getting up while lying down, Keep it alive in your heart, and you will be accomplish bound.

Your desired result will soon be in hand, this you must understand.

You can only give once you receive or get once you believe.

I do not have to say anything more for those who have journeyed on this road before.

But belief opens the door for those wanting something and it has not happened.

Keep what you want alive in your mind—yes, think about it all the time—and remember that faith is the fuel, my friend, for making your dreams come true.

Written by Nona Lang © 2012.

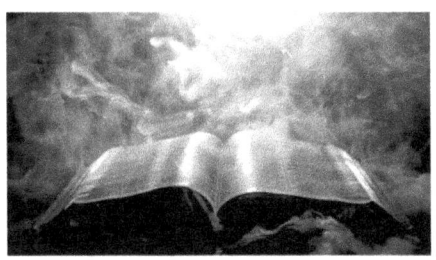

CHAPTER 9

GHOSTS OF THE PAST LEAVE THEM THERE.

Embracing the present moment is crucial. The past, with its weight and burdens, can hinder our progress. Living in the now and appreciating every opportunity is vital to our spiritual journey.

For believers, finding joy in beautiful things is essential. Imagine a world where everyone, without exception, followed YAH's commandments—a world of pure love and unending peace.

Life presents us with challenges, and it's crucial to confront them and seek YAH's powerful guidance. Avoiding our struggles only exacerbates them, and turning away from the Holy Spirit leads to spiritual emptiness. To grow spiritually, we must be ready to repent, accept salvation, and become a beacon of hope for lost people. We must be open to YAH's Word and follow it. This is the path to a purposeful and fulfilling life. It's a challenging journey, but with YAH's guidance, it's worth taking.

I strongly encourage you to explore the scriptures and find comfort in the Word of ELOHIM. Together, we can find the strength to overcome life's challenges and live more fulfilling lives.

"For brethren, ye have been called unto liberty; only use not liberty for an occasion to the flesh, but by love serve one another.

For all the law is fulfilled in one word, even in this "Thou shalt love thy neighbor as thyself."

But if ye bite and devour one another, take heed that ye be not consumed one of another, This I say then, Walk in the Spirit, and ye shall not fulfill the lust of the flesh.

For the flesh lusted against the Spirit, and the Spirit against the flesh: and these are contrary the one to the other; so that ye cannot do the things that ye would.

But if ye be led of the Spirit, ye are not under the penal law.

Now the works of the flesh are manifest, which are these; Adultery, fornication, uncleanness, emulations, wrath strife, seditions, heresies. Envying, murders, drunkenness, reveling, and such like: of which I tell you before, as I have told you in the past that they which do such things shall not inherit the Kingdom of Yahuah.

But the fruit of the spirit is love, joy, peace, long suffering, gentleness, goodness, faith.

Meekness, temperance: against such there is no penalty.

And they that are the messiah's have crucified the flesh with the affections and lusts.

If we live in the Spirit, let us also walk in the spirit.

Let us not be desirous of vainglory, provoking one another, envying one another." Galatians 5:13-26

As a person on a spiritual journey, it is vital to understand the concept of crucifying the flesh and walking in the Spirit. This means that we must refrain from indulging in anything that would harm our body or soul and instead focus on doing things that are beneficial for our spiritual growth and well-being. This includes reading the Word of YAH, forgiving and seeking forgiveness, and concentrating on healing and deliverance.

Walking in the Spirit is a gradual process that involves aligning our thoughts, actions, and desires with the guidance of the Holy Spirit. The Holy Spirit plays a crucial role in the lives of believers, and we can invite the Spirit to guide us through prayer and supplication. It is also important to remember that we should not rely solely on physical sustenance but on every Word that proceeds out of the mouth of YAH.

It can be challenging to resist temptations brought about by the lust of the flesh, lust of the eyes, and pride of life today. However, by nurturing our spirits with the Word of YAH and seeking the guidance of the Holy Spirit, we can overcome these challenges and live fulfilling lives.

"O ye sons of men, how long will ye turn my glory into shame? How long will ye love vanity, and seek after falsehood?" Psalm 4:2

"My people are destroyed for the lack of knowledge because thou hast rejected knowledge, I will also reject thee, that thou shalt be no priest to Me, seeing thou hast forgotten the law of thy Elohim, I will also forget thy children." Hosea 4:6

The food we eat profoundly impacts our physical and mental well-being. Similarly, the spiritual nourishment we provide to our souls affects our spiritual health. Just as unhealthy food can make our bodies sick, consuming ungodly things and neglecting our spiritual well-being can lead to a decline in our spiritual vitality and a disconnection from our divine purpose.

Regrettably, some individuals have unknowingly surrendered their rights and freedom by nourishing their souls with spiritual "junk food." As a result, they become spiritually unwell and trade eternal life for eternal death. Despite their appearance of being put together, they have fallen prey to the enemy's deception, losing their ability to live with wisdom, strength, and authority and becoming agents of darkness. It is of utmost importance to be vigilant of the spiritual nourishment we consume to protect our spiritual health and avoid falling into the enemy's snares.

"This knows also, that in the last days perilous times shall come.es shall come.

For men shall be lovers of their own selves, covetous, boasters, proud, blasphemers, disobedient to parents, unthankful, unholy.

Without natural affection, trucebreakers, false accusers, incontinent, fierce, despisers of those that are good.

Traitors, heady, high-minded, lovers of pleasure more than lovers of YAH.

Having a form of the worship of YAH but denying the power thereof: from such turn away. For of this sort are they which creep into houses, and lead captive silly women laden with sins, led away with varies lust. Ever learning and never come to the knowledge of the truth. II Timothy 3:1-7

"Man shall not live by bread alone, but by every word that proceeds out of the mouth of YAH." Matthew 4:4

We must not only prioritize respecting YAH and others, but also ourselves. Each of us is unique and valuable, and it's crucial to recognize and honor that. Unfortunately, many people struggle to break free from their past mistakes and habits, holding them back. It's crucial to leave the past behind and focus on moving forward positively, with the confidence that comes from self-respect.

As women, our unity is a powerful catalyst for change. Instead of getting caught up in gossip and criticism, let's unite to support the men in our lives. Together, we can make our world a better place.

It's not fair to blame all men for the actions of a few. While some men may participate in gossip, it's essential to acknowledge that women also play a role in driving positive change.

We must address issues like public nudity, which can be harmful and exploitative. While some individuals may feel compelled to expose themselves for their jobs, we must consider the impact on our souls and the harm it causes to ourselves and others. By respecting ourselves, we can earn the respect of others.

Let's not just remember but actively practice kindness and empathy towards ourselves and others as we strive to create a better world for everyone. In doing so, we foster a culture of understanding and compassion, which is the foundation of positive change.

"For what is a man profited, if he shall gain the whole world, and lose his own soul? Or what shall a man give in exchange for his soul?" Matthew 16:26

The mistreatment of women is degrading and harmful to every woman and girl. According to YAH, they should be cherished and not taken advantage of. Clear instructions are provided to married and single men, advising them to regard older women as mothers and younger women as sisters and to love their wives as they love themselves.

Women are also instructed on how to interact with men, to treat older men as fathers and younger men as brothers, and to show respect to their husbands. Older women are encouraged to focus on mentoring younger women to love and respect themselves, their spouses, and their children rather than solely concentrating on maintaining a youthful appearance.

Many women today seek love in the wrong places due to the absence of guidance from a positive male role model, which leads them to endure abusive relationships in their pursuit of genuine love.

Parents must educate their children about life, including matters related to sexuality, rather than relying on the media, which inundates children with sexual content and teaches them about using sex appeal to achieve their desires. Individuals who exploit their nude or partially naked bodies to deceive or promote products should cease this behavior, regardless of their gender.

People should not let the enemy steal their dignity for temporary pleasure or financial gain. Those who engage in such behavior should recognize that their actions lead others into sin and will be held accountable on the Day of Judgment. While we cannot control the thoughts of others, we are responsible for our actions and have been provided with the Master's Word without any excuses.

"If I had not come and spoken unto them, they had not had sin; but now they have no cloak for their sin." John 15:22

It's time to wake up and take action against the immoral and harmful practices being promoted in our society. Those who promote such practices are driven by greed and lust and don't care about the consequences of their actions. They lead people astray and blind them to the truth, which can ultimately destroy their lives.

As believers, we must separate ourselves from these practices and stand up for what is good and just. We must not support those who use cheap tricks to sell their products by appealing to our baser instincts. We must demand respect for ourselves and for others, especially in the media.

Male pastors, the hour has come for us to step forward and shoulder the responsibility for our communities. We are not just leaders, but role models for young men who often lack paternal guidance. We must extend our help to those who have been wounded by false pastors and have sought solace in the streets. It is our divine duty to venture into the streets and rescue the lost.

Let us not turn a deaf ear or a blind eye to the turmoil around us. We must exert ourselves to aid those in distress. The Almighty sees all, and He will pass judgment on those who perpetrate evil. Let us be a beacon of righteousness, inspiring others to follow suit. Together, we can effect change, shielding ourselves and our communities from harm.

Even though we as believers find ourselves at a crucial juncture we must address our society's unethical and harmful practices. Those who promote such practices are driven by unrelenting greed and selfish desires, often disregarding the consequences of their actions. They mislead others, distorting the truth and causing irreparable harm. It is not merely a choice but a necessity for us to take action to safeguard our society.

As individuals of faith, we must distance ourselves from these harmful practices and advocate for what is righteous and fair. We must reject those who use manipulative tactics to sell their products by appealing to our base instincts. It is crucial that we demand respect for ourselves and for others, particularly in the media.

The time has come for male pastors to step forward and embrace their responsibility to their communities. We are not just leaders but beacons of hope for young men who may lack paternal guidance. Our divine duty is to reach out to those who have been misled by false leaders and sought solace in the streets. We possess the power to make a meaningful impact and must extend our hand to rescue lost people.

We cannot turn a blind eye or a deaf ear to the suffering around us. We need to exert ourselves to assist those in distress. The Almighty sees all, and those who perpetrate evil will face judgment. Let us be a shining example of righteousness, inspiring others to do the same. We can effect change and protect ourselves and our communities from harm.

It is heartening to consider how we can unite to transform the world positively. We must teach our young men to care for one another, not just pastors, but all men. Similarly, as the backbone of our communities, women must do the same for our young women. While it may be challenging to make them listen or understand, we must make the effort because it is something we can change in this world.

We need more positive role models, both older and younger, who can guide the youth. It is disheartening to witness some young men wearing either too low or too tight pants, making it difficult for them to move freely, find employment, and provide for themselves and their families. We must show them a better way and encourage them to lead respectable lives by being true to themselves.

Regrettably, some men are tempted to exploit others with their bodies, and our responsibility is to hold them accountable and guide them toward a better path. We are our brother's keepers, and we must take an active interest in the children of the world and do what is right by them rather than simply politically correct.

Every individual has the potential to stand up, be a leader, and uphold what is just. We must encourage them to dress modestly and respect themselves and others. If they struggle to find employment, they can start by pursuing their talents and abilities legally and meaningfully. We cannot allow the trend of sagging pants to persist, and our mission is to spread awareness on this matter.

Acknowledging that we are not solitary beings in this world, but a collective force is crucial. We must unite our efforts to transform the world into a better place. Let us honor the real men and women who, through their daily actions, are making a positive impact.

Together, we can create a ripple effect of change that will resonate for generations.

"Turn, O backsliding children, saith Yahuah; for I am married unto you; and I will take you one of a city, and two of a family, and bring you to Zion: And I will give you pastors according to Mine heart, which shall feed you with knowledge and understanding." Jeremiah 3:15

"Because that, when they knew Yahuah, they glorified Him not as Elohim, neither were thankful; but became vain in their imaginations, and their foolish heart was darkened. Professing themselves to be wise, they became fools." Romans 1:21- 22

When someone walks around half-naked, thinking they look good, it is a deception by the enemy. People may not realize they are naked, and instead of being proud, they should be ashamed. Women who choose to dress this way should also feel embarrassed about wearing pants that expose parts of the body that should not be publicly exposed.

"Because thou sayest, I am rich, and increased with goods, and have need of nothing; and knowest not thou art wretched, and miserable, and poor, and blind, and naked: I counsel thee to buy of Me gold tried in the fire, that thou mayest be rich; and white raiment, that thou mayest be clothed, and thy shame of thy nakedness do not appear. And anoint thine eyes with eye salve that thou mayest see. As many as I love, I rebuke and chasten: Be zealous and repent." Revelation 3:17-19

Tattooing, a trend that has gained significant popularity, carries profound implications. It's not just about altering one's appearance but about inviting spiritual entities into our lives.

These markings can serve as a portal for malevolent spirits to attach themselves to unsuspecting individuals, altering their identity in ways they may not comprehend.

As believers, we must heed the warnings given in the Bible about the dangers of marking our bodies. YAH, our creator, has explicitly stated that we should not put marks on our bodies. By doing so, we are defiling the temple YAH created for us.

While tattoos may seem like a temporary fashion statement, they carry long-lasting consequences. They can become a source of regret and resentment, primarily when they represent people or things we no longer hold dear. Removing a tattoo can be financially burdensome, leaving many with a permanent reminder of their past choices.

It is still possible to abandon this practice. Even if you have already been marked up, you can still cancel the assignments of the demonic spirits through the blood of Jesus. You can also become a witness for YAH by warning others of the dangers associated with tattooing. Doing so can help prevent others from making the same mistake you did.

It is time to step back and reevaluate our choices. Let us not be swayed by fads and trends but instead honor our bodies as the temples they are. Remember, we are meant to be set apart and holy, not conforming to the world's ways.

"Ye shall not make any cuttings in your flesh for the dead, nor print any marks upon you: I am Yahuah." Leviticus 19:28

The things I mentioned above can lead to an empty life; It is only what we do for YAH that will remain forever.

"Where for I say unto you, All manner of sin and blasphemy shall be forgiven unto men; but the blasphemy against the Holy Spirit shall not be forgiven unto men." Matthew 12:31

Living a life of disobedience to our Creator can cause us to miss out on the things that truly matter. However, knowing the truth can empower us and lead us to a life of blessings and dignity. Even if we've spent a lifetime straying from the path, it's never too late to repent and turn our lives around. By uniting with other believers, we can collectively change the world and overcome spirits seeking to harm us. Remember, with Yahushua, we are more than conquerors.

"Who shall separate us from the love of the Messiah? Shall tribulation, or distress, or persecution, or famine, or nakedness, or peril, or sword?

As it is written, "For thy sake are we killed all the day long; we are accounted as sheep for the slaughter.

Nay, in all these things we are more than conquerors through Him that loved us." Romans 8:35-37

Many people believe they can engage in the same unwise behaviors and achieve different results. Some even think they can outwit the devil in doing evil, but this is impossible. Since the dawn of time, Satan has been leading humanity astray, and his deceptive ways persist to this day.

No individual can overcome Satan alone. He has been honing his deceptions for far longer than any of us. It is crucial to recognize that we are the ones who are enticed to commit wrongdoing, not the devil. Satan is the tempter, and he personifies evil itself.

"But every man is tempted, when he is drawn away of his own lust, and enticed." James 1:14

Let's remember the following: Satan's evil nature does not require him to actively think about doing wrong. His actions, from deceiving Adam and Eve to his ongoing efforts today, demonstrate his hatred for humanity. While our first parents set this pattern in motion, we continue it by disobeying our Creator. Rather than blaming Adam and Eve, we should acknowledge our contributions to the world's problems. Despite Satan's deceit, many have learned that he is not on our side. He is set on leading as many of YAH's creations to hell as possible. Satan's hatred for YHWH YAHUAH YAH YAHUSHUA is evident.

But through Yahushua, the Messiah, we can triumph over the enemy! Let's return to the old landmark, Yahushua, the Way, the Truth, and the Life. Yahushua is the Chief Cornerstone, the head of the Church, and our Messiah; He is the KING. HalleluYAH!

"Wherefore also as it is contained in scriptures, "Behold, I lay in Zion a Chief Corner Stone, elect, precious: and He that believeth on Him shall not be confounded."

Unto you therefore which believe He is precious: but unto them which be disobedient, "The Stone which the builders rejected, the same is made the head of the corner." 1 Peter 2:6-7

"For as the new heavens and the new earth, which I will make shall remain before Me, saith Yahuah, so shall your seed and your name remain." Isaiah 66:22

It is undeniable that Yahushua remains unchanged from yesterday, today and forever. He governs over all nations with unwavering confidence and authority, just as He did in the days of old. The enemy may try to conceal this truth, but the government is still firmly on YAH's shoulders, and nothing can change that.

"For unto us a child is born, unto us a child is given: and the government shall be upon His shoulder: And His Name shall be called Wonderful Counselor, of the Mighty El, of the Father of Eternity; The Prince of Peace." Isaiah 9:6

As believers, we should seek YAH's mercy in the present. If YAH ruled the world, the situation on Earth would be different. However, this will change when He returns at the appointed time. Laws contradicting YAH's Ten Commandments should never be passed in our governing bodies. If the world followed His commands, it would flourish, the land would heal, and people would live in peace.

"The righteous are in authority, the people rejoice: But when the wicked beareth rule, the people mourn." Proverbs 29:2

The truth needs to be preached to the earth's four corners. Yahushua said, 'If He is lifted up from the earth, He will draw all men to Himself.' People should not use statues of men, women, or animals as idols to be worshipped. Yahushua is King of the Jews and is only to be magnified and exalted "O Magnify Yahuah with me and let us exalt His Name together." Psalms 34:3

"As Moses lifted up the serpent in the wilderness, even so must the Son of man be lifted up: that whosoever believeth in Him should not perish but have eternal life. John 3:14, 15

"And I, if I be lifted up from the earth, will draw all men unto Me." John 12:32

Believers, let us spread the word of YAH; the world needs it! Walk in righteousness and teach the Holy Word of YAH to the children so they can pass it on. Acknowledge Yahushua as King of Kings, El of els, and Ruler of rulers. He is the Chief Cornerstone, the foundation of our faith, whom the builders, representing those who rejected him, had to go back and get to finish the building. We must do the same thing to live a prosperous life; we can do it with the help of Yahushua, THE Messiah/Christ help.

"Unto you therefore which believe He is precious: But unto them which be disobedient, "the Stone which the builders rejected, the same is made the head of the corner, and a stone of stumbling, and a rock of offense, even to them which stumble at the word, being disobedient: whereunto also they were appointed." 1 Peter 2:7- 8

As it was long ago, it remains steadfast in our day, brothers and sisters. We must stand up for the Word of YAH, especially in these times of unrest. Our Heavenly Father looks down and smiles upon His obedient sons and daughters. He is pouring out His choicest blessings in their lives. Remember, never be afraid to stand up for the truth and His Name, YHUH (Yahuah). He tells us in His Word that if we try to save our life, we will lose it, and if we lose our life for His sake, His Truth, we will save it, reaping the rewards of our steadfastness.

The verse Mark 8:35 says, "For whosoever will save his life shall lose it, but whosoever shall lose his life for My sake and the glad tidings, the same shall save it."

Be strong and courageous; nothing can thwart what YAH has ordained. Everything that is not of Him will ultimately fail. Just as it was in the past, so it is now - we must boldly uphold the Word of YAH, especially in these challenging times. Our Heavenly Father delights in His obedient children and will abundantly bless them. Stand fearlessly for the truth and the Name of YHUH (Yahuah).

Remember, those who try to save their lives will lose them, but those who lose their lives for His sake will find them. This is His promise to us in His Word.

"For whosoever will save his life shall lose it; but whosoever shall lose his life for My sake and the glad tidings, the same shall save it." Mark 8: 35

Let not your heart be troubled; neither let it be afraid, whatever is of YAH cannot be stopped, and whatever is not of Him shall come to nought.

"Let not your heart be troubled, neither let it be afraid." John 14:27

"And when the Chief Shepherd shall appear, ye shall receive a crown of glory that fadeth not away.

Likewise, ye younger, submit yourselves unto the elder. Yea, all of you be subject one to another, and be clothed with humility: for Yahuah resisted the proud, and giveth grace to the humble.

Humble yourselves therefore under the mighty hand of Yahuah, that He may exalt you in due time: Casting all your care upon Him; for He careth for you.

Be sober, be vigilant; because the adversary, your enemy, as a roaring lion, walketh about, seeking whom he may devour.

Whom ye resist steadfast in the faith, knowing that the same afflictions are accomplished in your brethren that are in the world.

But to Eloah of all grace, Who hath called us into His eternal glory by Yahushua, the m=Messiah, after that ye have suffered a while, make you perfect, establish, strengthen, and settle you.

To him be glory and dominion forever and ever." I Peter 5:4-11

Yahushua is the way to walk therein that leads to eternal life with our Creator. Beware of Satan, who seeks to capture as many souls as possible as he can. Hold on to your soul at all costs, and do not let the devil take it away. Forgiveness heals, and unforgiveness kills. Take your heart back and forgive; it leads to a peaceful life. Let us put our Creator first and let Him lead us. Keep love in your heart and trust in our Messiah, Yahushua. He will grace you with peace, prosperity, and good health. Come to Yahushua, cast all your burdens upon Him and let Him wash your sins away. He will give you strength and courage to overcome any obstacle. Yahushua is the King of Glory!

Let Him come into your heart and bring you through any life difficulties.

I Await My Tomorrow

How do I thank you for all you have done for me? You came to my rescue when you saw I had a need.

Before I could ask or even say please, you provided love for me, being a shoulder on which I could cry.

When my heart was in such deep pain, my mind was confused; I could not understand why all these things were happening to me.

You held my hands, looking into my tear-filled eyes, and gently wiped them away, yet you assured me it was okay to cry.

Rest your head on my shoulder, you said; the tears will only last a while.

One day, you will be able to look back at this and smile, but now you must endure; you said, YAH is in control, over us, He is head.

He did not come to earth but sent His Son Jesus, who His Holy Spirit led. He is the author and the finisher of our life story, which must be told.

You said it with faith, conviction, love, and authority—it was comforting and bold!

I could not help but take heed. You allowed me to borrow some of your strength and assured me you were there for me in words and deeds.

I rose from sorrow when I raised my head and looked into your warm, smiling face.

Now joy again lives in my soul, and love fills my heart.

During my trials and tribulations, you did not part. I am so glad I let you in. Thank you for Being a Friend!

Written by Nona McCollough © 2000

CHAPTER 10

WHY DO BAD THINGS HAPPEN TO GOOD PEOPLE

As humans, it is natural to feel concerned when we hear about the possible consequences of disobeying YAH's commandments. It is essential to remember that YAH disciplines those He loves. However, He desires to reward those who love, trust, and obey Him with the Kingdom, a Glorious Reward far exceeding our expectations. His commandments are not meant to restrict us, but to protect us from harm and to make us aware of the deceitful practices of the enemy. They are guides to a harmonious relationship with the YAH, the Creator, and a roadmap to a life filled with love, obedience, and kindness towards our fellowmen.

However, do not worry because Yahushua is on your side and is more powerful than anyone against you. Yahushua is the leader of all nations and supports everyone who believes in Him.

The Ten Commandments are essential rules from YAH. They teach us to obey our Creator, show love and respect to Him, and treat others with love and care.

This is especially important for families. It reminds us to teach our children to honor and respect their Creator and parents. This will lead to a long and happy life, and YAH will help in difficult times. YAH also wants us to love one another. The man and the woman will have to unite to defeat our common enemy, the Devil, and have peace on Earth.

Children who are not raised well or protected can have problems. If they are not taught about YAH and kept safe, they become vulnerable to Satan.

Worrying about the consequences of not following YAH's commandments is common, especially for believers, as YAH disciplines those he loves.

For those who do not know YAH yet, it's essential to know that YAH is love and always faithful and reliable. YAH is wise, always there, a loyal friend to all who will accept Him, and always with you.

YAH is full of mercy and grace. He is the healer, the deliverer, and the leader of all nations. He is the Rose of Sharon, the Truth, and the Light. YAH is the Good Shepherd, the True Vine, and the Living Water. He is the beginning and the end.

Yahushua can carry heavy burdens, calm troubled minds, heal broken hearts and give strength when you're weak. He is like the Lion of the tribe of Judah and the Lamb that was sacrificed before the world began. He is the King of Glory, and there is much more to know about Him. Most importantly, he loves your soul.

However, disobeying YAH's commandments can lead to negative consequences in a person's life, which is why knowing and following them is essential. The first commandment reminds us that YAH is our Creator, and we must respect and honor Him.

YAH is the highest ruler and King of all kings. It's foolish and dangerous to put anyone or anything before Him.

As a fellow woman, I understand the challenges and joys of motherhood, especially in nurturing our children and instilling in them the values of faith. It's not just a personal journey but a shared one we can all relate to.

Parents should be mindful of how they dress their children, as even the most minor child can be a target for predators. Telling young children that they are "sexy" takes away their innocence.

Above all, children are a precious gift, and we must protect and cherish them. Let's work together to create a world where our children can feel safe, happy, and loved.

"This also knows that perilous times shall come in the last days. Men shall be lovers of their own selves, covetous, boasters, proud, blasphemers, disobedient to parents, unthankful, unholy. Without natural affection, trucebreakers, false accusers, incontinent, fierce despisers of those that are good. Traitors, heady, high-minded, lovers of pleasure more than lovers of Yahuah. Having a form of the worship of YAH but denying the power thereof: from such turn away. For of this sort are they which creep into houses, and lead captive silly women laden with sins, led away with varies lust."

Ever learning and never coming to the knowledge of the truth. II

Timothy 3:1-7

"The steps of a good man are ordered by Yahuah: and He delighteth in his way." Psalms 37:23

"And for this purpose He is the mediator of the New Testament, that by means of death for the redemption of transgressions of the first Testament those which are called might receive the promise of eternal inheritance. For a covenant is, there must also of necessity be the death of that which ratifies." Hebrews 9:15-16

To be saved, one must be born again. No matter how well someone may appear to be doing in life, life outside of YAH is empty. Simply being a good person is not enough; one must confess their sins, acknowledge their need for a savior, and accept YAH's plan of salvation through His son, Yahushua.

"Yahuah so loved the world, that He gave His only begotten Son, that whosoever believeth in him should not perish, but have everlasting life." John 3:16

By accepting Yahuah's Son, Yahushua, we receive numerous blessings. We become eligible to receive His Spirit, the authority to operate in His name, His power, and anointing. Yahushua becomes our Savior and faithful friend who stands by us through thick and thin. Through Him, we gain the strength to overcome Satan's influence.

"Ye are My friends; if ye do whatsoever, I command you. Henceforth I call you not servants; for the servant knoweth not what his Master doeth: but I have called you friends; for all things that I have heard of My Father I have made known unto you." John 15:14- 15:

Yahushua, our mediator and lawyer, is more than just a figure of authority. He is also our loving provider, protector, healer, shepherd, bridegroom, deliverer, and the source of our peace. His love and forgiveness are unconditional, and when we forgive others, we open ourselves to receiving His boundless love and forgiveness.

Have they ever heard of the saying that someone is a 'lawyer in a courtroom'? Well, Yahushua operates similarly in His Supreme Court in Heaven. The unique aspect of Yahuah's Court is that Yahushua, our trusted judge, presides. In this court, justice is not just a concept but a living reality. No innocent person is ever found guilty, and no guilty person escapes justice. This assurance of fairness and justice should encourage us to turn to Him rather than trying to handle our affairs, which often leads to chaos.

If you wish to come before The Almighty Elohim in His Royal Court, it is crucial to examine your heart. Ensure it is pure and free from unforgiveness and evil. Only then will Yahushua take up your case and try the guilty party. Remember, self-examination is not just necessary but a crucial step when seeking acceptance from The Almighty Elohim.

"Examine yourselves, whether ye be in the faith: prove your own selves. No ye not your own selves how that Yahushua the Messiah is in you, except ye be reprobate? But I trust that ye now that we are not reprobates." II Corinthians: 13:5-6

When a person has a pure heart and follows the teachings of the Bible, their mind will be renewed, and the blood of Yahushua will cleanse their sins. On the other hand, if they have been wronged due to malice, envy, hatred, deception, manipulation, or coercion, they can bring their case before Elohim, the almighty God, and demand justice be served on their behalf. They have the right to demand that everything the enemy has taken from them be returned, at least double, and sometimes even sevenfold.

However, if a person suffers from disobedience, the accusations against them will not be justified, leading to deserved punishment. Still, when a believer repents and asks for mercy, which is essential, they can have confidence that YAH will grant His mercy that knows no bounds and forgive their sins; this is a testament to what Yahushua has already done for us.

"And the floors shall be full of wheat, and the vats shall overflow with wine and oil. And I will restore to you the years that the locusts have eaten, the cankerworm, My great army which I sent among you. And ye shall eat in plenty, and be satisfied, and praise the Name of Yahuah your Elohim that hath dealt wonderfully with you; And My people shall never be ashamed." Joel 2:25-26

Sometimes, justice can be delayed. The prosecuting attorney, Satan, relentlessly accuses believers, attempting to convince them that they are not entitled to fair compensation. However, ignoring his lies and continuing faith in YAH is crucial. Just like the persistent woman in the parable who approached the unjust Judge repeatedly until he finally granted her request, we too should persist in asking YAH for justice. We must keep our determination, knowing that YAH, the faithful Judge, will provide us with fair compensation.

"And there was a widow in that city: and she came unto him, saying, avenge me of mine adversary. And he would not for a while: but afterward he said within himself, Though I fear not Elohim, nor regard man; Yet because this widow troubleth me, I will avenge her, lest by her continual coming she weary me. And Yahushua said, "Hear what the unjust judge said? And shall not Yahuah avenge His own elect, which cry day and night unto Him, though He bear long with them. I tell you that He will avenge them speedily. Nevertheless, when the Son of Man cometh, shall He find faith on the earth?" Luke 18:3-8.

Let's revisit the story of Job, a man known for his just and upright character. Satan came to Yahuah to accuse humanity before Him, and Yahuah asked him if he had considered His servant Job. Satan replied that Job's faithfulness and love were due to Yahweh's favor and protection, saying that Job served Him because he had a hedge of protection around him.

"Now there was a day when the sons of Elohim came to present themselves before Yahuah and Satan came also among them.

And Yahuah said unto Satan, Whence comest thou? Then Satan answered Yahuah, and said, From going to and fro in the earth, and from walking up and down in it, Yahuah said unto Satan, Hast thou considered My servant Job, that there is none like him in the earth, a perfect and an upright man, one that feareth Elohim, and escheweth evil?

Then Satan answered Yahuah and said, doth Job fear Elohim for nought?

Hast not Thou made an hedge about him, and about his house, and about all that he hath on every side? Thou hast blessed the work of His hands, and his substance is increased in the land." Job 1:6-10

Yahuah allowed Satan to take everything from Job except his wife, whom Satan used to try to make him curse Yahuah.

"But put forth thine hand now, and touch all that he hath, and he will curse Thee to Thy face.

And Yahuah said unto Satan, Behold, all that he hath is in thy power; only himself put not thine hand. So Satan went forth from the presence of Yahuah." Job 1:12

Satan took Job's ten children and his livestock and covered his body with sores. However, Job remained faithful to YAH, even though he cried out, asking YAH to tell him what he had done wrong. Job's friends turned on him, and his wife told him to curse YAH and die, but Job remained faithful to YAH.

"Then said his wife unto him, Doest thou still retain thine integrity? Curse Elohim and die." Job 2:9 Finding peace when we encounter challenging situations without understanding why can be difficult. However, like Job, we can turn to YAH and ask for answers. YAH may challenge us with questions we cannot answer, but ultimately, his will is for our good. Trusting in YAH's plan requires humility, and we may feel overwhelmed. Nevertheless, even during trials, we can find hope and strength in serving him.

"Though He slay me, yet will I trust Him: but I will maintain mine own ways before Him. He also shall be my salvation: for a hypocrite shall not come before Him." Job 13:14-16

"If a man dies, shall he live again? All the days of my appointed time will I wait till my change come." Job 14:14

The story of Job is incredibly inspiring. Even though he endured immense hardships and suffering, he stayed faithful and humble. Eventually, his faith was rewarded when YAH blessed him with even greater abundance and happiness. Turning to YAH in humility and prayer can be comforting during tough times. It's also important to forgive those who may have wronged you. With faith and a compassionate heart, you can overcome any challenge.

"And Yahuah turned the captivity of Job when he prayed for His friends: also Yahuah gave Job twice as much as before."

Then came there unto him all his brethren, and all that they had been of his acquaintances before and did eat bread with him in his house; and they showed sympathy to him and comforted him over all the evil that Yahuah had brought upon him; every man also gave him a piece of money, and everyone an ear-ring of gold.

So Yahuah blessed the latter end of Job more than his beginning: for he had fourteen thousand sheep, and six thousand camels, and a thousand yoke of oxen, and a thousand she-assess. He also has seven sons and three daughters.

And he called the name of the first, Jemima, and the name of the second Kezia, and the name of the third was Keren-happuch.

And in all the land was no women found so far as the daughters of Job: and their father gave them inheritance among their brethren.

After this lived Job a hundred and forty years, and saw his sons, and his sons' sons, even four generations. So Job died being old and full of days." Job 42:10-17

To live a life free from bondage, we must seek deliverance. This deliverance is not only possible but also within our reach. We can achieve this through the shed blood of Yahushua, the Messiah, by repenting, doing better, correcting our mistakes to the best of our abilities, trusting, and believing in Him. The power of forgiveness, a key aspect of this journey, is not just a promise but a reality that can bring hope and reassurance to our hearts. If we forgive, we are forgiven and washed in His blood, making us whole.

As believers, we are not mere spectators in the battle against the devil and his demons. We have a significant, active role to play that can make a difference in this world. By standing firm in our faith, upholding the Laws of YAH (the Ten Commandments), and passing them on to the next generation, we actively contribute to the victory of light over darkness. Confession, repentance, and obedience are not just actions but powerful tools that can empower us in this battle. We are equipped with spiritual armor, including the Sword of the Spirit (YAH's Word) and the Buckle of Truth to face any challenge that comes our way.

Lying to a person does not help them to be better. The truth sometimes hurts feelings, but if it is accepted and the necessary changes are made, it can free a person. We must reiterate our dependence on YAH for healing, protection, provision, wisdom, love, and mercy. If we trust and obey Him, we become a part of His great family, a member of His body. This means we are not alone in our faith journey, but a loving and supportive community surrounds us. The mighty outpouring of YAH's Spirit will dwell within us, washing away our sins and making us brand new, forgiven, healed, and accessible.

As we give ourselves to YAH, He provides us with His Love and sweetness like honey in a honeycomb. It flows into our spirit and purifies our hearts. We can share His love with others who need it by showing kindness, forgiveness, and understanding.

YAH expresses His love through giving. For instance, we can receive His love by accepting His forgiveness and give His love by forgiving others. YAH will supply all our needs according to His riches in glory.

So, let us always rejoice in YAH! Receive Him today and experience the abundant life He offers. It pays to have faith in YAH and trust Him at all costs, for He will never disappoint us. This is because His plans, always for our good, are a beacon of hope even if we may not understand them now. HalleluYah! Receive Him and so be it!

I am not implying that bad things will never happen to believers, but by obeying YAH and rejecting the devil, they can prevent many such things from occurring to them and their families. Give it a try and see. Do not let the devil, the old serpent, use you. He is the true adversary.

Sexual Sins and Their Downfall

All other sins a person commits are outside the body, but whoever sins sexually, sins against their own body." 1 Corinthians 6:18.

It is essential to approach the sensitive topics of fornication, adultery, and homosexuality with empathy and understanding. These are issues that can profoundly impact people's lives and relationships. It's heart-wrenching to see how something as beautiful and natural as sex can be twisted and used to cause pain and destruction. The enemy preys on our natural desires, using them to lead us astray and cause us to sin against ourselves and others.

Fortification has destroyed so many people's lives when they decide to have sex outside of marriage, even though in today's society, it is a regular practice. But it can be hazardous, and a person can open themselves up to not only evil spirits when they are having sex this way from not only the person that they are having sex with but all the people they had sex with before them. And occur undesirable consequences.

Spiritual Adultery is a painful betrayal where a married person engages in sexual acts with someone other than their spouse. The emotional and spiritual consequences of this are profound. Even the act of lusting after someone other than your spouse is considered a betrayal of the heart and soul. These actions can cause significant harm to individuals and their relationships.

Homosexual relations are against YAH's original design for the man and the woman and will bring judgment to all who do such acts regardless of how much they say they love that person. Many feel this is not a sin and say I was born that way, and they genuinely believe this. However, they were not born that way but could have been carried by the mother wanting a child of a different gender, and her strong desire could have been transferred to the infant before birth. But this is the will of the mother or even the father, not YAH's. The enemy, knowing what the mother desires while carrying the fetus, can assign homosexual demons to be attached to the child when they are born. For this reason, a person will feel that they have been this way from birth when they actually have had this demon attached to them since birth.

The influence of that spirit becomes so familiar to them that they often think it is their own desire when, in fact, it is the desire of a demon. If they truly loved the person they say they love, they would respect them and not lead them away from YAH. This also applies to all unholy sexual acts. They are demoniac influenced.

It's crucial to approach these issues with compassion and understanding, recognizing the complexities and struggles that individuals may face. Instead of judgment, let's offer support and guidance to those facing these challenges. It is important to remember that everyone deserves love, respect, and understanding, regardless of their circumstances.

"But from the beginning of creation, 'God made them male and female.' 'Therefore a man shall leave his father and mother and hold fast to his wife, and the two shall become one flesh.' So they are no longer two but one flesh. What therefore God has joined together, let not man separate. "The two angels came to Sodom in the evening, and Lot was sitting in the gate of Sodom. When Lot saw them, he rose to meet them and bowed himself with his face to the earth and said, "My lords, please turn aside to your servant's house and spend the night and wash your feet. Then you may rise up early and go on your way." They said, "No; we will spend the night in the town square." But he pressed them strongly; so they turned aside to him and entered his house. And he made them a feast and baked unleavened bread, and they ate. But before they lay down, the men of the city, the men of Sodom, both young and old, all the people to the last man, surrounded the house. And they called to Lot, "Where are the men who came to you tonight? Bring them out to us, that we may know them." Mark 10:6-9

But because of the temptation to sexual immorality, each man should have his own wife and each woman her husband. I Corinthians 7:2

Instructions to believers and unbelievers, single people, married couples, and widows on how to avoid these temptations.

1. "Now for the matters you wrote about: It is good for a man not to marry.

2. But since there is so much immorality, each man should have his own wife, and each woman her own husband.

3. The husband should fulfill his marital duty to his wife and likewise the wife to her husband.

4. The wife's body does not belong to her alone but also to her husband. In the same way, the husband's body does not belong to him alone but also to his wife.

5. Do not deprive each other except by mutual consent and for a time, so that you may devote yourselves to prayer. Then come together again so that Satan will not tempt you because of your lack of self- control.

6. I say this as a concession, not as a command.

⁷ I wish that all men were as I am. But each man has his own gift from God; one has this gift, another has that.

⁸ Now to the unmarried and the widows I say: It is good for them to stay unmarried, as I am.

⁹ But if they cannot control themselves, they should marry, for it is better to marry than to burn with passion.

Thus, it is a wise choice to choose marriage over mere lust. However, it is essential to understand that marriage should not be solely based on physical desire. Both partners should feel empowered to carefully evaluate and ensure their compatibility in all aspects before committing to marriage. This decision should not be made lightly, as it shapes the course of their future. But if they do not have self-control, they should marry, for it is better to marry than to burn with passion. 1 Corinthians 7:9

They commit adultery with their eyes, and their desire for sin is never satisfied. They lure unstable people into sin, and they are well-trained in greed. They live under God's curse. II Peter 2:14

Before getting married, being fully committed and having a clear mindset is crucial. This will prevent the enemy from causing one to go astray. While marrying to avoid succumbing to lust is better than giving in to it, it's important to remember that marriage should not be solely based on physical desires. Both partners should thoroughly investigate and ensure that the other person is a suitable match in all aspects. Entering into marriage should not be taken lightly. Commitment and a clear mindset are vital to prevent straying from the path. Marrying to avoid lust is essential, but it's equally important to consider all aspects of compatibility. Marriage is a serious commitment, and thorough consideration is necessary before taking that step.

"They commit adultery with their eyes, and their desire for sin is never satisfied. They lure unstable people into sin, and they are well-trained in greed. They live under God's curse. II Peter 2:14

Adhering firmly to YAH's guidance is crucial to avoiding the enemy's deception. The enemy may tempt individuals into engaging in sinful behaviors, such as homosexuality, which contradicts YAH's divine plan for humanity. It is deemed a severe sin and an abomination to YAH. These inclinations may feel natural, but the enemy influences them and does not align with YAH's teachings. Acknowledging this and seeking repentance to evade severe judgment from YAH is imperative "If a man lies with a male as with a woman, both of them have committed an abomination; they shall surely be put to death; their blood is upon them." Leviticus 20:13

"Or do you not know that the unrighteous will not inherit the kingdom of God? Do not be deceived: neither the sexually immoral, nor idolaters, nor adulterers, nor men who practice homosexuality, nor thieves, nor the greedy, nor drunkards, nor revilers, nor swindlers will inherit the kingdom of God. And such were some of you. But you were washed, you were sanctified, you were justified in the name of the Lord Jesus Christ and by the Spirit of our God." 1 Corinthians 6:9-11 Just as Sodom and Gomorrah and the surrounding cities, which likewise indulged in sexual immorality and pursued unnatural desire, serve as an example by undergoing a punishment of eternal fire. Jude 1:7

The sexually immoral, men who practice homosexuality, enslavers, liars, perjurers, and whatever else is contrary to sound doctrine, 1 Timothy 1:10

"For this reason, God gave them up to dishonorable passions. For their women exchanged natural relations for those contrary to nature, the men likewise gave up natural relations with women and were consumed with passion for one another, men committing shameless acts with men and receiving in themselves the due penalty for their error. And since they did not see fit to acknowledge God, God gave them up to a debased mind to do what ought not to be done." Romans 1:26-28

It is essential to understand that YAH does not condone homosexual behavior or any sexual sins. If you are struggling with these issues, finding deliverance by recognizing the problem, denouncing it, and taking back control of your life through faith is possible. Demons can be cast out, and one can find freedom through Yahushua's sacrifice. He died to pay the sinful debt that we all owe one way or another. While believers may still face challenges, they can mitigate many of them by following YAH and rejecting the influence of the Devil.

My daddy wrote this poem for me when I was about sixteen, trying to figure life out and it is still on point today!

What to Do About It

During these days of indecision, in these times of strife and woe, there are so many isms going on until one wonders where to go.

Well, my friend, please let me help you.

Believe my friend, the words I say if you are puzzled or bewildered by so many isms along the way.

Now, what do I mean by all these isms?

What am I really trying to say?

Friend, one of these isms, is found in the movies.

The trash in the picture show books that folks will gladly sell you, even at the grocery store.

My friend, do not let the devil fool you; these folks are out to get your dough.

Follow Yahushua (Christ). That is what to do about it, for sure.

Now you will have to watch old Satan because that fellow knows his stuff.

He is the source of all these isms and will make you think he is awfully tough.

Now, you all have heard my story, and I pray you know just what I mean.

Without fear or contradiction, may you and Jesus make a team.

Without shame or reservation, say, LORD, you lead the way, and you will find your life much sweeter as you live from day to day.

Written by Walter McCollough Sr. © 1967.

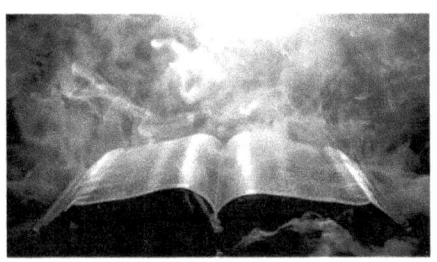

CHAPTER 11

OVERCOMING FEAR AND REJECTION AND LIVING AS YAH COMMANDS

If YAH, our Creator, had any weakness, rejection from His children, and them being held in captivity by the Devil because of sin, I feel I would be one of them. This causes humans to be rejected by Father Yahuah because they listen and obey the voice of His Satan and doom themselves to the eternal flames of hell.

Satan accuses us before the YAH throne of the very things He coheres to, manipulated, and encouraged people to do. YAH is not a lair, and He has to keep His Word. He is a KING!

YAH, knowing everything, the ending from the beginning had a plan to redeem believers' people who have been borne of His Spirit. Yah allows us to see, feel, know, and taste our new master, Satan. We discovered he was a hard taskmaster void of love or mercy.

Satan is unforgiving and relentless in his quest to steal, kill, and destroy humankind. In the fullness of time, when we could take no more, YAH sent His seed, wrapped it in the flesh, and placed it in Miriam, which redeemed humankind from the curse of the law that had been placed upon them because of Miriam and Joseph when they sinned in Paradise the Garden of Eden.

When they obeyed the voice of Satan and ate from the tree of good and evil, YAH had instructed them not to eat. They became a victim of death, and they fell to the will of Satan.

In their lost state, they were driven out of the garden, and an angel was placed there to guard the tree of life unless they ate of it and became cursed forever in that state. Then, the fullness of time came, and Yahushua, the Living Word, came down to earth wrapped in flesh to remind us of who He is and His power, love, grace, and mercy.

People who receive Yahushua, which Is YAH in the flesh, receive wonder-working power and can perform great miracles. He said we would do what He did and more because He would be in us. Not only did Yahushua turn wine into water and multiple five fishes and two loads of bread to feed five thousand people, but He did many more miracles.

Yahushua raised the dead, opened blind eyes, and enabled people with disabilities to walk and the dumb to talk. He also walked on water, calmed a storm, and so much more; if all He did were recorded, the world would not be big enough to house His records. As if that weren't enough, He went on to die for us and paid our debt of sin that we could not pay. It was not paid for with silver or gold but with His blood. But He did not stay dead; He rose in three days, returned to Heaven, and reclaimed His throne with all power in Heaven and the earth in His Hands.

No longer does YAH have to allow Satan to kill, steal, or destroy His people. He saves us and gives our soul back to us, and we must keep it at all costs.

Now, we once again could be called His children and, in the fullness of time, reign with Him.

Not only does Satan hate his followers, but he also hates YAH followers.

The Devil intends to steal blessings from believers, destroy their purpose and take their lives.

It does not matter to him how he does it. He will use every trick in the book to get them to disobey YAH laws, overlook His statutes, and forget His commandments.

The mind of the believer is where he operates to defeat them. He will first seek to deceive those asleep naturally or spiritually by planting lies in their mind, enticing and tempting people to disobey YAH.

Once the seeds of discord are planted, the enemy is well on his way to convincing people that they cannot trust YAH's love and care for them and that He will not supply all their needs according to His riches in glory. But He will. The Devil does not want believers to know this.

When people accept evil thoughts, they are set up and positioned to disobey Yah in hopes of significant gain, the same old trick he played on Adam and Eve.

The enemy tries his best to get believers to reject the word of YAH and believe that he can do better with their lives than YAH.

If you are being challenged in this area, this is a suitable time to ask YAH in the name of Yahushua to help you overcome unbelief.

When an evil thought is acted upon, if not corrected, it will bring in the spirit of death. This is why I am writing this book: to uncover some of Satan's plots and plans that he is using today to deceive many. What he is using on one may not be used on another, but rest assured of this one thing: no one is immune to him.

However, with the Word of Elohim and the blood of Yahushua, we can defeat him.

A person does not have to be tall to stand tall, nor do they have to have legs to walk, nor a tongue to talk. They do not have to have wings to fly, ears to hear, or eyes to see. It can all be done in the soul. They do not have to sit to be still or be loud to be heard. They do not have to be pretty to be beautiful, nor do they have to have a diploma to be innovative. They do not have to have muscles to be strong, and wrong feelings do not make it right. Just because they are smart does not make them wise. No one has to feel like forgiving to forgive, nor do they have to be rich to give or famous to live.

But if they have the things I mentioned, they can do anything through YAH that strengthens them.

"For as the body is one, and hath many members, and all the members of the body, being many, are one body: so also is the Messiah.

For by one Spirit are we all immersed into one body, whether we be Jews of Greeks, whether we be bond or free; and have been all made to drink into one Spirit.

For the body is not one member but many.

If the foot shall say, because I am not a hand, I am not of the body; is it therefore not of the body?

And if the ear shall say, because I am not the eye, I am not of the body? Is it therefore not of the body? If the whole body were an eye, where were the hearing? If the whole were hearing, where were the smelling?

But now hath Elohim set the members every one of them in the body, as it hath pleased Him. And if they were all one member, where were the body?

But now are they many members, yet but one body.

And the eye cannot say unto the hand, I have no need of thee: nor again the head to the feet, I have no need of you."

Nay, much more those members of the body, which seem to be more feeble, are necessary:

We must remember that the members of Yahushua's body should not fight each other. Fighting between believers only causes division, which is like a cancer cell turning against the body.

Unfortunately, millions of Church members are scattered and deceived, and as a result, the world no longer holds the church in the high regard it once did. When the world sees the church people acting powerless and seemingly without the authority that the church of old walked in, it's understandable why they lose their respect for the church.

Let's draw inspiration from the saints of old, who, through their unity and strength, left an indelible mark on their world and earned its respect.

Their example is not just a historical fact but a beacon of hope, reminding us of our immense potential as a unified assembly. When realized, this potential can inspire hope and bring about a positive change in our world.

In these challenging times, let's unite and set aside our differences. It's essential to acknowledge that hardships are unfolding on the earth and can be painful. However, they can also catalyze us to turn to prayer and worship.

As we're strengthened and uplifted, we can become powerful witnesses to others through our testimonies. Let's not just endure but praise YAH for the transformative power of these trials, which can make us stronger and more resilient!

Many will fall away, but we must remain steadfast. The true church will come together and stand. We have YAH's word, a steadfast and unchanging promise, that the gates of hell will not prevail. This is not just a hope, but our assurance, our strength, and our security.

"If I shut up heaven that there be no rain, command the locust to devour the land or send pestilence among My People."12:12-23

If My people, which are called by My name, shall humble themselves, and pray, and seek My face, and turn from their wicked ways; then will I hear from heaven, and will forgive their sin, and will heal the land." II Chronicles 7:13-14

"For I know the thoughts that I think toward you, saith Yahuah, thoughts of peace, and not of evil, to give you an expected end. Then shall ye call upon Me, and ye shall go and pray unto Me, and I will hearken unto you. And ye shall seek Me, and find me, and I will hearken unto you." Jeremiah 29:11-13

Believers can transform the world when we unite, repent, fast, and pray. Our savior, Yahushua, has reclaimed our rightful authority in the earthly realm from Satan. It is our calling to walk the path he has paved for us. YAH has placed He trusts us believers to carry out Yahushua's perfect works on this earth. His plan of redemption was set in motion long before our existence to rescue humanity from the adversary's influence.

Despite our disobedience, YAH chose to redeem us. Let us never forget the magnitude of Yahushua's sacrifice. He placed His seed in the woman Miriam, also known as Mary, and sent Yahushua, the Lamb, to pay the price for our sins. He did this even before humans had committed any sins.

According as he hath chosen us in Him before the foundation of the world, that we should be holy and without blame before him in love.

Having predestinated us unto the adoption of children by Yahushua the Messiah to Himself, according to the good pleasure of His will." Ephesian 1:4-5

In His wisdom, YAH bestowed upon us the Ten Commandments through Moses atop the mountains. These commandments, far from being outdated, are practical guidelines for our daily lives. They guide us to honor the Creator in Heaven and to treat our fellowmen with respect on earth. They are not just relics of the past but principles that, when ignored, can lead to dire consequences. Visiting any courtroom during sentencing might provide a sobering reality check for those who doubt their relevance. More often than not, the transgressions that led to the current predicament have violated one or more of these commandments, highlighting the importance of their adherence. Exodus 20:1-18 [1] And God spoke all these words:

[2] "I am the LORD your God, who brought you out of Egypt, out of the land of slavery.

[3] "You shall have no other gods before me.

[4] "You shall not make for yourself an image in the form of anything in heaven above or on the earth beneath or in the waters below.

[5] You shall not bow down to them or worship them; for I, the LORD your God, am a jealous God, punishing the children for the sin of the parents to the third and fourth generation of those who hate me,

[6] but showing love to a thousand generations of those who love me and keep my commandments.

[7] "You shall not misuse the name of the LORD your God, for the LORD will not hold anyone guiltless who misuses his name.

[8] "Remember the Sabbath day by keeping it holy.

⁹ Six days you shall labor and do all your work,

¹⁰ but the seventh day is a sabbath to the LORD your God. On it you shall not do any work, neither you, nor your son or daughter, nor your male or female servant, nor your animals, nor any foreigner residing in your towns.

¹¹ For in six days the LORD made the heavens and the earth, the sea, and all that is in them, but he rested on the seventh day.
Therefore the LORD blessed the Sabbath day and made it holy.

¹² "Honor your father and your mother, so that you may live long in the land the LORD your God is giving you.

¹³ "You shall not murder.

¹⁴ "You shall not commit adultery.

¹⁵ "You shall not steal.

¹⁶ "You shall not give false testimony against your neighbor.

¹⁷ "You shall not covet your neighbor's house. You shall not covet your neighbor's wife, or his male or female servant, his ox or donkey, or anything that belongs to your neighbor."

¹⁸ When the people saw the thunder and lightning and heard the trumpet and saw the mountain in smoke, they trembled with fear.
They stayed at a distance"

Due to humanity's sinful nature, they were unable to keep YAH's laws. Instead, they made idols with their own hands and worshipped them. This is the one thing YAH hates. He is a jealous Elohim who visits the iniquity upon the children of the third and fourth generations. Why should He like this? After all, it is in Him that we live, move, and have our being

"For in Him we live, and move, and have our being; as some of your poets have said, For we are His offspring." Acts 17:28

Remembering the Sabbath and keeping it holy can challenge many believers. While we can seek blessings from our Creator any day and at any time, it's crucial to remember that we must be vigilant against the adversary's deceptions that lead us astray from honoring the Sabbath. Despite the argument that Sunday is now considered a holy day, the seventh-day Sabbath holds a unique significance as the day hallowed and blessed by our Creator. It's vital to honor and respect this day with reverence, recognizing its spiritual importance and blessings. Though our busy schedules may make setting aside time for rest and worship difficult, remember that our Creator asks for just one day out of the six, He has given us for earthly tasks and enjoyment. We can experience intimate fellowship with our Creator by dedicating this special day to Him. Breaking away from our routines and obligations may be challenging, but worshiping our Creator and doing what He says is ultimately the most important thing we can do. Let's strive to honor Him by observing the Sabbath and keeping it holy, understanding that it is a particular time set apart by our Heavenly Father for our benefit and His glory

"And on the seventh day Elohim completed His work which He had made; and He rested on the seventh day from all His work which He had made. And Elohim blessed the seventh day and sanctified it: because that in it He rested from all His work which Elohim created and made." Genesis 1:33-34

Satan has also deceived YAH's people to break His first commandment by taking His name in vain and calling Him another name, as well as making idols by their own hands and worshiping them.

"The idols of the heathen are silver and gold, the work of men's hands. They have mouths, but they speak not; eyes have they, but they see not; They have ears, but they hear not; neither is there any breath in them. They that make them are like them; so is everyone that trusteth in them." Psalms 137:15-18

It is essential to recognize that YAH's Name is significant, and He intends us to call Him by His Name and His Son Yahushua by His Name. His Name appears over 6000 times in the Holy Scrolls, and He instructs us to call Him by His Name. Unfortunately, many people have been misled to believe that YAH's Name is too sacred to be spoken. This misconception has caused some individuals to dishonor our Creator by using titles and names that do not adequately represent Him. The church leaders must repent for leading their congregations astray and for any wrongdoings committed for personal gain. Additionally, adultery is a destructive sin that causes harm not only to the individuals involved but also to their families, often leading to dysfunction and division. Believers must recognize the damaging effects of adultery and avoid it at all costs.

"But the fearful, and unbelieving, and the abominable, and murderers, and whoremongers, and sorcerers, and idolaters, and all liars shall have their part in the lake which burneth with fire and brimstone: which is the second death." Revelation 21:8

Many people commit sins thinking that no one knows about them. However, YAH, our Creator, knows about everything we do, and we will be held accountable for our actions. If you are sinning, please repent and turn back to YAH. It is the only way to save your marriage and your family.

One common sin that the enemy is using to deceive and destroy lives is homosexuality. This sin is often caused by rejection or hurt from a different sex. If you are in a homosexual relationship, please repent and turn back to YAH. Homosexuality is against the will of our Creator and will lead us straight into hell if we don't repent.

If you love someone of the same sex, do not lead them to hell by doing things that YAH says not to do. This sin will cause you to experience rejection from those who walk in the truth. It is not that they reject you; they cannot accept what you are doing and be right with YAH.

We must respect ourselves and respect others by setting sexual boundaries, as YAH told us. We must obey Him, and He will act favorably on our behalf and remove feelings of rejection. Ultimately, it is not about what we think or say but what YAH says and feels about this critical subject. Let's examine His Words and thoughts about this.

"Thou shalt not lie with mankind, as with womankind; it is an abomination." Leviticus 18: 22

"Professing themselves to be wise, they became fools, And changed the glory of the incorruptible Elohim, into an image made like to corruptible man, and to birds, and four-footed beasts, and creeping things.

"Wherefore Yahuah also gave them up to uncleanness, through the lusts of their own hearts, to dishonor their own bodies among themselves: Who changed the truth of Yahuah into a lie and worshipped and served the creature rather than the Creator, Who is blessed forever.

For this cause Yahuah gave them up unto vile affections for even their women did change the natural use into that which is against nature: And likewise also the men, leaving the natural use of the woman, burned in their lust one toward another; men with men doing that which is indecent, and receiving in themselves that recompense of their error which was proper." Romans 1:22-27

My friends, it's crucial to understand that when people commit heinous acts, it's not a reflection of genuine love. It's a product of negative influences, not love. If they truly loved each other, they would prioritize and cherish each other's well-being. This behavior is not just a mistake but a grave offense to the divine. Failure to recognize this distinction-that it's not love, but lust - will lead to spiritual destruction. In His love, mercy, and desire for all to find salvation, the divine has forewarned us of this.

I trust that the enemy does not ensnare those who read this message. Will you consider changing your ways and being open to the guidance of the Spirit of the Divine? Let me restate: my intention in sharing this is not to condemn or judge you. It comes from a place of love, a plea for you to recognize the truth and turn away from this wrongdoing. Remember, only the Divine truly knows the state of a person's heart. We have all made mistakes but can find forgiveness and liberation through repentance.

"Know not that the unrighteous shall not inherit the kingdom of the Divine? Be not deceived: neither fornicators, nor idolaters, nor adulterers, nor homosexuals, nor self-abusers, Nor thieves, covetous, drunkards, revilers, or extortioners shall inherit the kingdom of the Divine."

And such were some of you: but now ye are washed, but now ye are sanctified, but now ye are justified in the Name of the Savior Yahushua, and by the Spirit of our Elohim." I Corinthians 6:8-11

Living in sin can be challenging and often makes one feel unworthy of love and acceptance. However, it's important to remember that YAH's love is boundless, and repentance is always an option. When we experience His love, we can let go of the spirit of rejection and realize that He cherishes us. This realization often comes through deep self-reflection, examining our actions and motivations, and acknowledging our need for His forgiveness. This introspection is a crucial step towards change.

Lying is a destructive force that not only harms us but also those around us, sowing seeds of confusion and deep-rooted mistrust in our lives. It's a habit that can be hard to break, but the significance of being truthful in every aspect of life cannot be overstated. YAH abhors dishonesty, and it's imperative to repent and seek forgiveness if we have strayed from the path of truth. This underscores the urgency to change our behavior, to strive for truthfulness in all our actions, and to repair the trust we may have broken.

"But the fearful, and unbelieving, and the abominable, and murderers, and whoremongers, and sorcerers, and idolaters, and all liars shall have their part in the lake which burneth with fire and brimstone. It's essential to recognize that engaging in occult practices such as sorcery, witchcraft, and black magic is contrary to the laws of YAH. Individuals involved in these activities risk rejection by YAH unless they sincerely repent.

The enemy employs unclean spirits to deceive and entrap individuals. These spirits assist witches in causing harm to people's souls. Seeking guidance from Satan, instead of turning to YAH, means consulting root workers rather than the church or holy prophets. Relying on horoscopes allows the enemy access to our lives and results in rejecting the Holy Spirit.

While Satan and his demons may not have the ability to foresee the future, they can manipulate circumstances to create the illusion that they can. They may not be able to read minds, but they can influence people by implanting thoughts and ideas. Engaging in these practices leads people away from their Creator and toward harmful spirits. We must rely solely on YAH through Yahushua.
The Devil has deceived humankind and led them into wickedness, causing YAH to regret creating them. YAH destroyed the First World with water but spared Noah and his family. YAH saw that man's wickedness was great on earth, and every thought in his heart was continuously evil. YAH regretted creating man on earth and chose to destroy him, along with beasts, creeping things, and birds of the heavens. gemstone: which is the second death." Revelation 21:8

But Noah found grace in the eyes of Yahuah." Genesis 6:5-8

"But the day of Yahuah will come as a thief in the night: in which the heavens shall pass away with a great noise, and the elements shall melt with fervent heat, the earth also and the works that are therein shall be burned up. Seeing then that all these things shall be dissolved, what manner of persons ought ye to be in all holy conduct and righteousness." II Peter 3:11-12

Before Yahushua was born, Yahuah accepted animal blood sacrifices for atonement, not human blood. Cain, who killed his brother Abel, was marked by Elohim. Elohim abhors murder. Yahuah tested Abraham by asking him to sacrifice Isaac but stopped him before any harm was done to his son. Yahuah disapproves of shedding innocent blood.

"And the Angel of Yahuah called unto him out of the heavens, and said, Abraham, Abraham: And he said, here am I. And He said, Lay not thine hand upon the lad, neither do thou anything unto him: for now I know that thou fearest Elohim, seeing thou hast not withheld thy son, thine only from Me. And Abraham lifted up his eyes, and looked, and behold behind him a ram caught in a thicket by his horns: And Abraham went and took the ram and offered him up for a burnt offering in the stead of his son." Genesis 22:11-13

Fourteen generations ago, YAH sent His only begotten son, Yahushua, to teach us about Him, pay our sinful debt, and bestow upon us eternal life. The idea of animal sacrifices to pay for our sins didn't sit well with Him. Why should innocent animals suffer for our mistakes? Instead, YAH chose to become human and sacrifice Himself for us. That's how much He loves us.

"To what purpose is the multitude of your sacrifices unto Me? Saith Yahuah; I am full of the burnt offerings of rams, and fat of fed beasts; and I delight not in the blood of bullocks, or lambs, or of the goats." Isaiah 1:11

The arrival of Yahushua, the man-child, was not just a defeat of Satan, but a profound testament to the unmatched power of Yahuah. His selfless act on the cross symbolized the triumph of light over darkness, inspiring awe and reverence. Let's unite to celebrate and honor YAH for this extraordinary gift.

YAH took on human form through Yahushua and filled Him with His Holy Spirit, an incorruptible seed. Miriam (Mary), Yahushua's mother, played a vital role in nurturing the world's savior.

Every woman should acknowledge her ability to bring forth Yahuah's Word. Each woman holds power, authority, a voice, and unique strength, serving as a channel for divine wisdom, a foe of Satan, a minister of the Holy Word, influences others through Teaching and example. You are precious, and no one should convince you otherwise.

YAH, the Living Word, is manifested in Yahushua, embodying Yahuah's Spirit, possessing free will, and described as Yahuah's only begotten Son, the woman's seed.

Yahushua's sacrifice, a monumental act, not only symbolized the end of blood sacrifices but also liberated us from the shackles of human traditions. This is a cause for immense celebration and a testament to the power of YAH's love.

"For Yahuah sent not His Son into the world to condemn the world, but that the world through Him might be saved." John 3:17

John the Baptizer was a forerunner of Yahushua, a voice that cried out in the wilderness: Repent.

"And he came into all the country about Jordan, preaching the immersion of repentance for the remission of sins; As it is written in the book of the words of Isaiah the prophet, saying, The voice of one crying in the wilderness, Prepare ye the way of Yahuah, make straight in the desert a highway for our Elohim. Every valley shall be exalted, and every mountain and hill shall be brought low, and the crooked shall be made straight and the rough places plain. And all flesh shall see the salvation of Yahuah." Luke 3:3-6

John was baptizing believers in the Jordan River when Yahushua, in His divine obedience, approached him to be baptized. Upon seeing Him, John recognized Yahushua and hesitated to baptize Him, feeling unworthy. He openly confessed his unworthiness, stating that he was not even fit to untie Yahushua's shoelaces. John believed that it was he who needed to be baptized by Yahushua. However, Yahushua, always obedient to the Father's will, instructed John to baptize Him to fulfill the scripture.

"Yahushua when He was immersed, went up straightway out of the water: and lo, the heavens were opened up unto Him, and He saw the Spirit of Yahuah descending like a dove, and lighting upon Him: And lo a voice from heaven, saying, This is My beloved Son, in Whom I am well pleased." Matthew 3:16 -17

Through baptism, we symbolize our beloved Yahushua's profound sacrifice, burial, and triumphant resurrection.

"Therefore we are buried with Him by immersion into death: that like as the Messiah was raised from the dead by the glory of the Father, even so we also should walk in newness of life. For if we have been planted together in the likeness of His death, we shall be also in the likeness of His resurrection:" Romans 6:4-5

Yahushua faced the devil's temptations in the wilderness but emerged victorious and sinless. He refused every advance made by Satan and resisted him at every turn. With Yahushua's help, we can also gain the strength to rebuke and resist the devil. We should learn from Yahushua's example and stand firm against the enemy's tricks.

"Again, the adversary taketh Him up into an exceeding high mountain, and showeth Him all the kingdoms of the world, and the glory of them; And saith unto Him, All these things will I give Thee, if Thou wilt fall down and worship me. Then saith Yahushua unto him, Get thee hence, Satan: For it is written, "Thou shalt worship Yahuah thy Elohim and Him only shalt thou serve. Then the adversary leaveth Him, and Behold, angels came and ministered unto Him." Matthew 4:8-11

"Submit yourselves therefore to Yahuah. Resist the adversary, and he will flee from you. Draw nigh to Yahuah, and He will draw nigh to you. Cleanse your hands, ye sinners: and purify your hearts, ye doubleminded." James 4:7-8

Satan continues to use the same tactics today. He leads people into temptation, especially when they feel vulnerable or have a challenging experience. Then he offers his help. However, we should not accept it. Why would we seek help from someone whose purpose is to tempt, steal, kill, and destroy us?

On the other hand, Yahushua lived a sinless life and grew strong in grace with both man and Elohim. He came to redeem and save humankind from their sins and the eternal death of the spirit, bringing the "marvelous light" that comes only from YAH.

"And Yahushua increased in wisdom and stature, and in favour with Yahuah and man." Luke 2:52

"For in that He Himself hath suffered being tempted, He is able to succor them that are tempted." Hebrews 2:18

It can be tough to face the same daily challenges, mainly when our weaknesses are being targeted. It can be challenging to resist our temptations, but it's important to remember that true strength comes from above. Let us seek wisdom to guide us better. Remember, YAH is the way, and He never gives a believer more than they can handle; you can find strength in this. HalleluYAH.

But the wisdom from above is first pure, then peaceable, gentle, and easy to be entreated, full of mercy and good fruits, without partiality, and without hypocrisy." James 3:1

"If any man lacks wisdom, let him ask of Yahuah, Who giveth to all men liberally, and upbraideth not; and it shall be given him. James 1:5

It is essential to have the whole armor of YAH and Yahushua's blood to stay protected and provided for in battles our natural eyes can't even see. YAH's Holy Spirit empowers us to resist the wiles of the Devil and stand firm. This steadfastness enables us to help others, and we must hold onto it tightly!

'Finally, my brethren, be strong in Yahuah and the power of His might. Please put on all of Elohim's armor; you may be able to stand against the adversary's wiles. For we wrestle not against flesh and blood, but principalities, against powers, against the world rulers of this darkness, against spiritual wickedness in high places." Ephesians 6:10-12

Remember this: Satan often tries to isolate people and use their past mistakes against them. He delights in bringing up past failures. But the next time Satan tries to remind you of your past, and you have repented of that mistake, confidently remind him that the Blood of Yahushua has covered your sins. Instead of dwelling on the past, whether good, bad, or ugly, focus on moving forward and wholeheartedly worshiping Yahushua. No matter your wrong if you come to Yahushua, repent, and worship Him in Spirit and Truth, Yahushua will forgive and save you."

"Brethren, I count not myself to have apprehended: but this one thing I do, forgetting those things which are behind, and reaching forth unto those things "which are before." Philippians 3:13.

For Elohim is a Spirit, and they who worship Him must worship Him in spirit and in truth." John 4:24

Confronting the challenges presented by evil in our world is a daunting task. However, we can find solace in the understanding that through repentance and salvation, we can overcome these challenges and embrace a new life filled with strength and authority. In the face of evil's relentless efforts, it is crucial to remember the importance of patience, both with ourselves and others, as we navigate these hardships. Equally important is seeking support from those around us and looking to YAH for peace and victory.

A Poem to Yahuah

After the first miracle, Yahuah, for me, that would have been enough,

But your son Yahushua went on to the cross to save your people who were lost.

Yahushua set the captive free, and I know, Dear Father, this included me,

He walked the water and calmed the sea,

For a long time, I was blind and could not

see, Your divine love you have for me.

It was by your son Yahushua's stripes I am healed, It was you father, Yahuah, who made me well.

Such good news I have to tell,

And give you my heart before the trumpets are blown,

And you roll away the sky like a scroll, as the Bible says.

Since I gave my heart to Yahuah, He has been so very sweet,

There is no one better Yahuah than you; through Yahushua, your Son that I could ever meet.

You have made me stronger and my life complete,

Like Mary, Yahushua, I will bow at your feet in heaven.

Thank you, Yahushua, for shedding your blood; oh, what love.

Thank you, Yahushua, for helping me understand,

And for every time you took me by the hand and led me through this land.

Thank you for all the times that I was in trouble, and you sent help on the double,

When I was afraid, and evil was near, Yahuah, you sent your Holy Spirit to remind me that I was not alone,

But through Yahushua, you were there.

When I wanted to give up, you let me know in you, I could trust,

When I let you in my heart, you proved to be more than just a friend,

When I was down, burdened with guilt and shame, with your love, my spirit you did lift.

When I wanted to do my own thing, love, grace, mercy, and truth abounded,

Showing me, it was like you, I was supposed to be.

You made the universe, the sun, and the moon, slung the stars across the sky,

And dried-up tears that fell from my eyes.

You made the earth, ocean seas, the cattle of a thousand hills, butterflies, and the bees,

With all my heart and in every way, thank you, Yahuah, for making me.

You gave me life and made me your bride; in your chariots of fire, I will someday ride,

Seated by your side.

I will walk the streets of gold. The pearly gates one day with my hands, I will hold,

And be seated along with my other sisters and brothers.

Through the blood of Yahushua and believing, dear Father, you made us able.

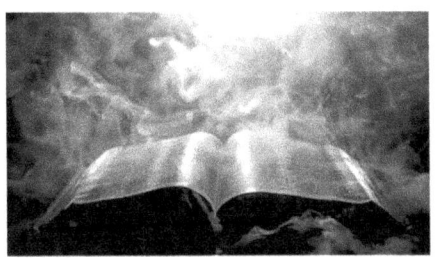

CHAPTER 12

TRUST THE TEACHINGS OF YAH-YAHUSHUA

In this chapter, we witness the true essence of YAH through His Son, Yahushua. Recognizing that YAH is not like humans, who can lie or change their minds, is crucial. He is unwavering in His ways and always faithful to His Word.

You might wonder who YAH-Yahushua is, and that's a valid question. Let's explore this journey of discovery together. Interestingly, this is the same question Pharaoh asked Moses when he was told to free YAH's people. Having questions and seeking understanding is normal, and I'm here to help you search for answers.

"1 And afterward Moses and Aaron went in and told Pharaoh. Thus saith the LORD God of Israel, Let my people go, that they may hold a feast unto me in the wilderness.

² And Pharaoh said, Who is the LORD, that I should obey his voice to let Israel go. I know not the LORD, neither will I let Israel go. Exodus 5:1-2

YAH sent ten plagues to convince Pharaoh to release His people, and you can read about them in Exodus Chapters 6 through 12

During a difficult time for the Egyptian people, Pharaoh made things more complicated for the Hebrews. They complained to Moses, feeling that despite witnessing the mighty works of YAH, he was making their situation worse. This is similar to many people today, who grow impatient and complain while waiting for YAH to act.

The situation worsened for the Egyptians, and Pharaoh eventually permitted YAH's people to leave. However, before this happened, YAH had to kill all the firstborns of the Egyptian people, including Pharaoh's son, before he allowed His people to leave.

"And it came to pass, that at midnight the LORD smote all the firstborn in the land of Egypt, from the firstborn of Pharaoh that sat on his throne unto the firstborn of the captive that was in the dungeon; and all the firstborn of cattle." Exodus 12:29 They left, carrying their belongings for the journey!

> [17] "And it came to pass when Pharaoh had let the people go, that God led them not through the way of the land of the Philistines, although that was near; for God said, Lest peradventure the people repent when they see war, and they return to Egypt:
>
> [18] But God led the people about, through the way of the wilderness of the Red sea: and the children of Israel went up harnessed out of the land of Egypt.

¹⁹ And Moses took the bones of Joseph with him: for he had straitly sworn the children of Israel, saying, God will surely visit you, and ye shall carry up my bones away hence with you.

²⁰ And they took their journey from Succoth, and encamped in Etham, in the edge of the wilderness.

²¹ And the LORD went before them by day in a pillar of a cloud, to lead them the way; and by night in a pillar of fire, to give them light; to go by day and night:

²² He took not away the pillar of the cloud by day, nor the pillar of fire by night, from before the people."

The Hebrew people, filled with joy at their liberation, were soon faced with what seemed like a dead end. It's a feeling all too familiar to believers when hope seems distant. Some may be tempted to give up, but those who believe in YAH can achieve victory. The story takes a thrilling twist as we explore what YAH did to Pharaoh and his army. When the Israelites thought they were safe, Pharaoh changed his mind and pursued them. In their panic and complaints, they yearned for familiarity with Egypt. Little did they know, YAH had a plan! Prepare to be surprised as we uncover what it was.

⁸ "And the LORD hardened the heart of Pharaoh king of Egypt, and he pursued after the children of Israel: and the children of Israel went out with a high hand.

⁹ But the Egyptians pursued after them, all the horses and chariots of Pharaoh, and his horsemen, and his army, and overtook them encamping by the sea, beside Pihahiroth, before Baalzephon.

¹⁰ And when Pharaoh drew nigh, the children of Israel lifted up their eyes, and behold, the Egyptians marched after them; and they were sore afraid: and the children of Israel cried out unto the LORD.

¹¹ And they said unto Moses, Because there were no graves in Egypt, hast thou taken us away to die in the wilderness? wherefore hast thou dealt thus with us, to carry us forth out of Egypt?

¹² Is not this the word that we did tell thee in Egypt, saying, Let us alone, that we may serve the Egyptians? For it had been better for us to serve the Egyptians, than that we should die in the wilderness. ¹³ And Moses said unto the people, Fear ye not, stand still, and see the salvation of the LORD, which he will shew to you today: for the Egyptians whom ye have seen today, ye shall see them again no more forever.

¹⁴ The LORD shall fight for you, and ye shall hold your peace.

¹⁵ And the LORD said unto Moses, Wherefore criest thou unto me? speak unto the children of Israel, that they go forward:

¹⁶ But lift thou up thy rod, and stretch out thine hand over the sea, and divide it: and the children of Israel shall go on dry ground through the midst of the sea.

¹⁷ And I, behold, I will harden the hearts of the Egyptians, and they shall follow them: and I will get me honour upon Pharaoh, and upon all his host, upon his chariots, and upon his horsemen.

¹⁸ And the Egyptians shall know that I am the LORD, when I have gotten me honour upon Pharaoh, upon his chariots, and upon his horsemen.

¹⁹ And the angel of God, which went before the camp of Israel, removed, and went behind them; and the pillar of the cloud went from before their face, and stood behind them:

²⁰ And it came between the camp of the Egyptians and the camp of Israel; and it was a cloud and darkness to them, but it gave light by night to these: so that the one came not near the other all the night.

²¹ And Moses stretched out his hand over the sea; and the LORD caused the sea to go back by a strong east wind all that night, and made the sea dry land, and the waters were divided.

²² And the children of Israel went into the midst of the sea upon the dry ground: and the waters were a wall unto them on their right hand, and on their left.

²³ And the Egyptians pursued and went in after them to the midst of the sea, even all Pharaoh's horses, his chariots, and his horsemen.

²⁴ And it came to pass, that in the morning watch the LORD looked unto the host of the Egyptians through the pillar of fire and of the cloud, and troubled the host of the Egyptians,

²⁵ And took off their chariot wheels, that they drive them heavily: so that the Egyptians said, Let us flee from the face of Israel; for the LORD fighteth for them against the Egyptians.

²⁶ And the LORD said unto Moses, Stretch out thine hand over the sea, that the waters may come again upon the Egyptians, upon their chariots, and upon their horsemen.

²⁷ And Moses stretched forth his hand over the sea, and the sea returned to his strength when the morning appeared; and the Egyptians fled against it; and the LORD overthrew the Egyptians in the midst of the sea.

²⁸ And the waters returned, and covered the chariots, and the horsemen, and all the host of Pharaoh that came into the sea after them; there remained not so much as one of them.

²⁹ But the children of Israel walked upon dry land in the midst of the sea, and the waters were a wall unto them on their right hand, and on their left.

³⁰ Thus the LORD saved Israel that day out of the hand of the Egyptians, and Israel saw the Egyptians dead upon the seashore." Why did I share this story with you? It demonstrated that YAH is faithful to His people and His Word, as shown in the Old Testament. Let's move to the New Testament to learn who YAH- Yahushua is. John the Baptist, a forerunner of Yahushua, bore witness to His authenticity and preached to people to repent. He informed believers of the coming Messiah, which was a noble assignment. While baptizing the people, he saw Yahushua coming and immediately acknowledged Him as the Lamb of Yahuah.

"And looking upon Yahushua as He walked, he said, Behold the Lamb of Yahuah!" John 1:36

'These things were said in Bethabara beyond Jordan, where John was immersing. The next day, John seeth Yahushua coming unto him, and saith, Behold the Lamb of Yahuah, which taketh away the sin of the world! This is He of whom I said, After me cometh a Man Who is preferred before me; for He was before me.

And I knew Him not: but that He should manifest to Israel, therefore am I come immersing with water.

And John bore record saying, I saw the Spirit descending from heaven like a dove, and it abode upon Him.

And I knew Him not: but He that sent me to immerse with water, the same said unto me, Upon whom thou shalt see the Spirit descending, and remaining on Him, the same is He which shall immerse you with the Holy Spirit.'

And I saw, and bear record that this is the Lamb of Yahuah! St John 1:28-33

"Elohim is not a man that He should lie; neither the son of man that He should repent: hath He said, and shall He not do it? Or hath He spoken, and shall He not make it good?' Numbers 23:19

To truly embrace Yahushua's teachings, believers are encouraged to approach with humility, acknowledging their shortcomings, seeking forgiveness and accepting salvation in Yahushua's name. It is also a time for them to partake in baptism and be open to receiving His Spirit. Through this process, Yahushua will help to transform their thinking, guiding them to adopt His mindset, resist negative influences, and release any harmful thoughts that may hinder their spiritual growth.

"And be not conformed to this world: But be ye transformed by the renewing of your mind, that ye may prove what is that good, and acceptable, and perfect will of Yahuah." Romans 12:2

YAH diligently watches over His Word to ensure its fulfillment. Every declaration by YAH will unquestionably come to pass; you can have complete confidence and trust in this. YAH watches over His Word to perform it. Everything YAH says will always come to pass; you can trust and believe this.

"So shall My word be that goeth forth out of My mouth: It shall not return unto Me void, but it shall accomplish that which I pleased, and it shall prosper in the thing whereto I sent it.' Isaiah 55:11

Yahuah, the Eternal, is always deeply concerned about the lives of believers, regardless of what they may be going through. He desires to be present with them in difficult times, to unite and celebrate with them when they overcome the enemy, Satan. We can always trust in the unbreakable unity and love of Yahuah and His Son, Yahushua, who are not just our guides but our spiritual family in every situation. Yahuah and His Son are one, and They also desire His children, His faithful servants, and His beloved sheep to be one with Him. Yahuah is the Good Shepherd who always lovingly looks after His flock.

"And the glory which Thou gavest Me I have given them; that they may be one, even as We are One:" John 17:22

Yahushua died and was raised three days later from the grave. Many people witnessed this. He did not leave us without comfort when He ascended back to Heaven. He sent His Holy Spirit to earth to teach us and help us remember everything He had taught us through His Word while He was on this earth.

But the Comforter, which is the Holy Spirit, whom the Father will send in My Name, shall teach you all things, and bring all things to your remembrance, what Yahushua taught us to know and trust His Father Yahuah. Yahushua is Love, peace, joy, faith, and hope; He also gives forgiveness and salvation. He is the only way to our Heavenly Father and the only way to eternal life.

YAH is Love, and who can teach us better than Love Himself? I love Him, don't you?

Yahushua tells us that we must love one another; this is how He has chosen to let others know we are His children.

"Take heed that ye do not your aims before men, to be seen of them; of them; otherwise ye have no reward of your Father in heaven.

Therefore when thou doest thine aims, do not sound a trumpet before thee, as the hypocrites do in the synagogues and in the streets, that they may have glory of men. Verily I say unto you, they have their reward.

But when thou doest alms, let not thy left hand know what thy right-hand doeth.

That thine alms may be in secret: and thy Father which seeth in secret himself shall reward the openly.

And when thou prayest, thou shalt not be as the hypocrites; for they love to pray standing in the synagogues and in the corners of the streets, that may be seen of men. Verily I say unto you, they have their reward.

But when ye prayest enter into thy room, and when thou hast shut the door, pray to thy Father which seeth in secret; and thy Father which seeth in secret shall reward thee openly.

But when ye pray, use not vain repetitions, as the heathen do; for they think that they shall be heard for their much speaking. Be not ye therefore like unto them; for your Father knoweth what you have need of, before ye ask Him. Mathew 6: 1-8 "After this manner therefore pray ye:

Our Father which art in heaven, hallowed be Thy name.

Thy kingdom come; Thy will be done in art as it is done in heaven.

Give us this day our daily bread. And forgive us our debts, as we forgive our debtors.' Mathew 6: 9- 12

Feeling hurt, angry, or resentful when someone hurts you is a normal part of the human experience. However, it's important to recognize that forgiveness is a powerful tool for healing. It may not be easy, but I encourage you to take the necessary steps towards forgiveness. Remember, holding onto resentment can be harmful, while forgiveness can bring profound healing and peace to your mind, body, and soul. Forgiveness is an inward journey that may take time, but the sooner you start, the better. It's a process that benefits the offended more than the offender. You'll know you've genuinely forgiven when you can think about their hurtful actions without feeling fear, shame, or pain.

"And lead us away from temptation and deliver us from evil: for Thine is the Kingdom, and the power, and the glory, forever.

For if ye forgive men their trespass, your heavenly Father will also forgive you.

But if ye forgive not men their trespass, neither will your heavenly Father forgive you your trespasses. Matthew 6:13-15

Believers of the Most High understand and know this: the one who made our eyes can see, and the one who made our ears can hear. YAH, the Hebrew name for God, knows if we love genuinely or just for show. As believers, we should give without expecting anything in return. We should give with a sincere heart, not to be seen by others or praised by them. If we do so, the praise from others will be our only reward.

"Understand ye brutish among the people: and when will ye be wise? He that planted the ear, shall He not hear? He that formed the eye, can He not see."

All honor and glory belong to Yahushua's Holy Name. That's why it's crucial to be saved, know His name, and walk in the authority that He gave back to believers over two thousand years ago.

The enemy, Satan, still tries to keep this truth hidden and instill fear in YAH's believers. But he no longer holds the authority to do so. This is one of his most significant secrets; he has lost his dominion over the Earth. HalleluYAH! It's crucial for believers to awaken to this truth, to recognize their victory over the enemy. Unless we do, he will continue his deadly game for souls on planet Earth. But we, as believers, have the power to overcome.

But there's Good News for those lost in this world. They can experience a spiritual rebirth, a transformation of their inner being, and be free today. First, they must confess that they need what Yah offers through Yahushua, our Savior. Repent, forgive, be forgiven, and be baptized and filled with the Holy Spirit of YAH.

YAH desires for all to repent and receive His forgiveness. When a person does this, it's a transformative act that liberates them from the burden of unforgiveness. The enemy may whisper that forgiveness is beyond our capacity, but YAH never asks us to do the impossible. Forgiveness is not a mere feeling but a powerful act of faith and obedience. Embrace forgiveness because YAH commands it and experience the freedom it brings.

Today, the enemy deceives people by tormenting them with unforgiveness. He sits on people's shoulders and says, "You can never forget what they did to you! How are you ever going to be able to forget that?" Well, of course, you will only remember if you develop amnesia.

When a believer chooses not to hold an offense, wrongdoing, or a hurtful act against the person who hurt them, YAH gives them the strength to forgive and clear themselves of guilt. YAH takes away the pain the offense caused and replaces it with peace. It's irrelevant whether they ever see that person again. The offense no longer inflicts pain. YAH's strength and truth prevail, making the Devil's lies futile.

A believer may remember the offense, but it no longer has the power to hurt them because they have surrendered it to Master YAH. Once the offense is truly given to YAH, it no longer bears its weight. This act of surrender brings a profound sense of relief and freedom. HalleluYah!

"I can do all things through the Messiah Who strengtheneth me." Philippians 4:13

Yahuah loves us all and is always there to guide and support us. Sometimes, we may not feel His presence, but we should know He always looks out for us. Even if we reject Him, He still cares for us in ways we may not fully comprehend. However, it's crucial to remember that we have a choice in how we live our lives. This choice empowers us, but it also comes with responsibility. Rejecting Him may lead us down a path that could be harmful in the long run, but it's our choice to make. Let's aim to show love and compassion towards ourselves and others and to always keep an open mind toward the possibility of growth and forgiveness

"Behold the fowls of the air: for they sow not, neither do they reap, nor gather into barns; yet your heavenly Father feedeth them. Are ye not much better than they?' Matthew 6:26

Yahuah's love for us is unwavering, always there to guide and support us. There may be times when we don't feel His presence, but we can be certain He is always watching over us. Even if we choose to reject Him, His care for us continues, often in ways we can't fully grasp. However, it's essential to recognize the power we have to shape our lives. This choice not only empowers us but also carries a significant responsibility. While rejecting Him may lead us down a harmful path, the decision is ours to make. Let's strive to demonstrate His love by showing compassion to ourselves and others, and by remaining open to the potential for growth and forgiveness. In these acts, we truly reflect His love.

"Lay not up for yourselves treasures upon earth, where moth and rust doth corrupt, and where thieves do not break through and steal: For where your treasure is, there will your heart be also." Matthew 6:19-21

It is crucial to recognize how worry and doubt can work against us. They divert our focus from finding solutions to our daily challenges. Satan understands that doubting in the Most High displeases Him by indicating a lack of faith. We should only anticipate receiving something from the Most High when we do not doubt. My husband often says, "When we doubt, we go without.

"But let him ask in faith, nothing wavering: for he, that wavers is like a wave of the sea driven with the wind and tossed. For let not that man think that he shall receive anything of Yahuah." James 1:6-7

When believers are worried, they must turn to prayer and place their trust in YAH. By believing in His faithfulness to His Word, we can find solace in knowing that He knows our needs and has provided guidance on how to receive them. His understanding of us surpasses our own, and we can rely on Him and His Word, which will endure even as Heaven and Earth pass away.

To live a victorious life, Yahushua taught His disciples and the multitudes to seek Him and put Him first. By letting His way be our way, He will provide everything we need.

"And He opened His mouth, and taught them saying,

Blessed are the poor in spirit; for theirs is the kingdom of Heaven.

Blessed are they that mourn because of sin; for they shall be comforted.

Blessed are the meek; for they shall inherit the earth.

Blessed are they who hunger and thirst after righteousness: for they shall be filled.

Blessed are the merciful: for they shall obtain mercy.

Blessed are the pure in heart: For they shall see Yahuah.

Blessed are the peacemakers: for they shall be called the children of Yahuah.

Blessed are they which are persecuted for righteousness sake: for theirs is the kingdom of Heaven'

Blessed are ye when men shall revile you, and persecute you, and shall say all manner of evil against you falsely, for my sake. Rejoice, and be exceeding glad: for great is your reward in Heaven: for so persecuted the prophets which were before you." Matthew 5:2-12

In times of worry, believers must turn to prayer and trust in YAH. By having faith in His Word, we can find comfort in knowing that He understands our needs and provides guidance to fulfill them. His understanding surpasses our own, and we can rely on Him and His enduring Word.

To lead a victorious life, Yahushua taught His disciples and the masses to seek Him and prioritize Him. By aligning our ways with His, He will provide everything we need. When believers are worried, they must turn to prayer and place their trust in YAH. By believing in His faithfulness to His Word, we can find solace in knowing that He knows our needs and has provided guidance on how to receive them. His understanding of us surpasses our own, and we can rely on Him and His Word, which will endure even as Heaven and Earth pass away.

To live a victorious life, Yahushua taught His disciples and the multitudes to seek Him and put Him first. By letting His way be our way, He will provide everything we need.

"Judah then, having received a band of men and officers from the chief priests and Pharisees, cometh thither with lanterns, torches, and weapons.

Yahushua, therefore, knowing all things that should come upon Him, went forth and said unto them, Whom seek ye?

They answered Him, Yahushua of Nazareth. Yahushua saith unto them, I am He. And Judah also, which betrayed Him, stood with them.

As soon then as He had said unto them, I am He, they went backward and fell to the ground.

Then He asked them again, Whom seek ye? And they said, Yahushua of Nazareth.

Yahushua answered, I have told you that I am He; If therefore ye seek Me, let these go their way:

That the saying might be fulfilled, which He spake, "Of them which Thou gavest Me have I lost none." John 18:3-9

He was taken from judgment hall to judgment hall, bearing the weight of the world's sins, including yours and mine. Satan believed he had the upper hand and sought to destroy Yahushua. Little did he know that Yahushua's blood would atone for the debt of sin owed by humankind since the time of Adam and Eve. This ultimate sacrifice granted freedom to all who believed in Him, empowering them to overcome the enemy.

Satan unjustly accused Yahushua of numerous charges and subjected Him to beatings, crucifixion, and even trials in hell.

However, these accusations were baseless, as the sins belonged to the entire world, including you and me, not Yahushua.

Before departing the realm of the dead, Yahushua took from Satan the keys of death. This act bestowed upon Yahushua gave Him power over hell and the grave. HalleluYah!"

"Behold what manner of love the Father hath bestowed upon us, that we should be called the children of Yahuah: therefore the world knoweth us not, because it knew Him not." 1 John 3:1

Yahushua rose from the dead with power and will return for his followers.

"If in this life only we have hope in the Messiah, we are of all men most miserable.

But now is the Messiah risen from the dead and become the first fruits of them that slept.

For since by man came death, by man also came the resurrection of the dead.

For as in Adam all die, even so in the Messiah shall all be made alive." I Corinthians 15:19-22

"Wherefore He said when He ascended up on high, He took captive captivity and gave gifts unto men.

(Now that He ascended, what is it but that He also descended first into the lower parts of the earth? He that descended is the same that ascended up far above all heavens, that He might fill all things). Ephesians 4:8-10

"For the Messiah also hath once suffered for sins, the just for the unjust, that He might bring us to Yahuah being put to death in the flesh, but quickened by the Spirit: By which also He preached unto the spirits in prison;" I Peter 3:18- 19

"And the great dragon was cast out, that old serpent, called the Devil, and Satan, which deceiveth the whole world: he was cast out into the earth, and his angels were cast out with him." Revelation 12:10

Yahushua, our Messiah and Savior, has paid the ultimate price to redeem us from sin. By embracing His teachings, we can attain everlasting life with Him. As Paul once said, placing our trust in Yahushua and following His teachings is the key to salvation. Reading this chapter in this book will demonstrate that Yahushua is not just trustworthy but fully capable of delivering you from the enemy. HalleluYah!

"If this gospel is untrue then we are as a people most misery. But if it is true and we endure YAH will give us a crown of glory!" 1Corinthians 9:17

One day, we will leave Earth. It is essential to come to terms with this reality and prepare to embrace eternity with Elohim, the Almighty God, by seeking forgiveness for our mistakes and embracing Yahushua's plan of Salvation. Our time on Earth is fleeting; even a lifespan of over a hundred years is brief in the grand scheme of eternity.

Reading this chapter in this book shows you that YAH-Yahushua teaching can be trusted and is more than able to deliver you from the enemy. HalleluYah!

I am Not in the Mood

I am not in the mood to be ruled or fooled by you, Satan.

Not by the drugs that you make in your labs, leaving me to pick up the tabs

Not by your alcohol that could take away my health, leaving me with nothing left.

Devil, I am just not in the mood to be used nor abused, not by sex or any other hoax.

I am just not pleased with your behavior.

I am sticking with Yahushua, the one who loves me, my Savior.

Written by Nona McCollough© 1999

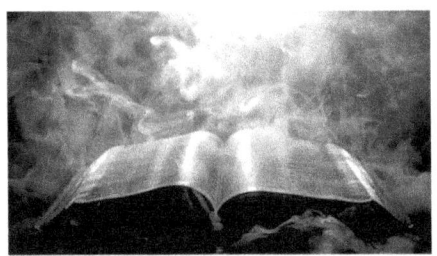

CHAPTER 13

ALL THINGS ARE POSSIBLE FOR THOSE WHO BELIEVE

The following Chapter will delve into the profound impact of Yahushua, the Messiah and the Son of Yahuah. His actions on Earth in human form were outstanding, remarkable, and awesome, and his influence continues to the present day. I want to demonstrate to believers the ways in which they, too, can carry out works similar to those of Yahushua and even surpass them in quantity, not quality, through the guidance of the Holy Spirit, who is also Yahuah.

Following Yahushua's resurrection and ascension, he bestowed upon us an invaluable gift that Satan attempted to conceal. On the Day of Pentecost, he sent his Holy Spirit to Earth, an event that reshaped our world, filling it with awe and wonder. It feels as though Yahushua is still present with us, albeit in Spirit, empowering us with His divine presence.

When Yahushua left Earth in bodily form, he did not leave us without hope. He restored authority to believers, reclaiming it from Satan, a truth that Satan desperately tries to conceal.

Satan's rule no longer prevails on Earth unless we willingly surrender to it. This restoration of authority should give us reassurance and confidence in our spiritual journey, empowering us to stand firm against the forces of evil.

Believers are no longer defenseless against our mortal enemy; we need not be at odds with one another. We have been gifted with the Holy Spirit and the power to genuinely forgive, love, and overcome the Devil and his followers. The gift of speaking in tongues, a spiritual language given by the Holy Spirit, is bestowed upon believers to confound the enemy and to show unbelievers the power of YAH. This gift allows believers to communicate uniquely with YAH and others who speak different languages, illustrating the universality of YAH's love and message.

Although various languages were spoken on Pentecost, people understood one another, transcending linguistic barriers. Believers have been graced with a powerful, extraordinary, and precious gift - the ability to communicate and understand each other by interpreting the Holy Spirit.

We need to remain united in matters concerning Yahushua. YAH's Spirit once again reigns supreme on Earth, just as when Yahushua was in bodily form. He operates through every believer's Spirit, body, mind, heart, and life. YAH is the ultimate authority of the nations, and the government is upon His shoulders, a metaphor that signifies His ability to bear the weight of responsibility. He told us to cast our burdens upon Him because He cares for us.

Believers in Yahuah are His people and the power of the Holy Spirit that He has given us enables us to be witnesses for Him, sharing His love, teachings, and miracles with the world.

And when the day of Pentecost was fully come, they were all with one accord in one place.

Suddenly there came a sound from heaven as of a rushing mighty wind, and it filled all the house where they were sitting.

And there appeared unto them cloven tongues like as of fire and rested upon them.

And they were all filled with the Holy Spirit and began to speak with other tongues, as the Spirit gave them utterance. Acts 2:1-4

I want to share what the Scriptures say about specific works believers can perform. But before that, let me tell you about a parable that Yahushua gave to His disciples. Through this parable, you will understand why some people are healed and receive the benefits of salvation while others do not.

"And He began to teach by the seaside: and there was gathered unto Him a great multitude so that He entered into a ship, and sat in the sea, and the whole multitude was by the sea on the land.

And He taught them many things by parables and said unto them in His doctrine.

Hearken; Behold, there went out a sower to sow;

And it came to pass, as he sowed, some fell by the wayside, and the fowls of the air came and devoured it up.

And some fell on stony ground, where it had not much earth; and immediately it sprang up, because it had no depth of the earth.

But when the sun was up, it was scorched; and because it had no root, it withered away.

And some fell among thorns, and the thorns grew up, and choked it, and it yielded no fruit.

And others fell on good ground, and did yield fruit that sprang up and increased, and brought forth some thirty and some sixty and some a hundred.

And He said unto them, he that hath ears to hear, let him hear.

And when He was alone, they that were about Him with the twelve asked of him the parable. And He said unto them,

Unto you it is given to know the mystery of the Kingdom of Yahuah: but unto them that are without, all these things are done in parables:

In order that, seeing they may see, and not perceive, and hearing they may hear, and not understand; lest at any time they should be converted, and their sins should be forgiven them.

And he said unto them, Know ye not this parable? And how then will ye know any parables?

The sower soweth the word,

And these are they by the wayside, where the word is sown; but when they had heard, the adversary cometh immediately, and taketh away the word that was sown in their hearts.

And these are they likewise which are sown on stony ground; who, when they have heard the word immediately receive it with gladness;

And have no root in themselves, and so endured but for a time; afterward, when affliction or persecution ariseth for the word's sake, immediately they are offended.

And these are they which are sown among thorns; such as hear the word.

And the cares of this age, and the deceitfulness of riches, and the lust of other things entering in choke the word, and it becometh unfruitful.

And these are they which are sown on good ground; such as hear the word, and receive it, and bring forth fruit, some thirtyfold, some sixty, and some a hundred." Mark 4:1-20

To receive YAH's Word, one must be willing to listen and possess a heart with a strong desire to understand Yahushua, the Word of Yahuah.

The journey to understanding YAH's Word in today's world may seem complex, but it all begins with a profound transformation, a rebirth that enables us to house the Spirit of our Creator. This divine intervention, a direct and miraculous act of YAH, equips born- again believers with a unique understanding and interpretation of His Word, allowing them to perceive, discern, and comprehend the truth guided by the Holy Spirit of YAH.

Without this divine intervention, those lost in their sins may benefit from the Word without truly dedicating their heart and soul to YAH, ultimately using it for personal gain. Their lack of a proper understanding of the Word's purpose leaves them unable to correct, heal, rebuke, or lead to righteousness and chastisement, deliver the captive, or make a person accessible. However, when the transformative power of YAH's Word is embraced, profound changes can occur, empowering us to live a purposeful and righteous life.

A world of blessings unfolds when a believer's heart is genuinely aligned with YAH, free of self-interest, and filled with love for Him. This authentic commitment enriches their lives and empowers them to share these blessings with others, fostering a sense of joy and fulfillment in our shared journey. They become vessels of YAH's grace, continuing Yahushua's work by healing the sick, raising the dead, and guiding the lost through the power of YAH's Word and Spirit, creating a sense of community and belonging in our shared mission.

By doing so, they bless themselves and help others be ready for their blessings. Let us consider the story of the woman with the issue of blood, a compelling testament to the transformative power of YAH's Word. Despite her physical ailment and societal barriers, her faith in YAH and her determination to touch the hem of Yahushua's garment led to her healing. This story, among other examples of such individuals, shows us how YAH's Word transforms lives and enables us to participate in this transformative journey.

"A certain woman, which had an issue of blood twelve years, And had suffered many things of many physicians, and had spent all that she had, and was nothing bettered, but rather grew worse. When she heard of Yahushua, came in the press behind, and touched His garment. For she said, if I may touch but His clothes, I shall be whole. And straightway the fountain of her blood was dried up; and she felt in her body that she was healed of the plague. And Yahushua, immediately knowing in Himself that power had gone out of Him, turned about in the press, and said, Who touched My clothes? And His disciples said unto Him, Thou seest the multitude thronging Thee, and sayest Thou, who touched Me? And He looked around about to see her that had done this thing. But the woman fearing and trembling, knowing what was done in She came and fell down before Him and told Him all the truth. And he said unto her, Daughter, thy faith hath made thee whole; go in peace and be whole of thy plague." Mark 5:25-34

Countless stories bear witness to the fact that faith can move mountains and heal the sick. One such powerful story is about a woman who, despite being afflicted by a blood issue, was made whole by the miraculous touch of Yahushua. Her unshakeable faith and confidence in Yahushua's healing power made all the difference, reassuring us of His unwavering love and care.

Today, we are blessed with the opportunity to connect with our Messiah on a personal level. He is not distant or unreachable, but rather, He eagerly awaits our invitation into our hearts through repentance, confession, and understanding of His true nature. Just as the woman in the story had unwavering faith, He desires our faith. Your faith, like hers, has the power to touch the Messiah's heart and bring about the healing you seek.

While there are countless stories like this, each one a testament to the incredible power of faith, I am compelled to share with you a man's story. He was healed and delivered, even though it seemed he did nothing to warrant it. Remember, it is your faith that moves YAH, and with unwavering confidence, you, too, can move mountains and experience the miraculous healing power of Yahushua. HalleluYah!

"And they came over unto the other side of the sea, into the country of the Gadareness. And when he was come out of the ship, immediately there met him out of the tomb a man with an unclean spirit. Who had been dwellings among the tombs and no man could bind him, no, not with chains. Because that he had been often bound with fetters and chains, and the chains had been plucked asunder by him, and the fetters broken in pieces: neither could any man tame him.

And always night and day, he was in the mountains, and in the tombs crying and cutting himself with stones. But when he saw Yahushua afar off, he ran and worshipped Him And cried with a loud voice, and said, what have I to do with thee, Yahushua, thou son of the Most High El? I adjure thee by Elohim, that thou torment me not. For He said unto him, come out of the man, thou unclean spirit And he asked him what is thy name? And he answered, saying, my name is Legion: for we are many. And he besought him much that He would not send them away out of the country. Now there was there nigh unto the mountain a great herd of swine feeding. And all the demons besought Him saying; Send us into the swine, that we may enter into them. And forthwith Yahushua gave them leave. And the unclean spirits went out and entered into the swine; and the herds ran violently down a steep place into the sea, (they about two thousands, and were choked in the sea.

And they that fed the swine fled and told it in the city, and in the country. And they went out to see what it was that was done. And they come to Yahushua, and see him that was possessed with demons, and had had the legion sitting and clothed, and in his right mind; they were afraid." Mark 5: 1-15

This story is about a powerful transformation. There was once a man who suffered in isolation, tormented by demons. However, his spirit found freedom when our Savior heard his cries and came to his rescue. With Yahushua's authority and support, the man was liberated from the demons that had held him captive for so long.

This story is a testament to the strength of faith and the possibility of deliverance. Always remember, you are never alone. Yah is always watching and listening. If you ever feel caught in the grip of darkness, take comfort in knowing that Yahushua is here, ready to offer His help and deliverance. He does not discriminate and is always prepared to embrace your soul with His Holy Spirit. Feeling overwhelmed and lost at times is a natural response to life's challenges, temptations, and loneliness.

However, remember that everything is possible for those who believe. If you have ever turned away from the light, it's never too late to turn back and embrace Yahushua. He is here to comfort troubled hearts, free you from oppression and rejection, and allow you to return to the light. Always remember that Yahushua's compassion knows no bounds, and He is always prepared to help those in need.

I Am Trying

Sometimes, I speak when I should listen.

Sometimes, wrong things make my eyes glisten

But I am trying! Sometimes,

I run when I should be still.

And hear what YAH says and do His will But

I am trying!

Sometimes, I mean when I want to be sweet and when I should be kind.

But I am trying!

Sometimes, I get into things I should not

And trouble is what I got.

But no matter what, I am going to keep on believing,

I am going to keep on

trying!

Written by Nona McCollough© 1996

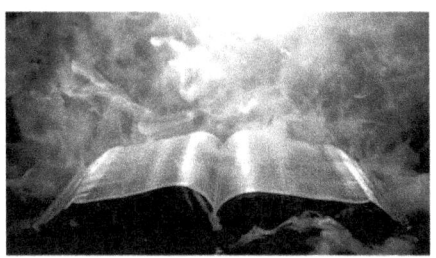

CHAPTER 14

YAHUSHUA VICTORY OVER HELL AND THE GRAVE

Yahushua, the Anointed One, upheld His anointing on earth through unwavering obedience to the Father and the fulfillment of His divine purpose. Despite facing trials in every form, He emerged triumphant and untainted by sin. His victory over temptation stands as a beacon of hope and a testament to His strength, inspiring awe and reverence in us.

Throughout His earthly mission, Yahushua accomplished His task by willingly offering His life as a sacrifice, paying the debt of humanity's disobedience. Only through the unblemished blood of the Lamb of Yahushua could the power of sin be overcome, liberating humankind in a way that animal sacrifices could never achieve. This act of Yahushua's love, sacrifice, and unselfishness should fill our hearts with profound gratitude and humble us before His immense love and power.

Despite Satan's relentless attempts to hinder the birth, crucifixion, and resurrection of the Messiah, he was defeated every time. Yahushua triumphed and ascended to the Father's right hand with all power, grace, and truth. His mercy endures through all generations.

⁴⁵ Now from the sixth hour until the ninth hour there was darkness overall the land.

⁴⁶ And about the ninth hour Jesus cried out with a loud voice, saying, "Eli, Eli, lama sabachthani?" that is, "My God, My God, why have You forsaken Me?"

⁴⁷ Some of those who stood there when they heard that, said, "This

Man is calling for Elijah!"

⁴⁸ Immediately one of them ran and took a sponge, filled it with sour wine and put it on a reed, and offered it to Him to drink.

⁵⁰ The rest said, "Let Him alone; let us see if Elijah will come to save Him."

⁵¹ And Jesus cried out again with a loud voice and yielded up His spirit.
⁵² Then, behold, the veil of the temple was torn in two from top to bottom; and the earth quaked, and the rocks were split,

⁵³ and the graves were opened; and many bodies of the saints who had fallen asleep were raised;

⁵⁴ and coming out of the graves after His resurrection, they went into the holy city and appeared to many.

⁵⁵ So when the centurion and those with him, who were guarding Jesus, saw the earthquake and the things that had happened, they

feared greatly, saying, "Truly this was the Son of God!" Matthew 27:45-54

His mercy is still enduring upon all who will receive Him.

"He, seeing this before, spake of the resurrection of the Messiah, that His soul was not left in Sheol, neither did His flesh see corruption."

This is Yahushua hath Yahuah raised up, whereof we all are witnesses. Therefore, being by the right hand of Yahuah exalted and having received of the Father the promise of the Holy Spirit, he hath shed forth this, which ye now see and hear. For David is not ascended into heavens: but he saith himself, "Yahuah said unto my Eloah, Sit Thou on my right hand Until I make Thy foes Thy footstool. Act 2:31-35

Yahushua's resurrection is a beacon of hope and brings salvation to the world, embracing all, regardless of location or circumstances. The Word is a testament to Yahushua's victory over death, hell, and the grave and is a gift to all who believe and accept it. It affirms the universal love and acceptance of Yahushua.

The transformative power of love, a new paradigm bestowed upon us by YAH in His mercy through Yahushua, is the key to embracing this profound salvation and creating a better world for all. Love, as the guiding principle, not only illuminates the path to salvation but also empowers each of us to be agents of positive change.

While we cannot possess the absolute power that belongs to YAH, which is beyond our human comprehension and control,

He releases a portion of it to us through the blood sacrifice of His only begotten Son, Yahushua. This is a testament to His boundless love and mercy, as he eagerly awaits people to come to Him and receive what was theirs from the beginning, providing a comforting assurance of His unfailing love. To receive this salvation, believers must actively follow YAH-Yahushua's guidance. He has provided clear instructions on approaching Him, such as placing trust in Him and acknowledging Him in all aspects of life. He promises to guide their path and lead them to everlasting life, free from pain, suffering, and death, in His eternal kingdom.

"Trust in Yahuah with all thine heart; and lean not to thine own understanding. In all thy ways acknowledge Him, and He shall direct thy paths." Proverbs 3: 5- 6

When you give your heart to Yahushua on your life journey, get ready to receive abundant love, wisdom, peace, knowledge, forgiveness, strength, courage, and power. Trust and obey Yahushua, and He will take care of everything else. Let us give Him the glory and witness the King of Glory, Yahushua, in all His glory!

"I am Yahuah: that is My Name: and my glory will I not give to another, neither my praise to graven images." Isaiah 42:8 Who is the King of Glory? Yahuah of hosts, He is the King of glory. Selah!" Psalms 24: 10 Believers, it's crucial to remember that your choices and actions hold immense significance. They are not just a means to an end but the very key to achieving the right results. Your ability to discern and act wisely is not a burden but a source of empowerment directly linked to your relationship with the Almighty Creator, Yahuah.

Rest assured; you will never be misguided if you seek His guidance and follow His instructions. We no longer rely solely on our understanding thanks to Yahushua, our Savior and guide. We now have a written record of the Word given to us through the Apostles and Prophets, and even more importantly, Yahushua speaks to us through His Holy Spirit, the Truth. Do you remember when Pilate asked Yahushua what Truth was? Yahushua had already told him that He was the Truth. Let's not just give thanks and praise but do it with joy and gratitude by saying HalleluYah!

"Pilate therefore said unto Him, Art Thou a King then? Yahushua answered, Thou sayest it, for I am a King. To this end was I born, as for this cause came I into the world, that I should bear witness unto the Truth. Everyone that is of the truth heareth My voice.

Pilate said unto Him, What is Truth? And when he hath said this, he went out again unto the Jews, and said unto them, I find in Him no fault. But ye have a custom that I should release unto you one at the Passover: will ye therefore that I release unto you the King of the Jews?" (scriptures)

Then cried they again, saying, Not this man, but Barabbas. Now Barabbas was a robber" John 18:36-39

I am genuinely thankful for the love that YAH has shown me. His Love inspires me to love Him, and it warms my heart to hear others express their love for Him. Let us all rejoice in His love. "HalleluYah!"

"For as the new heavens and the new earth, which I will make shall remain before Me, saith Yahuah, so shall your seed and your name remain." Isaiah 66:22

YAH, through Yahushua, has revealed His profound desire for humankind. Have you ever wondered what Yahuah wants to give to His creation? It is the gift of eternal life – a testament to His boundless love – offered to all willing to accept Him. Love, the essence of Yahuah, is the path to everlasting life. There is no one better to guide us on this Spirit journey than Love Himself – the Almighty Elohim, who is YAH.

"A new commandment I give unto you, That ye love one another; as I have loved you, that ye also love one to another. By this shall all know that ye are My disciples if ye have love one to another." John 13:34- 35

As believers, we can confidently rely on the Holy Spirit to work in us according to YAH's will. While understanding conversion is essential, being filled with the Holy Spirit is crucial. When filled with the Holy Spirit, we yield ourselves to YAH and receive His empowerment to do His work. However, being filled with the Holy Spirit does not necessarily mean we are walking in the Spirit; hidden inner sins can lead to the loss of our souls, a consequence we must be acutely aware of. On judgment day, instead of welcoming us, YAH may say, "Depart from Me, you workers of iniquity," even if we have done great works on earth and in the church. Believers need to be vigilant against deceptive spirits.

"But ye are not in the flesh, but in the Spirit, if so be that the Spirit of Yahuah dwell in you. Now, if any man does not have the Spirit of the Messiah, He is none of His. And if the Messiah be in you, the body is dead because of sin; but the Spirit is alive because of righteousness." Romans 8:9-10

"But He shall say, I tell you, I know you not whence ye are; depart from me, all ye workers of iniquity. There shall be weeping and gnashing of teeth, when ye shall see Abraham, and Isaac, and Jacob, and all the prophets, in the Kingdom of Yahuah, and you yourselves thrust out.

"And they shall come from the east, and from the west, and from the north, and from the south, and shall sit down in the Kingdom of Yahuah. And behold, there are last which shall be first, and there are first which shall be last." Luke 13:27-30

The life of Yahushua, the embodiment of the Spirit of YAH, is a prime example of teaching through demonstration, fellowship, and mighty acts empowered by the Holy Spirit. Even though Yahushua, the son of Yahuah, experienced immense suffering, his disciples, initially frail and limited, were transformed after being filled with the Holy Spirit. This transformation is a testament to the impact of Yahushua's life and teachings, offering hope and empowerment to all. HalleluYAH! "But ye shall receive power after the Holy Spirit comes upon you: and ye shall be witnessed unto me both in Jerusalem, and in all Judea, and Samaria, and in unto the uttermost part of the earth." Act 1:8

"And when the day of Pentecost was fully come, they were all with one accord in one place. Suddenly, a sound from heaven, like a rushing mighty wind, filled the house where they were sitting. And appeared unto them cloven tongues like as of fire, and rest upon each of them. And they appeared unto them cloven tongues like fire and rested upon each of them. And they were filled with the Holy Spirit, and began to speak with other tongues, as the Spirit gave the utterance." Act 2:1-4

"Thinkest thou that I cannot now pray to My Father, and He shall presently give Me more than twelve legions of angels?" Matthew 26:53

Remember the importance of "keeping your peace," as our beloved Savior Yahushua emphasized. It is not just about appearing calm on the outside but about finding inner peace through trusting in Him. If you haven't already, I encourage you to open your heart to Him. When we humbly confess our sins, He forgives and purifies us. Embracing Him, confessing our wrongdoings, seeking forgiveness, and committing to live by His teachings bring His blessings and His Holy Spirit into our lives. The Holy Spirit empowers us, enabling us to be effective witnesses in Yahushua's name.

Yahuah's name is a label and a Mighty Tower of Refuge. The righteous find solace, safety, and profound peace in His name. Through His love, He takes our sins upon Himself and bestows upon us His righteousness. Let's rejoice in His name, HalleluYah.
Understanding what YAH's name is essential.

"Then said Yahushua, Father forgive them; for they know not what they do. And they parted His raiment and cast lots." Luke 23:34

The wicked rulers were oblivious to the fact that their evil deeds would also adversely affect them, and even Satan himself did not fully comprehend the consequences of his actions when he orchestrated the crucifixion of our Savior. If he had known, he would never have led to the death of our Messiah. Satan would not have used humans to torture the Son of YHUH - Yahuah.

Furthermore, he would not have had Him beaten, as it was through
His suffering that we find healing. Let us praise YHUH - HalleluYah!

"But we speak the wisdom of Yahuah hidden in a mystery, which Yahuah hath ordained before the ages unto our glory: Which none of the rulers of this age knew: for had they known it, they would not have crucified the King of Gory." 1 Corinthians 2:7- 8

Through the sacrifice of Yahushua, a human being, Yahuah found pleasure, and Satan was defeated. As a result, born-again believers have been granted authority over the enemy, just as it was in the time before the fall in the Garden of Eden. Let us join together in celebration and praise Yahuah! HalleluYah! "Surely he hath borne our pains and carried our diseases; yet we did esteem Him stricken, smitten of Elohim, and afflicted. But He was wounded for our transgressions, He was bruised for our iniquities; the chastisement of our peace was upon Him; and with His stripes, we are healed."
Isaiah 53:4-5

Notes

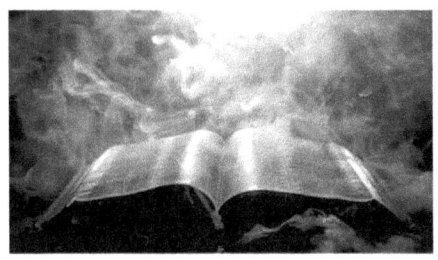

CHAPTER 15

CHOOSE THIS DAY WHOM YOU WILL SERVE

The remarkable accomplishments of Yahushua during his time on Earth is truly captivating and awe-inspiring. As a human being, he displayed an unparalleled level of righteousness and obedience to the will of Yahuah, which is undeniably remarkable. Despite facing numerous challenges and temptations, he remained steadfast in his commitment to follow the Law of Elohim. This is a testament to his divine nature and a powerful reminder of our potential to emulate him. It's essential to remember that despite the efforts of Satan and his followers undermine our faith by suggesting our unworthiness and incapability to meet Yahuah's expectations; this message is untrue and should be disregarded.

[12] "For we wrestle not against flesh and blood, but against principalities, against powers, against the rulers of the darkness of this world, against spiritual wickedness in high places." Ephesians 6:12

We are grateful that YAH had a plan to save us from our sins and shortcomings. He chose to come to Earth as a human being, born of Miriam and live among us as one of us. Yahushua embodied

YAH's grace and mercy; his birth was a testament to our Creator's infinite love for us. Through Yahushua, YAH showed us that even in our imperfections, we are still beloved and capable of doing great things. Yahushua's life and teachings continue to inspire and guide us, and we can take comfort in knowing that he is always with us, offering his love and support as we navigate this world.

"Who was born, not of blood, nor the will of man, but of Yahuah. And the Word was made flesh, and dwelt among us, (and we beheld His glory, the glory of the only begotten of the Father), full of grace and truth." John

The birth of Miriam's son, Yahushua, marked the ultimate triumph over evil. Through unwavering obedience to the Father, Yahushua vanquished Satan and granted humanity redemption, even in the face of the cross.

In a betraying act, Judas guided Roman soldiers to arrest Yahushua. When they confronted Him, stating "Yahushua of Nazareth," they were overpowered and fell to the ground. Yahushua willingly allowed his arrest after this demonstration of divine power, eventually facing Pontius Pilate.

Satan's influence persists, affecting innocent individuals striving to lead virtuous lives and follow YAH's commandments. Those who seek not to harm are frequently the primary targets of the Devil's evil intentions.

"The wicked watcheth the righteous, and seeketh to slay him. Yahuah will not leave him in his hand nor condemn him when. Wait on Yahuah, and keep his way, and He shall exalt thee to inherit the land: when the wicked are cut off, thou shalt see it. I have seen the wicked in great power and spreading himself like a green bay- tree. Yet he passed away, and lo, he was not: yea, I sought him, but he could not be found."

Mark the perfect man and behold the upright: for the end of that man is peace." Psalms 37:32-37

"Satan hates people, and he turns them against one another. It isn't very smart for anyone to do this. Do not be deceived into thinking that Satan loves you because he is incapable of love. He cannot forget his doom, and he wants to take as many souls as possible with him to hell. Satan despises Elohim Almighty God, who is also known by various names such as YHUH, YAHUAH, YAH, YAHUSHUA, or JESUS. These names represent different aspects of God's character and relationship with us. Yahushua's victory over Satan is a testament to His power and love. HalleluYAH!

YAH, in His infinite love and mercy, took our unworthiness and made us worthy to receive Him and everlasting life. This was made possible through His son Yahushua's sacrificial death on the cross, which paid the 'sin debt.' The 'sin debt' refers to the consequences of our sins that we cannot pay on our own. Therefore, Yahushua did it for us. Oh, what Love!

Below are poems in this chapter that reflect a different spiritual condition or struggles in which a person may find themselves. This poem is not just words on a page but a tool for spiritual reflection and transformation. They are meant to resonate and speak to the heart of anyone challenged in this area and guide them on their spiritual journey to deliverance and victory. If you resonate with any of these conditions, take them to heart, let them rest in your spirit, and allow YAH to make the change in you that you have been waiting for. There is hope for the drug dealers. I was inspired to write this poem on their behalf.

A Drug Dealer's Prayer

YAH, forgive me for all my wrongs. I'm away from home all the time, into the wee hours of the night, not doing right but wrong.

YAH, I still feel you near, and I know your love is so dear to your daughters and sons.

I am thinking about what I have done, causing many tears and holding people with fear.

I am dreading tomorrow that it will only bring sorrow.

Heavenly Father, day after day, I want to be free. Will you save me?

My prayer in Yahushua's name is, will you hear this sinner's prayer?

I have been pushing drugs to take care of my needs, doing all these evil deeds.

Yahushua, will you help me? It has been a hard fight; show me the light.

There is no rest for the weary when I'm not doing right. I was dodging bullets with no name.

I am tired of the drug game, and I must be insane. How could I have been so lame? Even after all the money I have made in my own life, I cannot save.

I can take no pride in the lives I helped wreck.

In my own life, I've made such a mess. When you are not on my side, there is no place I can hide.

Always looking over my shoulder, day after day, my heart grows colder, trying not to be afraid of sending others to an early grave.

No longer hearing the babies cry, I ask myself why, in and out of jail, getting thrown into the hole of such a tiny cell.

With all the money I've made, half the time, I can't make bail; these attorney fees are more than I can bear. They take my money and put me back on the street, helping me to live a life of defeat.

I want to straighten up my act and stop dealing drugs, putting monkeys on people's backs and destroying others' lives.

YAH, please help me; Momma's heartbroken, and Daddy does not speak.

I do not have any friends even after all the people I meet.

Yahushua, will you help me get my life on the right track?

I'm tired of sleepless nights and want to get it right.

Fathers and mothers are hurting themselves and their children because of the drugs I sell, sending souls to hell.

Disrespecting your law of love, YAH, I must admit, it's a terrible sight.

I know you do not like it, not one little bit; thank you for every time a bullet was shot at me, and I was not hit.

This horrible life, I want to quit. Thank you for the mercy that I do not deserve.

Now, it is you I want to serve, even though I have helped kill hundreds for the dollar bill.

Is this my destination? Has my fate been sealed? Do I have to go to hell?

YAH, will you give me another chance? I will start my life over. I want to do better.

Please allow me to make things right. I have learned that the end does not justify the mean.

Forgive me for all my sins. In Yahushua's name, I ask.

Written by Nona McCollough © copyrights 1997

There is Hope; Believe and Receive It!

CHAPTER 16

THE POWER OF MEDIATION, PRAYER, AND FASTING

Connecting with your spiritual side and overcoming life's challenges is crucial. Quieting our minds and focusing on the Creator can bring deep peace and connection with the divine mind, body, and soul. It's important to note that the more Believers in Elohim, the Almighty God, gives up on the world the more YAH they get.

Meditation, fasting, and prayer profoundly impact our physical, psychological and spiritual well-being. By practicing these techniques, we can cultivate a more peaceful mindset and bring positive changes into our lives.

Meditating on the positive aspects of life is essential, guided by The Word of Elohim. Reacting without much thought is common in our daily lives, and it can be challenging to maintain a positive outlook when faced with adverse situations. However, through prayer, we can find the strength to stay positive and manifest the desired outcomes in our lives.

Belief in YAH is paramount. I urge you to trust Him, acknowledge Him for His provisions and praise Him for His abundant blessings. Fasting is also a powerful tool for enhancing mental, spiritual, and physical health. If you're new to fasting, start with shorter periods, prepare yourself by cultivating a positive mindset, and reduce your consumption of sweets, caffeine, meats, and processed foods. Stay hydrated and drink plenty of water during your fast.

Remember, Yahushua is always with you, and prayer can bring healing, peace, deliverance, and salvation. He eagerly awaits your request when it is done with a sincere heart to build and not destroy. Believe that all things are possible with Him, and you will manifest the good things in your life.

The power of meditation, fasting, and prayer can help you find the inner peace and strength you need to overcome life's challenges. Then shall thou delight thyself in Yahuah; and I will cause thee to ride upon the high places of the earth and feed thee with the heritage of Jacob, thy father: for the mouth of Yahuah has spoken it." See Isaiah 58:

Fasting is a practice connected to a range of health and spiritual benefits. There are various types of fasting, each with its distinct approach and potential advantages.

Intermittent fasting involves cycling between periods of eating and fasting, typically fasting for 16-18 hours and consuming food within an 8-hour window. It has been associated with improved insulin sensitivity, weight management, and increased cellular repair.

Water fasting is a more extreme form of fasting in which one abstains from all food and only consumes water for a set period.

This method is believed to lead to deep detoxification, heightened mental clarity, and cellular regeneration, but it requires careful consideration and preparation. The Daniel Fast is a unique dietary approach that involves abstaining from specific foods such as meat, dairy, refined sugars, and processed foods. This fast brings about nutritional changes, fosters spiritual focus, encourages reliance on plant-based foods, and promotes improved digestion.

When it comes to fasting within a marriage, mutual agreement is crucial. Both partners should decide together whether to engage in sexual activity during the fasting period. If one partner is not willing to fast or abstain from sex, it is advisable to wait until both are on the same page. There are specific principles for married individuals regarding fasting, sex, and prayer.

PRINCIPLES FOR MARRIAGE

[1] Now concerning the matters about which you wrote: "It is good for a man not to have sexual relations with a woman." [2] But because of the temptation to sexual immorality, each man should have his wife and each woman her husband. [3] The husband should give to his wife her conjugal rights, and likewise the wife to her husband. [4] For the wife does not have authority over her own body, but the husband does. Likewise, the husband has no authority over his body, but the wife does. [5] Do not deprive one another, except perhaps by agreement for a limited time, that you may devote yourselves to prayer; but then come together again, so that Satan may not tempt you because of your lack of self-control." Remembering that it's best to reach an agreement

with your partner before fasting in a marriage is important. "Abstaining from sex is permissible for some time if you both agree to it and if it's for prayer and fasting - but only for such times. Then come back together again." 1 Corinthians 7:5

A POWERFUL TOOL

Fasting and prayer are such powerful tools.

Breaking the powers of Satan to rule

This tool moves the chains of oppression and breaks the yokes of bondage and injustice.

Do away with greed and let those who are captive go free.

It helps you to overcome burdens and every gesture of contempt.

Put an end to evil words. so that the word of YAH can be heard.

It keeps you strong and well.

Heals your every disease if in your heart you can believe.

Written by Nona McCollough © Copyright 1995

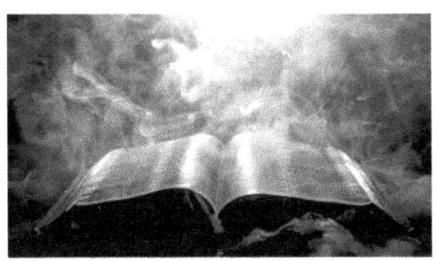

CHAPTER 17

WHAT IS THE HEAVENLY FATHER'S AND HIS SON'S NAME

It can be a challenging and confusing experience to seek the truth about faith and spirituality. I understand that the abundance of misinformation and deception can make it hard to connect with your Creator. But please know that you are not alone. Many have walked the same path and found clarity and comfort by embracing the name of Yahuah, the Hebrew name for God, and His son Yahushua, the Hebrew name for Jesus. These names hold profound spiritual significance and are believed to carry the essence of their divine beings. I understand that faith and belief are required to follow this path. Still, the good news is that Yahushua has already paved the way for believers by paying the debt humankind owed YAH and defeating the enemy of all believers.

Overcoming the lies and deception sown by 'the enemy' can be daunting, but believers must open their hearts and minds to the truth. Each time we lend an ear to these falsehoods, our hearts grow callous, making it more challenging to embrace the truth. However, as you delve into this chapter, I hope it will serve as a key to unlock your heart, allowing you to welcome Yahuah, our Creator, and His Son Yahushua, The Messiah, our Savior.

Take solace in knowing that Yahuah, the Father, has vested all power in Heaven and Earth in the Hands and the Name of His Son Yahushua. I hope this chapter will guide your quest to uncover the proper names of our Creator and His Son. 'Unearthing your truth' refers to deep introspection, seeking divine guidance, and aligning your beliefs and actions with the teachings of Yahuah and Yahushua. This chapter will set you on the right path, empowering you to unearth your truth. I urge you to persist in your search for truth with an open heart and mind.

I understand that accuracy is vital in all aspects of translation and interpretation, especially when dealing with this crucial issue. Any errors in translation or interpretation can have severe consequences and significantly impact people's lives. Inaccuracies in these processes can lead to misunderstandings and misinterpretations of the spiritual teachings. That is why it is essential to prioritize accuracy in all translations and interpretations.

If you're wondering where to find the truth hidden from the Christian world, please start at the beginning. It can be surprising to learn that the proper names of the Heavenly Father and His Son, Hebrew, had been transliterated into English names due to historical and cultural factors. The Old Testament Sacred Scrolls were written in Hebrew by the Prophets, and the New Testament Scriptures were written by the Apostles in Hebrew, Arabic, and Greek.

It can be perplexing and raise many questions about why the names were changed. You have every right to ask these questions and seek answers. I encourage you to continue studying and praying to discover the truth.

"Draw not nigh hither: put off thy shoes from off thy feet; for the place whereon thy standest is holy ground." Exodus 3:5

During the intimate exchange between YAH and Moses, YAH entrusted Moses with a significant task-to tend to the burning bush. In a personal and direct manner, YAH instructed Moses to return to Egypt and deliver his brethren. Curious, Moses sought the Name of the One he was conversing with. In response, Elohim, the eternal and unchanging, revealed His Name in Hebrew as "AYAH ASHER AYAH," meaning "I WILL BE WHO I WILL BE."

Furthermore, Elohim disclosed His eternal Name, "YHUH" or "Yahuah," when the Hebrew vowels Yod Heh Vav Heh were added. In Hebrew, the letter A takes the sound of Ar, and the letter He takes the sound of A.

"And Elohim said moreover unto Moses, Thus shalt thou say unto the children of Israel, Yahuah, the Elohim of your fathers, the Elohim of Abraham, the Elohim of Isaac, and the Elohim of Jacob, hath sent me unto you: this is My name forever, and this my memorial unto all generations. Exodus 3:15

The name, Yahuah, is a strong tower: the righteous runneth into it and is safe." Proverbs 18:10.

Some people avoid using the Savior's Name for fear of criticism, but Yahuah gave us love, power, and a sound mind, and not the spirit of fear.

"For Yahuah hath not given us the spirit of fear; but of power, and of love, and of a sound mind." II Timothy 1:7

Miriam Yahushua's mother was introduced to her son as the world's savior before His birth. An angel of Yahuah, who also spoke to her husband in a dream, gave her this name.

"Now the birth of Yahushua the Messiah was on this wise; when His mother Miriam was espoused to Joseph before they came together, she was found with child of the Holy Spirit. Then Joseph, her husband, being a just man and not willing to make her a public example, was minded to put her away privily. But while he thought on these things, behold, the angel of Yahuah appeared unto him in a dream, saying Joseph, thou son of David, fear not to take Miriam thy wife' for that which is conceived in her is of the Holy Spirit. And she shall bring forth a Son, and thou shall call His Name Yahushua: for He shall save His people from their sins." Matthew 1:18-21

YAHU-shua" means "YAH is salvation" or "Yahuah saves." King David, a man after Elohim's heart, referred to Him as "Yahuah." It is important to note that David never knew The Creator as "Jehovah" or "Lord," as the English language did not exist during his time. Similarly, neither did his son, King Solomon, who was known to be the wisest man of all time. Both of these men saw "Yahuah" in a vision, where He appeared to them and gave them wisdom and revelation, and they both wrote about the visions they saw. The writings and books of King David were quite prophetic and informative, with David being inspired to declare:

"But let the righteous be glad. Let them rejoice before Elohim: yea, let them exceedingly rejoice. Sing unto Elohim, sing praises to His Name: Extol Him that rideth upon the heavens by His Name YAH, and rejoice before Him." Psalms 68:3- 4

"Yahuah is my shepherd; I shall not want. He maketh me to lie down in green pastures; He leadeth me beside the still waters.

He restoreth my soul; He leadeth me in the paths of righteousness for his Name sakes.

Yea though I walk through the valley of the shadow of death, I will fear no evil; for Thou art with me; thy rod and Thy staff Thy comfort me?

Thou preparest a table before me in the presence of my enemies; Thou anointed my head with oil; my cup runneth over.

Surely goodness and mercy shall follow me all the days of my life; and I will dwell in the house of Yahuah forever. Psalms 23

Remember the powerful transformation of Saul, later known as Paul, who was on his way to persecute believers when he encountered Yahushua. He was thrown off his horse and blinded. When asked about the one who did this, Yahushua asked Saul, "Why do you persecute me?" Saul responded, "Who are Thou?" This divine intervention changed Saul's life forever, leading him to become one of the most influential figures in Christianity.

Yahushua replied, "I am Yahushua of Nazareth whom Thou persecutes." This was spoken in Hebrew, as English did not exist in Yahushua's time on earth. It is essential to recognize the significance of these names and their impact on our faith as seekers of truth. As compassionate individuals, we are called to be aware of the falsehoods and to seek the truth.

Those who honor Yahushua's name may experience greater glory and splendor in their worship. It's worth noting that Yahushua instructed Paul to preach in his name, setting an excellent example. As a community, let us strive to show compassion and sympathy to those who may not share the same beliefs and focus on the message of love and peace that Yahushua preached, uniting us all.

"AND Saul yet breathing out threatening's and slaughter against the disciples of Yahushua, went unto the high priest. And desired of him letters to Damascus to the synagogues, that he found any of this way, whether they were men or women, he might bring them bound unto Jerusalem. And as he journeyed he came near to Damascus; and suddenly there shined round about him a light from heaven: And he fell to the earth, and heard a voice saying Saul, Saul, why persecutes thou Me? And he said Who art Thou Sire? And Yahushua said I am Yahushua of Nazareth Whom thou persecutest; it is hard for thee to kick against the pricks." Acts 9:1-5

Apostle Paul said to King Agrippa: "At midday, O King, I saw in the way a light from Heaven, above the brightness of the sun, shining round about me and them which journeyed with me.

And when we were all fallen to the earth, I heard a voice speaking unto me, and saying In the Hebrew tongue, Saul, Saul, why persecutest thou Me? It is hard for thee to kick against the pricks.

And I said, Who art Thou Sire? And He said I am Yahushua of Nazareth Whom thou persecutest." Acts 26:14- 15

"And except those days be shortened, there should no flesh be saved: but for the elect's sake those days shall be shortened." Matthew 24:22

The Son, Yahushua, came to Earth in His Father's Name, Yahuah. He is our Salvation. YAH-Yahushua protects those who belong to Him and is always there to help in times of trouble. When believers embrace Yahuah and keep His word in their hearts, His Name is sealed and written on their foreheads.

"And I looked, and lo, a Lamb stood on Mount Zion and with Him a hundred forty-four thousand, having His Name and His Father's Name written in their foreheads." Revelation 14:1

Those who acknowledge and honor the name of Yahuah can receive blessings such as protection, provision, and exaltation. Those who are aware of His name and accept it can dwell in His secret place and live under the shadow of the Almighty Elohim.

"He that dwelleth in the secret place of the Most High shall abide under the shadow of the Almighty.

I will say of Yahuah, He is my refuge and my fortress: my El; in Him will I trust.

Surely he shall deliver thee from the snares of the fowler, and from the noisome pestilences.

He shall cover thee with his feathers, and under His wings shall thou trust: His truth shall be thy shield and buckler.

Thou shalt not be afraid for the terror by night; nor for the arrows that flieth by day. Nor for the pestilence that walketh in darkness; nor for the destruction that wasteth at noon day.

A thousand shall fall at thy side, and ten thousand at thy right hand; but it shall not come nigh thee.

Only with thy eyes shalt thy see the reward of the wicked. Because thou hast made Yahuah which is My refuge, even the Most High my habitation;

There shall no evil befall thee, neither shall any plague come nigh thy dwelling. For He shall give His angels charge over thee, to keep thee in all thy ways.

They shall bear thee up in their hands, lest thou dash thy foot against the stone.

Thou shalt tread upon the lion and adder; the young lion and the dragon shalt thy trample under feet.

Because he hath set his love upon Me, therefore will I deliver him: I will set him on high because he hath known My Name.

He shall call upon Me, and I will answer him; I will be with him in trouble; I will deliver him and honour him.

With long life will I satisfy him and shew him My salvation." Psalms 91

"But we all, with open face beholding as in a glass the glory of Yahuah, are changed into the same image from glory to glory, even as by the Spirit of Yahuah." 1 Corinthians 3:17- 18

It's important to understand that YAH, the God of justice and love, is unwavering in His promises. He has made it clear in His Word that He will warn His true apostles and prophets before taking action. If you stand with them, you will be safe. In the challenging times ahead, it's crucial to comprehend Yah and His perfect plan for His people. While it may be tempting to refer to Him as Jehovah, Jesus, or the Lord, none of these are His proper Name. His Name is YHUH (YAHUAH), and it's important to start addressing Him as YAH. By doing so, when difficulties arise, you can call upon the Name Yahuah and find safety, for His Name is a strong tower, and the righteous run into it and are safe. Understanding the significance of Yah's Name is crucial before it's too late. I implore you to call Him by His Name, Yah, today.

Remember that whoever calls upon the Name Yahuah will find safety in the days ahead. Allow the Holy Spirit to open your spiritual eyes and ears so you can find joy in the Rock of your salvation, knowing that His eternal Word cannot fail.

However, be cautious, as not using His correct Name could have serious consequences. We must always be mindful that the adversary will stop at nothing to hinder us from realizing the enduring power of the Name of Yahuah. He may attempt to persuade us that we have all we need and that there is no need for further growth. However, we must prioritize our journey of continuous, unceasing development and productivity. Like an aging tree that ceases to bear fruit, we must avoid becoming stagnant. We must persist in moving forward, ceaselessly seeking the truth that Yahuah wants us to uncover. It is crucial always to remember that there is liberation in the presence of the Spirit of Yahuah, a guiding and supporting force constantly with us on our spiritual journey.

Deliverance

Deliverance is bestowed when sought with sincerity, but what does this mean to a trembling soul in need of love?

Bitter, anguish, and distressed, running out of time, powers of fear gripped their mind: this is what you must do.

Turn to Yahushua, and he will be waiting for you. You can trust him He always listens for your voice; He hears you even before you speak.

Repent, give up the pride of life, the lust of the eyes, the lust of the flesh, rejoice, and have faith; there is help for the lost, weary souls.

Come humble yet boldly before YAH's throne through Yahushua, Yahuah's son, and you will receive love, mercy, forgiveness, and grace there. You will find hope and strength to run your race.

Written by Nona Mccollough © 1997

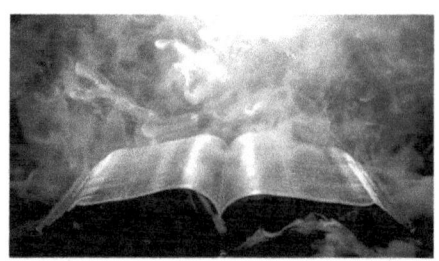

CHAPTER 18

WHAT IS LOVE?

Dear USA and the world, I am grateful for all the help and support you have given me. Your Love and kindness have made a difference in my life, and I am so thankful for everything you've done for me. Thank you once again for your kindness and generosity.

Sincerely,
Nona McCollough Lang

To know Love, one must experience its warmth and acceptance, gentleness, faith, courage, strength and forgiveness, chastisement, mercy, grace, and victory.

"Yes, a person must know Love to give true Love. Love is many things, but it is not selfishness, a liar, or a failure. People do not have to be afraid to love because they think it will fail them. Love never fails. It has the power to transform, heal, and bring hope. This is the Love we should strive to give and receive.

This Love only comes from above, and Yahuah's grace and mercy provide this Love to each living soul. He gave His only begotten son to preserve this Love, and I want to let you know this and share it with you. My encounters with Yahuah have been profound, and they have shaped my spiritual journey. I want to share these experiences with you so that you, too, can feel the presence of His Love in your life.

There is nothing like the Creator telling you, "I LOVE YOU."

Honestly, I tell you because He has told me so on multiple occasions, and even though I am now more accustomed to hearing it, it still makes me feel undone. I remember He first told me in Baton Rouge, Louisiana. I had left California to go home. It was where I wanted to spend the rest of my life and be laid to rest at home in a little village on the skirts of Baton Rouge called Scottland Ville, where I was born to Walter and Iree Loud. My sister always told me it was a good night between my mom and dad when they conceived me. My sister Frances is a beacon of loving herself. I digress. Let me continue. This declaration of Love from the Creator was a turning point in my life, a moment of profound realization and acceptance of myself.

I left everyone behind and went to another state and city, Baton Rouge, Louisiana. The people there treated me well. I was waiting for my social security benefits to be released, and the time was almost up for them to be released. After being abused, both physically and mentally, I went into a deep depression and suffered both physically and mentally. But by the grace of YAH and my faith in Him, I was getting along and saving money by sharing my poetry and receiving donations. I managed to obtain this by putting my feelings into words, expressing my emotions, and putting the words on decorative paper. When I realized my poetry was encouraging and uplifting to me, I made up my mind to share it with others. Writing became my passion and a way of escaping the mundane things of life. It became a way of life and support, and my life changed.

The Holy Spirit began to teach and lead me as requested, and I learned about free will, which led me to write many psalms and poems. This was the beginning of my learning of free will. Self-discovery was where I began learning about myself and how to realize and control my emotions. I knew that forgiveness was available, and I knew it was possible because I had forgiven many offenses others had done to me. But I never really considered the depth of how much I needed it myself. I was no Saint. I realized this after the fact. It was and is humbling to know that my Heaven Father had already forgiven me even before I asked, which made me fall in Love with Him all over again. By the Love of my Heavenly Father, I was strengthened and sought to follow my dreams. One was to go to my birthplace, which I had not walked on since childhood and had no recall of. Long story short, so I did. The process of forgiveness was not easy, but it was transformative. It allowed me to let go of the past and embrace a new beginning in my spiritual journey.

I sold everything I did not want, caught a bus, and went to Louisiana, hoping to find Love and peace. After arriving, I went to a spouse abuse shelter after being advised by Carolyn, who was headed farther down South. What a miracle and a blessing to meet her as we rode together on the bus, sharing our war stories. Following her advice, I called the shelter and told them my story. They met me at the bus station, and it became a private affair, and I was cautious not to tell anyone of it. After processing, I received some toiletries, a towel, and a few stuffed animals. I chose a fury gray cat that I called Fat Cat because it was so fat. Fat became my comforting friend who I could trust with all my secrets. Something that I had not had since I was a child before I learned that Jesus was a constant companion.

I spent a lot of time crying needles, to say and feeling lost. However, Yah strengthened me, and soon, I was well enough to leave and get a small apartment. I went to a church that I found in the Yellow Pages to celebrate and see if anyone had some items they wanted to eliminate that I so badly needed. The night's service was also good, and the people were warm and accepting of me. Many offered me household gifts, and some gave me cash. They would clash the catch in my hand, and it to me as though it was a private expression of Love for me. I just remembered getting my check and buying a Blue Toyota wagon.

I told the Pastor and the members of his church my story and warned them of what YAH had told me to say to them. The warning was Crack was on the way and that they should fast and pray to save them from its danger, for it had not yet hit the beautiful city's streets.

Yes, I enjoyed Baton Rouge and its people, and the food was good, too. It reminded me a lot of the city I had just left and how it was before Crack hit its streets. The people were receptive, but they did not truly realize the devastation this drug could cause to their city.

I made a few friends, but I still felt lonely. It was my first time away from family, but I was a loner, so it did not bother me; this is what I thought. As time went on, the lonely only grew. Even though I felt comfort and Love in the church, I had to go home to my tiny apartment alone. I continued to go out and share my poems and meet many people. The church became a significant part of my life, providing me with a sense of community and belonging that I had been missing.

Yes, I enjoy sharing my poems, which is why I share some of them from time to time in this book.

One particular night, I went to church. The service was good, as was the message about forgiveness and our need for it. I was convicted and moved to pray when the altar call came. The message made me reflect on the power of forgiveness in our lives and how we all need it to give and receive. Forgiveness is a powerful tool for healing and growth, which we should all strive to practice.

Little did I know that night that I would meet Jesus there. I stood at the altar one second and on the floor the next, just that quick. As I lay there trying to figure out what just happened to me, a sweet and low voice said, "I love you." It was the voice of the Lord that I later learned was Yahuah. Oh, my, what love the Father has bestowed upon those who love him and ones who do not. I did and love Him even to this day, and I always will. That night, the tears flowed as I walked out of the church. I do not know how I got off the floor.

I was sobbing so hard. All I knew was someone helped me, and I walked out of the church that stormy night. The wind was blowing, the lightning flashed, and the rain poured down, and I was crying uncontrollably, releasing the pain I had bottled upside in me from feeling unworthy of Love. After all, I had been told and shown this by others, but now, I was experiencing the Love of the Heavenly Father overwhelmed me. The Holy Spirit drove me home that night. I shall never forget it. It was pouring down rain that night. The traffic was heavy, and I was bawling from hearing and feeling YAH's Love for me. He accepted me as I am, was my thought. Regardless of my failures and sins, He still loved me and showed me that night.

For me, Love begins with forgiveness, starting with the forgiveness of others and forgiving oneself. This level of experiencing Love is so fulfilling. This Love became accessible by accepting Yahushua's blood sacrifice to pay the sin debt we humans owed.

I must testify that YAH is loving and kind to me. HalleluYAH, How many know what I am speaking of?

I obtained This Love, wisdom, knowledge, kindness, and faith from knowing YAH's Love; even though He chastisement those He loves for correction, which is sometimes necessary, to keep us on the right road, it is so worth it!

Salvation is something that I desire not only for myself but for others as well.

Love is what hate is not. In this transformative chapter on Love, we discover that without faith, hope, and Love, it is impossible to please YAH. Hope, a beacon of light, fortifies our faith, and faith, in turn, strengthens our Love. Yet, Love reigns supreme among these three. It is the catalyst for peace on earth and the key to salvation.

Let us cultivate a spirit of gratitude in all aspects of our lives, acknowledging the boundless Love of our Messiah.

The Divine Word, Yahushua, guides us to express gratitude in all things, forgive all things, let go of the past, and move forward in His ways. His teachings testify to His divine Love and forgiveness, offering us reassurance and Love in all circumstances.

We all have been deceived by the enemy at one time or another by someone who says they love us. Yet Love is the way to defeat the enemy's tricks. Loving YAH with all one's heart, obeying Him, and being grateful in all things, knowing everything works together for the good of those who love YAH and are called according to His purpose Yahuah is the judge; He has made it plain in His Word what is acceptable to Him and what is not. He showed us this through the example of His Son Yahushua's works. He came down to earth and dwelt among us. He taught His disciples how to love and left records that have survived even to this day.

The defining characteristic of a true disciple is the genuine expression of love (agape) for others, mirroring the sacred affection one has for the Heavenly Father Himself. This love for others fosters a sense of connection and value within the spiritual community.

Yahuah so loves the world that He gave His only begotten Son, who shared it with the world. He taught it to His disciples and shared it with them and the world before his death, and He is still showing it to this very day to all who will receive Him. Not only did he tell them what would happen to Him for their sakes, but He told them He would go away, and they did not have to worry or be afraid. He was going to prepare a place for them, and while he was away from them in the body, He was going to send His Spirit to dwell in them so they could continue His works on the earth.

Yahushua told them that He would come back and receive them unto Himself.

"Love Yahuah thy Elohim with all thy heart, and with all thy soul, and with all thy strength, this is the first commandment. And second is like unto it: "Thou shalt love thy neighbor as thyself." There are none other commandments greater than these. Mark 12:30-31

When we, as believers, wholeheartedly practice the powerful gift of love, it can significantly enhance our lives and positively impact the world. Our actions can inspire, serve as a beacon for others to follow, a testament to our faith, and a witness for Yahushua, the world's Savior. In doing so, we become the salt of the earth and a city set on a hill that cannot be hidden.

"Ye are the salt of the earth: but if the salt has lost its savor, wherewith shall it be salted? It is thenceforth good for nothing, but to be cast out, and to be trodden under foot of men." Matthew 5:13

Navigating in a world of hate and self-indulgence can be challenging, and some might wonder how to do it. As I mentioned earlier, one way is to experience a spiritual rebirth and receive the guidance of Yahuah through Yahushua. Allowing Him to fill you with love, mercy, wisdom, and truth and following the teachings of Yahushua, shared by His apostles and prophets, can help you overcome these challenges and become a witness to His power.

How can one do this in a world full of hate and self-indulgence, one may ask? As I stated before, one must be born again and receive the Spirit of Yahuah through Yahushua. They must allow Him to lead, guide, and fill them with His love, mercy, wisdom, and truth as they follow the teachings of Yahushua given to them through His apostles and prophets. As a witness, they will become more than conquerors.

"Be ye followers of me, even as I also am of the Messiah." I Corinthians 11:1

In I Corinthians Chapter 13, the Apostle Paul beautifully explains the essence of love. This profound teaching can transform your and people's lives worldwide if they are open to receiving and embracing it.

"Though I speak with the tongues and of angels, and have not love, I have become a sounding brass or a tinkling cymbal. And though I have the gift of prophecy and understand all mysteries, and all knowledge; and though I have all faith so that I could remove mountains and have no slope, I am nothing.

And though I bestow all my goods to feed the poor, and though I give my body to be burned, and have not love, it profited me nothing. Love suffereth long and is kind; love envieth not; love vaunteth not itself is not puffed up. Doth not behave itself unbecomingly, seeketh not her own, is not easily provoked, thinketh no evil. Rejoiceth not in iniquity, but rejoiceth in the truth.

Beareth all things, believeth all things, hopeth all things, and endureth all things. Love never faileth: but whether there be prophecies, they shall fail; whether there be tongues, they shall cease; whether there be knowledge, it shall vanish away. For we know in part, and we prophesy in part, but when that which is perfect is come, that which is in part shall be done away.

When I was a child, I spoke as a child; I understood, But when I became a man, I put away childish things. For now, we see through a glass, darkly, but then face to face: Now I know in part, but then shall I know even as I am known. And now abideth faith, hope, love, and these three: but the greatest of these is love." I Corinthians Chapter 13

This, friends, is something the Devil does not want people to know. He wants people to be burdened and yoked to every evil work.

Yahushua said, "Take My yoke upon you and learn of Me because His yoke is easy, and His burdens are light," oh, what love. "Let not your heart be troubled; ye believe in Yahuah, believe also in Me. In My Father's house are many mansions, and I tell you, I must go to prepare a place for you.

And if I go and prepare a place for you, I will come again and receive you unto Myself; that where I am there ye may be also. Yahushua saith unto him, I am the way, the truth, and the life: no man cometh unto the Father, but by Me." John 14:1-3

The profound love that Savior Yahushua had for His followers demonstrates the love during His arrest, even up to His death on the cross. He had His current disciples and those who would come after them in mind. His prayer for all of us before His arrest is a testament to this love.

"These words spake Yahushua, and lifted up His eyes to heaven, and said, Father, the hour is come; glorify Thy Son, that Thy Son also may glorify Thee: As thou hast given Him power over all flesh, that he should give eternal life to as many as Thou hast given Him. And this is life eternal, that they might know that Thou only art the true El, and Yahushua the Messiah, Whom Thou hast sent. I have glorified Thee on the earth: I have finished the work which

Thou gavest me to do. And now, O Father, glorify thou me with Thine own self with the glory which I had with thee before the world was. I have declared Thy Name unto men which Thou gavest Me out of the world: Thine they were, and Thou gavest them to me, and they have kept Thy Word. Now they have known that all things whatsoever Thou hast given Me are of Thee. For I have given them the words which Thou gavest me, and they have received them and have known surely that I came out from Thee, and they have believed that Thou didst send me. I pray for them; I pray not for the world, but for them which Thou hast given me, for they are Thine. And all Mine are Thine, and Thine are Mine, and I am glorified in them. And now I am no more in the world, but these are in the world, and I come to Thee.

Holy Father, take and keep through Thine name those whom Thou hast given Me, that they may be one, as We are. While I was with them in the world, I kept them in thy Name: those that thou gavest me I have kept, and none of them is lost, but the son of perdition; in fulfillment of the Scripture.

And now come I to Thee; and these things I speak in the world, that they might have My joy fulfilled in themselves. I have given them Thy Word, and the world will hate them, because they are not of the world, even as I am not of the world.

I pray not that Thou should take them out of the world but that Thou shouldest keep them from the evil one. They are not of the world, even as I am not of the world. Sanctify them through thy truth: because Thy Word is truth. As Thou hast sent me into the world I also sent them into the world. And for their sakes I sanctify Myself, that they also might be sanctified through the truth.

Neither pray I for these alone, but for them also which shall believe on me through their Word;

That they all may be one; as thou, Father, art in me, and I in Thee, that they may also be one in Us: that the world may believe that thou hast sent me.

And the glory which thou gavest me I have given them; that they may be one, as We are One: I in them, and Thou in me, that they may be made perfect in unity; and that the world may know that thou hast sent me, and hast loved them, as thou hast loved me.

Father, I will that they also, who thou hast given me, be with me where I am; that they may behold my glory, which thou hast given me: for thou lovest me before the foundation of the world.

O righteous Father, the world hath not known Thee, and these have known that Thou hast sent me. And I have declared unto them Thy Name and will declare it; that the love wherewith Thou hast loved Me may be I them, and I in them." John 14

Oh, what love does the Father have for the Son, and the Son has for us? We can trust YAH's love through Yahushua the Word; whatever What He says will not return void, no matter what the Devil says.

'In the beginning was the Word, and the Word was with Yahuah, and the Word was Yahuah. The same was in the beginning with Him. John 1:1- 2

YAH's Holy Spirit continues to guide and teach His people today, empowering them to heal the sick and perform extraordinary miracles. This includes opening the eyes of the blind, unstopping deaf ears, and even raising the dead. YAH's love is limitless and everlasting.

If you have not already, I wholeheartedly encourage you to open your heart to Yahuah and become one of His children. Surrender your life to Him and let His love flow through you.

If you obey Him, you will undoubtedly experience the countless benefits of His love and mercy. Always remember that Yahushua is alive and gave His life so you can live. His love is constantly in the lives of all who will accept and receive Him by faith, and there is no greater love than the love of Yahuah.

IF HUMANS MADE YAHUSHUA KING OF EARTH

On the sabbath day, we all would rest; no more failures, no need for any test. All the hungry people would be fed; he would heal all the sick and raise the dead.

There would be no hate, his love would take its place, and there would Be no lying, cheating, stealing, or killing to pay bills. Yet every thirsty, hungry soul would be fed from his bread from heaven and his living water.

His love will rule the land, and we will all walk hand in hand; his Holy Spirit will enable us to understand. No one will challenge his commands.

We would all live in peace, and the color of man's skin would be obsolete.

We would live without defeat, like the rainbow colors, which are beautiful to behold.

YAH's light would shine in each soul, and no sorrowful cry would be heard. Only the sound of laughter and praise, saying glory to the king, is YAH's Holy Word; with everyone free, there would be no such thing as slavery. And everyone would wear his signet ring if humankind made Yahushua king.

Written by Nona McCollough © 1998

Believe

It only happens once you believe. It is independent of what you see now.

Let me encourage you to take the faith route. Don't waste precious time with unbelief and doubt.

In life, every dream is attainable when you decide what you want. It is wise not to waver, stay focused and steadfast, and be on the right path.

Get a firm image in your mind and think about it constantly.

Keep it alive in your heart when you get up and lie down, and you will be accomplished bound.

Your desired result will soon be in hand, and you must understand it. You can only give once you receive or get once you believe.

For those who have journeyed on this road before, I do not have to say anything more.

But for those who have been waiting and have not heard of it, belief opens the door to your heart, and remember, faith is the fuel to making your dreams come true.

Now, it is all up to you, depending on what you say and do.

Written by Nona Lang © 2012

YOU CAN TRUST THE LOVE OF YAHUAH BECAUSE IT NEVER FAILS!

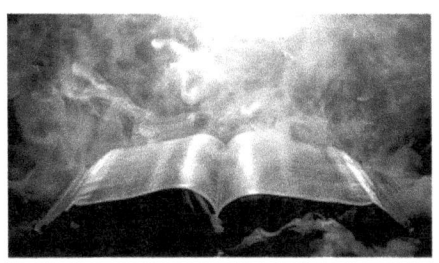

CHAPTER 19

THE RAPTURE DECEPTION

Many people may feel overwhelmed with fear during challenging times on Earth and lose hope. Additionally, some individuals may abandon their faith due to the mistaken belief that they will be taken up in the rapture before the great tribulation and spared from experiencing worsening conditions on Earth. This misconception may lead to deception and disillusionment.

"Men's hearts failing them for fear, and for looking after those things which are coming on the earth: for the powers of heaven shall be shaken." Luke 21:26

I understand this can be a sensitive topic, and I intend to approach it with compassion and sympathy. It's important to remember that many people worldwide, including many of you, share the belief in the church being raptured before the great tribulation. This shared belief can be a source of unity and strength, even in the face of differing interpretations. However, some view this as a false doctrine perpetuated by the enemy to deceive people. This can be a problematic and unsettling thought, and I want you to know that.

I am here to offer support and understanding. In this chapter, I will share information that might help shed light on this topic and provide comfort during these uncertain times.

"But what I do, that I will do, that I may cut off occasion from them which desire occasion; that wherein they glory, they may be found even as we.

For such are false apostles, deceitful workers, transforming themselves into the apostles of the Messiah. And no marvel; for Satan transformeth himself into an angel of light.

Therefore, it is no great thing if his ministers also be transformed as the ministers of righteousness, whose end shall be according to their works." I Corinthians 11:12-15

In Matthew Chapter 24, we are reminded of the signs that will precede Yahushua's return and the gathering of His Bride. It's crucial to recognize these signs unfolding around us. Wars, rumors of wars, and earthquakes in various places are becoming more frequent. Time is accelerating, making it challenging to discern the seasons. As prophesied, families are turning against each other. As Daniel prophesied, the definitive sign of the impending tribulation is the establishment of the abomination that causes desolation. This is a clear and unmistakable indicator that believers must heed and prepare for. "And Yahushua went out and departed from the temple: and His disciples came to him for to show Him the buildings of the temple.

And Yahushua said unto them, See ye not all these things? Verily I say unto you, "There shall not be left one stone upon another that shall not be thrown down."

And as he sat upon the Mount of Olives, the disciples came unto

He privately, saying; Tell us when shall these things be? And what shall be the sign of Thy coming and of the end of the age? And Yahushua answered and said unto them, Take heed that no man deceive you. For many shall come in My name, saying, I am the Messiah; and shall deceive many. And ye shall hear of wars and rumors of wars: see that ye be not troubled; for all these things must come to pass, but the end is not yet.

For nation shall rise against nation, and kingdom against kingdom: and there shall be famines, and pestilences, and earthquakes, in various places.

All these are the beginning of the Plagues.

Then shall they deliver you up to be afflicted and shall kill you: and ye shall be hated of all nations for my Name sake.

And then shall many be offended and shall betray one another. And many false prophets shall a rise and shall deceive many.

And because apostasy shall abound the love of many shall grow cold. But he that shall endure unto the end, the same shall be saved.

And the glad tidings of the Kingdom shall be preached in all the world for the witness unto all nations; for a witness unto all nations; and then shall the end come.

"Where ye therefore shall see the abomination of desolation, spoken of by Daniel the prophet, stand in the holy place, (Whoso readeth, let him understand)

Then let them which be in Judea flee into the mountains: Let him which be on the housetop not come down to take anything out of his house:

Neither let him which is in the field return back to take his clothes. And woe unto them that are with child, and them that give suck in those days!

For then shall be great tribulation, such as was not since the beginning of the world to this time, nor ever shall be. And except those days should be shortened, no flesh should be saved, but those days shall be shortened for the elect's sake.

Then if any man shall say unto you, Lo here is the Messiah, or there; believe it not. For there shall arise false Messiahs, and false prophets, and shall show greatsigns and wonders; insomuch that, if possible, they shall deceive the very elect. Behold, I have told you before.

Wherefore if they shall say unto you, Behold, He is in the desert; go not forth: behold, He is in the secret chambers; believe it not.

As the lightning cometh out of the east, and shineth even unto the west; so shall the coming of the Son of Man be. For wherever the carcass is the eagles will be gathered together. Immediately after the tribulation of those days shall the sun be darkened, and the moon shall not give her light, and the stars shall fall from heaven, and the powers of the heavens shall be shaken:

And then shall appear the sign of the Son of Man in Heaven: and then shall all of the tribes of the earth mourn, and they shall see the Son of Man coming in the clouds of heaven with power and great glory. And He shall send His angels with a great sound of a trumpet, and they shall gather together His elect from the four winds, from one end of heaven to the other." Matthew 24

As a devout believer, we will be saved from Yahuah's wrath. However, we cannot ignore the fact that the entire world will fall prey to Satan's deceitful ways and will have to endure a time of great tribulation. According to Matthew 24:29, after the great tribulation, our Messiah Yahushua will appear to take His saints and engage in warfare against the Devil and his followers. Do not be deceived by any other notion. Pray that you will be among those who are saved and ready for His coming. Pray for the strength to stand firm in your faith and trust that YAH has prepared your place in His Kingdom.

"Watch ye therefore, and pray always, that ye may be accounted worthy to escape all these things that shall come to pass, and to stand before the Son of Man." Luke 22:36

Please pay close attention to Apostle Peter's impactful preaching on the day of Pentecost. He explains that the Book of Joel, one of the oldest scriptures in the Old Testament, provides critical insights into what will occur before Yahushua's return to Earth. This profound understanding can significantly enhance your grasp of the Bible. Don't miss out on this fantastic chance to deepen your knowledge of the scriptures.

"And on My servants and on My handmaidens, I will pour out in those days of My Spirit; and they shall prophesy: And I will show wonders in the heaven above, and signs in the earth beneath; blood, and fire, and pillars of smoke: The sun shall be turned into darkness, and the moon into blood, before that great and notable day of Yahuah come: And it shall come to pass that whosoever call upon the Name of Yahuah shall be saved." Acts 2:16-21

Our Master will not appear until the signs in Joel Chapter Two occur. This "notable day" in Acts Chapter 2 is called a terrible day in Joel Chapter Two and verse 31.

"And I will show wonders in the heavens and in the earth, blood, and fire, and pillars of smoke.

The sun shall be turned to darkness and the moon into blood before the great and terrible day of Yahuah comes. Joel 2:30-31

Have you ever considered what would happen if the Messiah didn't return before the significant tribulation period? It's a worrying thought. Do you feel confident that you and your family would be able to survive this challenging ordeal for seven years? If you're uncertain, you're not alone. It's time to take action and find a ministry with a vision to help you prepare for safety and survival. Remember, you can be safest in the Name of Yahuah and Yahushua's direct, perfect will.

So, what are you waiting for? Without a vision, people will perish. Let's work towards a safe and secure future today, guided by our unwavering faith and trust. The Name, Yahuah, is a strong tower: the righteous runneth into it and is safe. Proverbs 18:10

YAH, a God of justice and love, is steadfast in His promises. He reveals in His Word that He will warn His true apostles and prophets before Taking action. If you align with them, you're safe. But it's crucial to understand YAH and His perfect plan for His people in the challenging times ahead. It might be tempting to call Him Jehovah, Jesus, or the Lord, but none of these are His true Name. His Name is YHUH (YAHUAH), and you should start calling Him YAH. This way, when difficulties come, you can call upon the Name Yahuah and be saved, for His Name is a strong tower, and the righteous run into it, and they are safe. Grasp the importance of YAH's Name before it's too late. I urge you to call Him by His Name, YAH, today.

Remember, whoever calls upon the Name Yahuah shall be saved in the days ahead. Let the Holy Spirit open your spiritual eyes and ears so you can rejoice in the Rock of your Salvation, knowing that His eternal Word cannot fail. But be warned, not using His correct Name could lead to dire consequences. "And it shall come to pass that whosoever shall call on the Name of Yahuah shall be saved." Acts 2:21

THE DOOR

I stood there staring at the door

There was that knock again

The one that I've heard

So many times before

I started to open it up

But I hesitated

I said to myself

I'll open it later

But the gentle rapping persisted

The more it persisted, the more I resisted

But finally, I gave in, and I am so glad I did.

The guest who was knocking turned out to be my best friend.

Written by Nona Mccollough © 1997

CHAPTER 20

LIVE A VICTORIOUS LIFE WHILE HERE ON EARTH

As people of faith, we find great comfort and solace in embracing the joy and fulfillment that come from humbling ourselves under the mighty hand of YAH through Yahushua. His name, a symbol of love and compassion, draws us into His eternal family, bringing us a sense of security, power, strength, wisdom, peace, love, joy, health, and wealth. Our genuine delight in YAH is met with His blessings, fulfilling the deepest desires of our hearts. HalleluYAH!

When we draw joy from our relationship with YAH, the enemy is forced to retreat, acknowledging YAH's unwavering faithfulness to those who worship, honor, and praise Him. The blessings YAH has for His people go beyond our wildest imagination. Trusting Him and faithfully following His commandments fortifies our strength and determination. Our devotion to YAH shatters the enemy's hold, leading us to eternal bliss in Heaven.

Yahuah, in His boundless wisdom, has chosen to reveal His profound truths to us through His Spirit. His Spirit, an illuminator of all things, including the deepest mysteries of Yahuah, guides us on our spiritual journey.

Just as no one knows a person's thoughts except their own Spirit within them, similarly, no one comprehends the thoughts of Elohim except the Spirit of Elohim. The wonder and excitement await those who love Him as they eagerly anticipate the unimaginable blessings and joys.

Now we have received, not the spirit of the world, but the Spirit which is of Elohim; that we might know the things that are freely given to us of Yahuah." I Corinthians 2:9-12

YAH, the source of all power and love, desires a rich and fulfilling life for everyone and is always ready to bless us abundantly. Let us unite against the evil schemes of Satan, who seeks to harm every person on this planet. YAH eagerly awaits our prayers and calls us to stand together, fortified by His strength, against Satan's deceptions.

Satan has always opposed our Messiah, Yahushua, but he cannot overcome Yahushua's power. Through His sacrifice, Yahushua has gained all power in Heaven and Earth. He is our advocate, our defender, and our hope. He will return for those who eagerly await Him, bringing an end to Satan's reign.

YAH is always on humanity's side; we should never forget that. Yahushua is still healing and delivering people and their families. Trust Him and take a firm stand for YAH-Yahushua by living a life that reflects His teachings, by praying without ceasing, and by sharing His love with others.

YAH, the embodiment of love and wisdom, loves and treasures each one of us. He sees all the good we do, but it saddens Him when we do not obey and trust Him. To please Yahuah, we need faith, a beacon of hope in our lives. Hebrews Chapter 11 provides an excellent example of faith and how to obtain it. YAH desires all of us to have faith in His Word and to live by it, inspiring us to a life of hope and purpose.

Faith is the substance of things hoped for and the evidence of things not seen. For by it the elders obtained a good report.

"Through faith, we understand that through the ages were ordained by the Word of Elohim, so that things which were not in evidence, are now seen coming to pass." Hebrews 11:1-3

"But without faith, it is impossible to please Him; for He, that cometh to YAH must believe that He is and that He is a rewarder of them that diligently seek Him." Hebrews 11:6

Having faith is crucial in life and can sometimes be challenging to maintain. However, unwavering trust is essential when you genuinely believe and ask for blessings. Yahuah seeks believers to believe in Him, even when the results are not immediately visible. It is vital to have trust, wait for His response, and be guided by His Holy Spirit. Take solace in the assurance that Yahuah will answer your prayers and fulfill your heart's desires in His perfect timing.

"But let him ask in faith, nothing wavering: for he, that wavereth is like a wave of the sea driven with the wind and tossed. For let not that man think that he shall receive anything of Yahuah. A doubleminded man is unstable in all his ways." James 1:7-8

"The eyes of Yahuah are in every place, beholding the evil and the good. "Proverbs 15:3

Elohim, our compassionate and loving God, finds joy in seeing His people express love and kindness towards one another. He is not a distant deity but a constant presence, always listening with open ears and watching with open eyes, ready to support us in our times of need. His son Yahushua is also filled with love and compassion, longing for people to return to Him. He continuously reaches out to those who have wandered, welcoming them with open arms. When we approach Yahushua with a repentant heart, He forgives us and lovingly releases us from our burdens, casting them as far as the East is from the West. He wants us to understand that we don't have to carry our burdens alone - we can always bring them to Him. He can handle everything and wants us to have faith and trust in Him. I have personally experienced His love and compassion, and I can assure you that He is always there for us, ready to help us in our time of need. "He hath not dealt with us after our sins, nor rewarded us according to our iniquities. For as the heaven is high above the earth, so great is His mercy toward them that fear Him. As far as the east is from the west, so far hath he removed our transgressions from us." Psalms 103: 10-12

It is a common struggle to resist the temporary pleasures of sin, even when we're aware of the negative consequences. We all yearn for a life free from pain or discomfort, but often, hidden sins prevent us from experiencing true fulfillment. In the midst of these challenges, it's crucial to remember that hope always exists. The Word for Believers provides a remedy for these struggles. We must recognize the significance of our spiritual well-being, which is just as vital as our physical health. Yahushua is the path to finding peace and healing for both.

"Casting down imaginations and every high thing that exalteth itself against the knowledge of Yahuah and bringing into captivity every thought to the obedience of the Messiah. And being in readiness to revenge all disobedience when your obedience is fulfilled." 2 Corinthians 10:5-6.

Many individuals are drawn into harmful behaviors such as drug abuse, alcoholism, pornography, and gambling as a way to cope with inner pain. It's crucial to recognize that seeking relief from these vices is often temporary, and the pain resurfaces when they sober up or face the consequences.

Undoubtedly, mistakes made in youth, unhealthy relationships, and involvement in harmful activities can attract negative influences. These influences can make life even more challenging by bringing about theft, death, and destruction. Nevertheless, there is hope. People can find comfort and support through faith and a closer relationship with Elohim, the Almighty God. If you're seeking this kind of relationship, you must relinquish worldly desires and earnestly pursue a connection by faith with YAH through His son Yahushua.

"Mortify therefore your members which are upon the earth fornication, uncleanness, inordinate affection, evil concupiscence, and covetousness, which is idolatry." "For which things` sake the wrath of Yahuah cometh on the children of disobedience." Colossians 3:5-6

Throughout history, our adversaries have sought to harm humanity through our weaknesses. They prey on our minds, luring us into disobedience, fear, worry, pride, and arrogance. But we know that a higher power has already determined the time, place, and circumstances to overcome these adversaries. We can be renewed, strengthened, and guided by placing our unyielding trust in this power. Those attuned to this power can discern its guidance and follow it, while those who are not will falter. Although the process may be complex, it can lead to liberation from the chains of sin and the influence of our adversaries. Renewing one's spirit involves shedding the burdens that weigh us down and gaining the strength to resist temptation and bring the flesh under submission. We have been given a strategy to defeat our adversaries - an approach that promises clarity and peace. We are urged to focus on positivity instead of dwelling on negative thoughts that our adversaries try to instill in us. Our adversaries seek to fill our minds with thoughts of failure and wrongdoing, taking advantage of every misstep. We are reminded to guard our hearts and minds against these harmful thoughts, assured that a peace that surpasses understanding will protect us.

"Finally, brethren, whatsoever things are true, whatsoever things are honest, whatsoever things that are lovely, whatsoever things that are of a good report; if there be any virtue, and if there be any praise, think on these things." Philippians 4:7-8

It is essential to remember that what we choose to focus on can profoundly affect our lives. When we allow the Holy Spirit to lead us, we are not relinquishing control but gaining a divine compass. This empowerment is crucial as we follow YAH's guidance and strive to embody the mind of Yahushua within us.

When believers humbly present themselves before YAH and make themselves available to Him, incredible things can happen through them, rendering the enemy powerless and displaying the strength and resilience their faith bestows upon them. YAH promises to raise believers at the right time if they remain humble and faithful to His word. This requires faith, patience, and trust in YAH's plan. We must not race ahead of Him but allow Him to work on our behalf, through us, and for us.

YAH is always by our side; his love and compassion are constant and reassuring, guiding us through every challenge and offering comfort and security amid uncertainty. "Likewise, ye younger, submit yourselves unto the elder. Yea, all of you be subject one to another, and be clothed with humility: for Yahuah resisteth the proud, and giveth grace to the humble. Humble yourselves therefore under the mighty hand of Yahuah, that He may exalt you in due time: Casting all your care upon Him; for He careth for you. Be sober, be vigilant; because the adversary, your enemy, as a roaring lion, walketh about, and seeking whom he may devour: Whom resist steadfast in the faith, knowing that the same afflictions are accomplished in your brethren that are in the world." I Peter 5:5-9

It is crucial to pause each day and acknowledge the blessings bestowed upon us by our Divine Creator and Savior, Yahushua. It's disheartening that some individuals believe they can navigate life's journey without His presence, yet life is a delicate and unpredictable gift. We have all felt the pain of losing someone dear, and the thought of enduring eternal suffering is a weighty burden. Our Creator, YAH, has meticulously designed each of us with a unique purpose and sent us to this world to learn and grow. He hopes that we can discern right from wrong and strive to bring goodness into our lives and the lives of others.

Life's journey may be fraught with complex challenges and hardships, but it's crucial to remember that every experience, no matter how difficult, is an opportunity for personal growth. While some individuals may find it hard to fully embrace this concept, we are always endowed with the power to make positive decisions and lead a life of significance. Let us all find solace and guidance in our faith, knowing that our Creator is steadfast by our side, supporting us every step of the way.

It is essential to set aside a moment each day to recognize and be grateful for our Creator and Savior, Yahushua, who has blessed us with the precious gift of life. It's saddening that some people believe they can navigate through life without His presence, but life is fragile and uncertain. We have all experienced the pain of losing someone we care about, and the thought of facing eternal suffering is a heavy burden to bear.

Our Creator, YAH, has meticulously crafted each of us with a unique purpose and sent us to this world as His living masterpieces to learn, grow, and spread His light. He yearns for us to discern right from wrong and strive to infuse our lives and the lives of others with goodness, like a beacon in the darkness. We may encounter complex challenges and hardships, but it's crucial to remember that every experience is an opportunity for growth. While some individuals may struggle to grasp this idea entirely, we always have the choice to make positive decisions and live a meaningful life. May we all find solace and guidance in our faith and always remember that our Creator is by our side every step of the way.

"Be not deceived; Elohim is not mocked: for whatsoever a man soweth, that shall he also reap." Galatians 6:7

It's a sobering thought that our sojourn on Earth is temporary, a truth that becomes clearer as we journey through life. It's essential to grasp the fleeting nature of our time here. We're informed that we're gifted with approximately seventy years of life. Yet, even if we were to stretch our lifespan to over a century, it would still be a brief moment in the vast expanse of eternity. "The days of our years are three score years and ten; and if by reason of strength they be fourscore years yet is their strength labour and sorrow; for it is soon cut off, and we fly away." Psalms 90:10

Let's remember to appreciate each day, acknowledge our limitations, be grateful for our spiritual body, which is not confined by the limitations of our physical body, and praise YAH for this blessing.

"We know that if our earthly house of this tabernacle were dissolved, we have a building of Elohim, a house not made by hands, eternal in the heavens. For in this we groan, earnestly desiring to be clothed upon with our house which is from Heaven:

If so be that being clothed we shall not be found naked. For we that are in this tabernacle do groan, being burdened: not for that we would be unclothed, but clothed upon, that mortality might be swallowed up of life. Now He that wrought us for the same-same thing is Elohim, Who also hath given unto us the pledge of the Spirit." 2 Corinthians 5:1- 5

The deceptive tactics of the enemy have undeniably influenced humankind, causing concern and doubt. Despite the daunting nature of this battle, it's vital to remember that the truth is revealed to those with pure hearts. There's still hope for redemption, even for those who have been spiritually misled. Recognizing the need for a Savior and placing unwavering faith in Yahushua is crucial. Embracing YAH's teachings and accepting His Holy Spirit offers strength, comfort, and a deep connection with the Creator. Remember, you do not have to face this journey alone - there is always hope for a brighter future.

"All things were made by Him, And without Him was not anything made that was made. In Him was Life; and the life was the light of men." John 1:3-4

"But as it is written, Eye hath not seen, nor ear heard, neither have entered the heart of man, the things which Elohim hath prepared for them that love Him. But Yahuah hath revealed them unto us by

His Spirit: for the Spirit searcheth all things, yea, and the deep things of Yahuah." I Corinthians 2:9-10

Receiving the gift of speaking in tongues with evidence is not a passive act, but an active one. It involves seeking, asking, and persisting until the Holy Spirit of Yahuah, which is His perfect will for His people, is received. This process is not dependent on one's life journey, circumstances, or the world's opinion, but on the individual's earnest desire and faith.

YAH's Holy Spirit provides believers with more than just the ability to speak in tongues. It bestows upon them love, wisdom, forgiveness, strength, and revelation. He is The Teacher, and when He enters a believer, they are not just witnesses, but bold witnesses for the Messiah. Believers will perform miracles, discern the thoughts of those who are secretly opposed to them, and have authority over Satan and his demons. They will teach others that Yahushua came into the world not to condemn it but to save, heal, and deliver it.

This is the power that resides within each and every one of us, believers in the Christian faith. Yahushua, our loving Savior, rewards those who seek Him diligently. He yearns for a personal relationship with His creation, with every believer. There is no reason for anyone to be lost. By receiving His Holy Spirit, we, His chosen ones, are equipped with powerful weapons to safeguard our spiritual, mental, and physical well-being. Learn these weapons and how to use them to fight the unseen enemy. The Devil is still a real and present being, but remember, the Light, the True Light of the world, Yahushua has already overcome Satan, our adversary and the prince of darkness.

Yahushua, the world's Light, and YAH, our guiding force, are accustomed to bringing Light into the darkest areas of people's lives. They want to shine this Light into the hearts of His true disciples—those who are called, chosen, and ordained to carry out His work here on earth. From the start, He wants to work through you and me to accomplish His plan for the human family. Remember, the victory over darkness has already been won, and we are the bearers of this victorious Light. "This then is the message which we have heard of Him, and declare unto you, that Yahuah is light, and in Him is no darkness at all. If we say that we have fellowship with Him and walk in darkness, we lie and do not tell the truth:

But if we walk in the light, as He is in the light, we have fellowship on with another, and the blood of Yahushua the Messiah, His Son, cleanseth us from all sin. If we say that we have not sinned, we deceive ourselves, and the truth is not in us. If we confess our sins, YAH is faithful and will forgive **us and cleanse us from all unrighteousness**." "If we say we have not sinned, we make Him a liar, and His word is not in us." 1 John 1:5-10

It is crucial to remember the powerful message conveyed by Yahushua through his Apostles about putting on His complete armor to defeat the devil. Life's challenges can be daunting and intimidating, but we are not alone in this struggle. Our spiritual community has found strength and comfort in the armor of Elohim, and so can you. The Helmet of Salvation is not just an item of protection; it also provides comfort and assurance. It safeguards our thoughts and reinforces our identity as part of a spiritual army, keeping our minds focused on truth and righteousness. The breastplate of righteousness is indispensable because humans often lack righteousness.

However, we have been granted righteousness through the grace of Yahushua, who bore our sins and bestowed His righteousness upon us. The Shield of Faith is not only for defense but also for personal empowerment. It guards against the enemy's attempts to undermine our faith and symbolizes our active participation in our spiritual journey.

The Buckle of Truth is vital for exposing the enemy's lies, keeping us grounded in truth, and protecting us from straying from the path of righteousness. Shod your feet with the 'Gospel of Peace' for safe passage through life's challenges. The Gospel offers peace and security, allowing us to walk securely despite the enemy's attempts to disrupt our journey. Lastly, the 'Sword of the Spirit,' the Word of Elohim, is both a defensive and offensive weapon, essential in a world where truth can be hard to discern. Equipping ourselves with this spiritual armor is not just a choice but a necessity for standing firm against the enemy and winning spiritual battles. Remember that with Yahushua's armor, you can face any battle with confidence and faith instead of uncertainty. When you put on the whole armor of Elohim and welcome His power, you will emerge victorious.

"Finally, my brethren, be strong in Yahuah, and in the power of His might. Put on the whole amour of Elohim, that ye may be able to stand the wiles of the adversary. For we wrestle not against flesh and blood, but against principalities, against powers, against the world-rulers of darkness, against spiritual wickedness in high places. Wherefore take unto you the whole armor of Elohim that ye may be able to withstand in the evil day, and having overcome, to stand.

Stand therefore having your loins girt about with truth and having on the breastplate of righteousness; And your feet shod with the preparation of the glad tiding of peace. Above all, taking the shield of the faith, wherewith ye shall be able to quench all the fiery darts of the wicked. And take the Helmet of salvation and the sword of the Spirit, which is the word of Yahuah. Praying always with all prayers and supplication in the Spirit and watching thereunto with all. The power of fasting and prayer in defending ourselves against the adversary. As discussed before, we can overcome the enemy by abstaining from food and coming together in prayer. During this fast, we don't need to express specific requests or desires; instead, we put our trust in Yahuah to use our sacrifice of fasting according to His will.

In turn, He tells us in Isaiah 58, verses 8-12, what He will do for us due to our faithfulness and obedience to Him. I understand that giving can be a sensitive topic for many, especially when there are concerns about corruption or uncertainty about where the contributions are going. Given the challenges that can arise, it's natural to have doubts and reservations about tithing.

However, it's important to remember that giving is not just charitable; it holds significant power against our challenges and adversities. It is a way to take control of our blessings and stand against the negative influences that might threaten our prosperity. If you ever feel uncertain, remember that Yahuah invites us to 'prove Me now herewith,' offering us the opportunity to test His faithfulness. He will always guide and support you in your acts of giving.

"Bring ye all the tithes into the storehouse, that there may be meat in My house, and prove Me now herewith, saith Yahuah of hosts if I will not open you the windows of Heaven, and pour you out a blessing, that there shall not be room enough to receive it. And I will rebuke the devourer for your sakes, and he shall not destroy the fruits of your ground; neither shall your vine cast her fruit before the time in the field, saith Yahuah of hosts. And all nations shall call you blessed: for ye shall be a delightsome land, saith Yahuah of hosts." Malachi 3:10-11

"Give, and it shall be given unto you; good measure, pressed down, and shaken together, and running over, shall men give into your bosom. For with the same measure that you use withal it shall be measured to you again." Luke 6:38

Let us focus on the positive impact of our actions on our spiritual journey. As we strive for salvation and embrace the Holy Spirit, we can experience significant personal growth. Let's keep pushing forward and strengthen our connection with our higher power. "I press toward the mark for the prize of the high calling of Yahuah in Yahushua, the Messiah." Philippians 3:14

It's crucial for all of us to be accountable for our actions, whether they are good or bad. Engaging in a life of wrongdoing without remorse can lead to serious consequences. Even the most righteous individuals can falter at times, but those who choose to do wrong will ultimately face their downfall. It's our responsibility to choose the right path and seek forgiveness when we make mistakes. Sin can lead to a tragic end, but there's always a beacon of hope shining. Through the gift of YAH, we can not only find forgiveness but also have the promise of eternal life with Him.

YAH has given us His word, and if we open our hearts to Him and accept His love, He will come and dwell within us, making us more than conquerors. Therefore, let's strive to do good and seek forgiveness whenever we fall short, knowing that YAH is always there to guide us on the right path. "For the wages of sin is death, but the gift of Yahuah is eternal life through Yahushua the Messiah our Saviour." Romans 6:32

Life can be filled with unexpected twists and turns, but I want to remind you that you are never alone. Yahushua's commitment to guiding His people through life's difficulties can provide immense comfort and assurance. He will never abandon or forsake any believer. It's a promise that even our dearest friends and family may be unable to make. Please remember that Yahushua is here for you today, just as He has been.

"For all the promises of Yahuah in Him are yea, and in Him are true, unto the glory of Yahuah.' I Corinthians 1:20 Yahushua told us that he was going away to prepare a place for us and one day He would return and receive us to Himself. Do you believe this? "In My Father's house there are many mansions: and I tell you, I must go and prepare a place for you. And if I go and prepare a place for you, I will come again and receive you unto Myself; that where I am, there you may be also. And whither I go, ye know, and the way ye know." John 14:2-4

After His resurrection, Yahushua spent time with His disciples before ascending to Heaven. They watched in awe as He was taken up into the clouds, forever imprinting the power of faith and its limitless possibilities in their hearts.

"Two men standing by spoke and asked them why they were standing here gazing into the sky. The same Yahushua you see going up is returning just as He left."

"And while they looked steadfastly toward heaven as He went up, behold, two men stood by them in white apparel; Which also said, Ye men of Galilee, why stand ye gazing up into heaven? This same

Yahushua, which is taken up from you into heaven, shall so come in like manner as ye have seen Him go into heaven." Act 1:10-12

"Teaching them to observe all things whatsoever I have commanded you, and lo, I am with you even unto the end of the age." Matthew 28:20

Heaven, a place of pure beauty and grandeur, is a realm where every believer is liberated from the schemes of Satan. The Holy City, with its twelve pearl gates and streets of pure, transparent gold, is a sight to behold. The twelve foundations, adorned with stunning stones, are a testament to the rewards of obedience to YAH. In Yahuah's Holy City, there is no need for sun or night; every tear will be wiped away, leaving no room for sorrow.

Obedience to YAH is not just a duty but a powerful weapon; by embracing it, we can gain the abundant benefits YAH graciously offers His people. "The River of Life" and "The Tree of Life" will provide us with nourishment and healing. The tree bears twelve different fruits, which ripen each month. We will not be mere spirits hovering around heaven but known as we are. It is essential to get it right now and not fall for the lies the enemy wants to feed us. HalleluYah!

"And he showed me a pure river of water of life, clear as crystal, proceeding out of the throne of Yahuah and of the Lamb. In the midst of the street of it, and on either side of the river, was there the tree of life, which bare twelve manners of fruits, and yielded her fruit every month: and the leaves of the tree were for the healing of the nations. And there was no more curse: but the throne of Yahuah and of the Lamb shall be in it; And His servants shall serve Him. And they shall see His face; And His Name shall be in their foreheads. And there shall be no night there; and they need no candle, neither light of the sun; for Yahuah Elohim giveth them light: and they shall reign for ever and ever."

"And he said unto me, These sayings are faithful and true: And Yahuah the Elohim of the holy prophets sent His angel to show unto His servants the things which must shortly be done." Revelation 22:1-6

Let us strive to follow Yahuah's commandments with a heart full of compassion and understanding, knowing that from within us will flow rivers of living waters. Let us hold onto hope for the day when believers gather in Heaven, finding unity and solace around His table. Yahushua will again offer his unwavering support to humanity, strengthening our bond. There, we will drink from the "River of Life" and partake of the "Tree of Life," reconnecting with the spiritual nourishment that has been kept from us since the time of the Garden of Eden. It is crucial to show empathy and concern for all individuals, especially those led astray, believing they can find safety outside of Yahuah. It is not just important, but a duty to approach those who may reject His teachings with love and understanding, as they may be suffering difficulties. Remember that every individual's journey is unique, and they may need our compassion and support.

"And behold, I come suddenly; and My reward is with Me, to give every man according as His work shall be. I am the first and the last, the beginning and the end. Blessed are they that do his commandments that they may have rights to the tree of life and may enter in through the gates into the city. For without are dogs, and sorcerers, and whoremongers, and murders, and idolaters, and whosoever loveth and maketh a lie. I Yahushua have sent mine angel to testify unto you these things in the assemblies. I am the offspring of David, and the bright and morning star.

And the spirit and the bride say come and let him that heareth say Come. And let him that is athirst come. And whosoever will let him take the water of life freely." Revelation 22:12-17

Let's be ever mindful in our efforts to avoid self-destruction, harming our planet and causing harm to others. It's crucial to pray for those who seek safety outside of Yahuah's guidance. We must always remember that without Yahuah's protection, there are sinful and abominable conditions that lead to much suffering. Seeking His protection is our anchor in this turbulent world. Our journey to follow Yahuah's commandments is ongoing. Following His teachings and commandments will give us spiritual shields and guidance, leading us away from sin toward a life of righteousness and peace. As we strive to follow Yahuah's commandments, we will experience an outpouring of living waters from within us. We must patiently await the day when we sit with other believers in Heaven around His table, and Yahushua will join us for a meal. We will have the opportunity to drink from the "River of Life" and eat from the "Tree of Life," which has been withheld since the Garden of Eden. Accepting the Holy Spirit will lead to an outpouring of living waters from within us, filling us with eternal joy and satisfaction.

Sweeter Than Honey,
In The Honeycomb

This poem is about the love of Yahushua. Will you taste and see how sweet He is? Taste of Him today!

He is sweeter than Honey in the honeycomb; he can warm any cold, aching heart. Let him warm your heart today. His love is more powerful than anything else.

If you let him in your heart, I caution you, everyone will know. You will not be able to keep it to yourself, but as you let him in and give him praise, your spirit will rise higher and higher.

His love is peace in the valley; where the still waters flow, His love will pick you up when you feel low.

His love is like a rainbow in the sky after it has rained for forty days and forty nights. His passion is like the way a dove shines in the sunlight.

His love is like the smell of a flower in bloom. Let Yahushua into your heart; He will fill each room. Grace is His, and it is unmerited favor.

Let Yahushua into your heart right now and accept him as your Savior today. You will be so thrilled that you did. HalleluYah!

Written by Nona McCollough © 2000

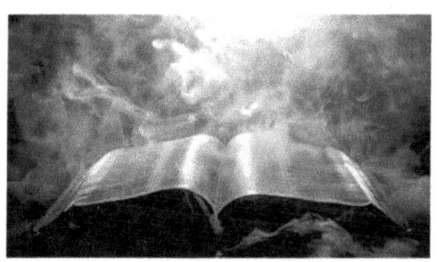

CHAPTER 21

YAHUSHUA HAS DEFEATED THE ENEMY CALLED DEATH

I shall never forget that night when I had to fight the spirit of death for a mother of three, who I met on Highway 99 after leaving the Twenty Grand Club in San Jose. This is a prime example of why we should always be ready for YAH's use and how YAH will use us if our heart is right with Him. Even though I did not know he would use Jacuba, my husband and I were far from it that night, but we quickly adjusted that and got it right. We were in our early 30s and had been married for three years.

We are still trying to figure out how to serve YAH and yet be able to enjoy some of the things that pleased us. I love to dance, and I would often go out on the weekend before I got married. I would go to the Collins Club and let the music take me away after a long week on my job at Lytton Gardens, where I worked the night shift. Many fellows would say I would rather see you dance than eat. I would always slip out about an hour before closing time at the Club, and no one was the wiser for it. I did this to avoid being bombarded with questions about who would take me home after the Club closed. Some fellow I danced with brought me drinks and planned to take me home. Wait, I digress back to the night on Highway 99, where I came face to face with the spirit of death.

Jacuba, my husband, and I often argued when we went to the Club because of the attention I would get. That night, we decided to go to separate clubs, and when closing time came, he would pick me up at the Club where I was, the Twenty Grand that night, where Jacuba dropped me off. I would be back about two, he said. I kiss him before getting out of His Blue and silver Dodge Van. Okay, I love you I said, walking off, hearing him say I love you too. Be back at 2 am, he said as he drove off.

As usual, I was having a great time when we saw each other simultaneously at about midnight when Jacuba walked into the Club. I was sitting at my table with a couple of drinks on it. I had one I had not drunk; the other was on my table. Jacuba walked over to the table where I was sitting and picked up the full drink, saying good, I will take this one as he sat down to let the other fellows know her man was there. The whole mood of the Club changed for me as I watched the crowd and a few of the guys slipping in a quick wink. Jacuba caught one of them winking and finished the other drink, sitting it back on the table and saying, "Let's go. I am not ready, I replied; it's only 12 am. Let's go now he said, and when he used that voice, I knew I had better listen. I had felt his fury before, and I sad to say I reluctantly rose, grabbed my purse, and headed for the door. When we got outside, he began to scold me, saying I know you were in there shaking your butt. I was just dancing, I rebutted, getting into the Van. He continued scolding me, trying to make an excuse for forcing me to leave early. I sit there silent, thinking about the good time I was having and trying not to argue back with him. It was not worth it when suddenly we bumped into a shiny yellow and gold Cadillac. We didn't hit it hard. It was only a bump, and it didn't look like any damage was done. Look what you done made me do Jacuba said. I didn't do anything I said, that was you. Suddenly, a short, well-dressed Hispanic man emerged from the Cadillac. He was agitated, talking under his breath, and he walked to the back of his vehicle to assess the damage when a young Hispanic lady who looked like she was about 17 years old also got out of the vehicle. That was quite too sprang into action. For what was she getting out of her vehicle? I thought, opening my door to join my husband, but she walked up and stopped me. Will you help her she said, pointing to the woman in the back of the Cadillac who looked delirious. What's going on? I said." She is overdosing on heroin. I cannot be here. I am a minor, and if the police see me, I will be arrested and have to go to jail. I have to leave, she said frantically." I turned to look at the woman in the back of the Cadillac, and when I turned back the young lady was running away and disappeared into the night. I stood there in shock as I focused on the woman in the back of the Cadillac whose eyes were rolling around in the back of her head. I opened the back door, and I got in the vehicle.

I began trying to talk with her, but she was not coherent and hardly breathing. I tried shaking here, but that didn't work. Frantic, I got out of the man's vehicle and ran to my husband, saying there was a woman in the back seat and she was dying. What? Jacuba said, focusing on the back seat and the woman sitting there. She has to get to the hospital right now, I said assertively. The man said I would not take her anywhere until I got this settled about my vehicle; it had a small dent. Then I told Jacuba we would have to take her, and you all could work that out later. But the man refused, so I said to Jacuba that we would have to take her, and Jacuba, seeing the seriousness of the matter, got her out of the man's vehicle and placed her frail body in our Van, laying her down in the back. After laying her down, the man approached the Van and continued to badger Jacuba. I was in the back of the Van trying to revise the lady when I saw a tiny cross about her neck. I grabbed her hand and began praying for her. I told her that the one that cross about her neck represented was the only one who could help her now.

"If you can hear me, please squeeze my hand to let me know you can hear me, "I continue, and she softly, faintly, and gently made an impression upon my hand. I barely felt it, but that was enough and boosted my faith it was then I began praying for her when I heard the most detestable horrible sound I had ever heard before, and since then, growling at me with so much strength and power. I jumped back and hit my head on top of the Van. When I was able to recapture my wits from what had happened, I realized it was a demon speaking through her, trying to scare me and make me leave her alone. Yes, she was marked for pick up that night to go to hell, and I was interfering. Come on, let go! I yelled at Jacuba as he got back into the Van. Guess what? It would not crank after several attempts. I frantically told Jacuba she was dying. I could see we were losing her, and we had to get her to the hospital. if the man did not drive his car, we would drive, and this is exactly what Jacuba told the man who wasn't having that. He was in love with his vehicle. Get her back in my vehicle. I will drive. said the man, who seemed to be returning to his senses. We got her to the hospital right on time.

The Doctor said that in a few more minutes, she would have died. Relieved, I flopped down on the hospital chair while Jacuba thanked the Doctor. Can I see her I said, looking up at the doctor.

He motioned for the nurse to take us to her room. There she lay weak but coherent, barely able to speak above a whisper, but her eyes told it all. She had a grateful look in her eyes, and she tried to thank us. I told her there was no need. She mumbled 'I have three children, and you saved my life."

I told her that God did it and that she had three children and herself to live for. She nodded, her head up and down slowly like it took all her strength exhausted from the ordeal, as if to say yes. I hugged her and gave her hand a final squeeze, and we left her room only to find out that my purse and Jacuba wallet were in our Van, and we had left it unlocked.

You have to get my next book, YAH, say the same to find out what happened next. But the point here is YAH used us that night to help save a soul. Not because we were perfect but because Yahushua Is. Yes, death is real, but so is Yahuah, and only He has the power over death, hell, and the grave. No one is leaving Earth before their time. I want to take a moment at this point to empathize with those of you who have experienced the loss of a loved one. It's never easy to cope with the emotions that come with such a significant loss. My heart goes out to you, and I want you to know that your feelings are valid and understandable. Losing someone close to you can be incredibly challenging, and it's normal to feel a wide range of emotions, including loneliness, pain, anger, guilt, confusion, resentment, and heartache. These feelings can be overwhelming, and taking the time to process and accept them is necessary. It's important not to blame yourself or anyone else for the loss. Remember, death is ultimately in the hands of a higher power, and it was never intended for humanity to have to face it. The concept of death entered our world due to the choices made in the Garden of Eden, and since then, it has been a difficult and painful reality for us all. I offer my deepest condolences to those of you who are struggling with the loss of a loved one. Please know that you are not alone, and it is alright to seek comfort and support during this difficult time.

The LORD God took the man and put him in the Garden of Eden to work it and take care of it.

[16] And the LORD God commanded the man, "You are free to eat from any tree in the garden, [17] but you must not eat from the tree of the knowledge of good and evil, for when you eat from it you will certainly die."

[19] The LORD God said, "It is not good for the man to be alone. I will make a helper suitable for him."

[20] Now the LORD God had formed out of the ground all the wild animals and all the birds in the sky. He brought them to the man to see what he would name them; and whatever the man called each living creature, that was its name.

[21] So the man gave names to all the livestock, the birds in the sky, and all the wild animals. But for Adam, no suitable helper was found.

[22] So the LORD God caused the man to fall into a deep sleep, and while he was sleeping, he took one of the man's ribs and then closed up the place with flesh.

[23] Then the LORD God made a woman from the rib he had taken out of the man, and he brought her to the man.

²⁴ The man said, "This is now bone of my bones and flesh of my flesh; She shall be called 'woman,' for she was taken out of man."

²⁵ That is why a man leaves his father and mother and is united to his wife, and they become one flesh.

²⁶ Adam and his wife were both naked, and they felt no shame. Genesis 2:15-25 Yahuah commanded the man and the woman to rule over the Earth. He warned them about the existence of an adversary but also promised them that as long as they obeyed His instructions, they had no reason to be afraid. Yahuah did not want them to be acquainted with evil or to endure its harmful consequences, which the adversary could exploit to injure them and their descendants. He intended for them to thrive, govern, and cherish the Earth and its creatures, which He had created explicitly for them and their future generations.

However, the narrative takes a turn when the man and the woman disobey Yahuah's commandments, leading to dire consequences. "God blessed them and said to them, "Be fruitful and increase in number; fill the earth and subdue it. Rule over the fish in the sea, the birds in the sky, and every living creature that moves on the ground." Genesis 1:28

"But you must not eat from the tree of the knowledge of good and evil, for when you eat from it you will certainly die." Genesis 2:17

Despite having an abundance of food at their disposal, the man and the woman chose to disobey YAH and ate from the tree he had forbidden. This act of disobedience was a strategic move by Satan, his first attack, which led to their expulsion from the Garden of Eden. While it may have appeared as a victory for

Satan, YAH had a plan. However, Adam and Eve were not exempt from the consequences of their disobedience.

The Fall

³ Now the serpent was more crafty than any of the wild animals the Lord God had made. He said to the woman, "Did God really say, 'You must not eat from any tree in the garden'?"

² The woman said to the serpent, "We may eat fruit from the trees in the garden,

³ but God did say, 'You must not eat fruit from the tree that is in the middle of the garden, and you must not touch it, or you will die.'"

⁴ "You will not certainly die," the serpent said to the woman.

⁵ "For God knows that when you eat from it your eyes will be opened, and you will be like God, knowing good and evil."

⁶ When the woman saw that the fruit of the tree was good for food and pleasing to the eye, and also desirable for gaining wisdom, she took some and ate it. She also gave some to her husband, who was with her, and he ate it.

⁷ Then the eyes of both of them were opened, and they realized they were naked; so they sewed fig leaves together and made coverings for themselves.

⁸ Then the man and his wife heard the sound of the LORD God as he was walking in the garden in the cool of the day, and they hid from the LORD God among the trees of the garden.

⁹ But the LORD God called to the man, "Where are you?"

¹⁰ He answered, "I heard you in the garden, and I was afraid because I was naked, so I hid."

¹¹ And he said, "Who told you that you were naked? Have you eaten from the tree that I commanded you not to eat from?"

¹² The man said, "The woman you put here with me—she gave me some fruit from the tree, and I ate it."

¹³ Then the LORD God said to the woman, "What is this you have done?" The woman said, "The serpent deceived me, and I ate."

¹⁴ So the LORD God said to the serpent, "Because you have done this, "Cursed are you above all livestock and all wild animals! You will crawl on your belly and you will eat dust all the days of your life. ¹⁵ And I will put enmity between you and the woman, and between your offspring and hers; he will crush your head, and you will strike his heel."

¹⁶ To the woman he said, "I will make your pains in childbearing very severe; with painful labor you will give birth to children. Your desire will be for your husband, and he will rule over you."

¹⁷ To Adam he said, "Because you listened to your wife and ate fruit from the tree about which I commanded you, 'You must not eat from it,' "Cursed is the ground because of you; through painful toil you will eat food from it all the days of your life.

¹⁸ It will produce thorns and thistles for you, and you will eat the plants of the field.

¹⁹ By the sweat of your brow you will eat your food until you return to the ground, since from it you were taken; for dust you are and to dust you will return."

²⁰ Adam[c] named his wife Eve because she would become the mother of all the living.

²¹ The LORD God made garments of skin for Adam and his wife and clothed them.

²² And the LORD God said, "The man has now become like one of us, knowing good and evil. He must not be allowed to reach out his hand and take also from the tree of life and eat and live forever."

²³ So the LORD God banished him from the Garden of Eden to work the ground from which he had been taken.

²⁴ After he drove the man out, he placed on the east side [of the Garden of Eden cherubim and a flaming sword flashing back and forth to guard the way to the Tree of Life. Genesis 3

Even though YAH banished the man and the woman from the Garden He gave them a promise that one day a deliverer will come who would break the yoke that was placed on them by Satan and humanity will be able to have fellowship and redemption once again.

15 "And I will put enmity between you and the woman, and between your offspring[a] and hers; he will crush your head, and you will strike his heel." Genesis 3:15

Then, the journey of Mankind being separated from YAH began, and so did Satan's authority over humanity. Even though Adam and Eve did not die the day that physically, but a spiritual death occurred and separated them from YAH.

Satan's plan to destroy humanity raised up its ugly head again when He causes Adam and Eve's son Cains, Abel's brother, to rise up against him and murder him.

Cain Kills Abel

¹ "The man lay with his wife Eve, and she was going to have a child and she gave birth to Cain. She said, "I have given birth to a man with the help of the Lord."

² Next she gave birth to his brother Abel. Now Abel was a keeper of sheep, but Cain was one who worked the ground.

³ The day came when Cain brought a gift of the fruit of the ground to the Lord.

⁴ But Abel brought a gift of the first-born of his flocks and of the fat parts. The Lord showed favor to Abel and his gift. ⁵ But He had no respect for Cain and his gift. So Cain became very angry, and his face became sad.

⁶ Then the Lord said to Cain, "Why are you angry? And why are you looking down?

⁷ Will not your face be happy if you do well? If you do not do well, sin is waiting to destroy you. Its desire is to rule over you, but you must rule over it."

⁸ Cain told this to his brother Abel. And when they were in the field, Cain stood up against his brother Abel and killed him.

⁹ Then the Lord said to Cain, "Where is Abel your brother?" And he said, "I do not know. Am I my brother's keeper?"

¹⁰ The Lord said, "What have you done? The voice of your brother's blood is crying to Me from the ground.

¹¹ Now you are cursed because of the ground, which has opened its mouth to receive your brother's blood from your hand.

¹² When you work the ground, it will no longer give its strength to you. You will always travel from place to place on the earth."

¹³ Then Cain said to the Lord, "I am being punished more than I can take!

¹⁴ See, this day You have made me go away from the land. And I will be hidden from Your face. I will run away and move from place to place. And whoever finds me will kill me."

¹⁵ So the Lord said to him, "Whoever kills Cain will be punished by Me seven times worse." And the Lord put a mark on Cain so that anyone who found him would not kill him.

¹⁶ Then Cain went away from the face of the Lord, and stayed in the land of Nod, east of Eden." Genesis 4

The act of disobedience to YAH and the heed given to the words of Satan had profound consequences. It introduced sin into the world, leading to the downfall of the first family and impacting the world as a whole. With this choice of following and obeying Satan instead of YAH, humanity unknowingly handed over control to him. Satan, with his power to take human lives at his discretion, used death as a tool. However, it was ultimately under YAH's supreme authority that he wielded it to bring people to Him and combat evil and sin. Despite the world's people becoming increasingly sinful and consumed by evil thoughts, YAH's authority remained unchallenged. In His all-knowing nature, YAH was deeply saddened by humanity's wickedness. He considered wiping them out, along with all living things, through a flood. However, YAH had a plan for redemption, a plan that Satan would not be able to thwart. Noah, a righteous man, was chosen by YAH to save humanity along with his family. This is his remarkable story.

¹ "And it came to pass, when men began to multiply on the face of the earth, and daughters were born unto them,

² That the sons of God saw the daughters of men that they were fair; and they took them wives of all which they chose.

³ And the LORD said, My spirit shall not always strive with man, for that he also is flesh: yet his days shall be an hundred and twenty years.

⁴ There were giants in the earth in those days; and also after that, when the sons of God came in unto the daughters of men, and they bare children to them, the same became mighty men which were of old, men of renown.

⁵ And God saw that the wickedness of man was great in the earth, and that every imagination of the thoughts of his heart was only evil continually.

⁶ And it repented the LORD that he had made man on the earth, and it grieved him at his heart.

⁷ And the LORD said, I will destroy man whom I have created from the face of the earth; both man, and beast, and the creeping thing, and the fowls of the air; for it repenteth me that I have made them.

⁸ But Noah found grace in the eyes of the LORD.

⁹ These are the generations of Noah: Noah was a just man and perfect in his generations, and Noah walked with God.

¹⁰ And Noah begat three sons, Shem, Ham, and Japheth.

¹¹ The earth also was corrupt before God, and the earth was filled with violence.

¹² And God looked upon the earth, and behold, it was corrupt; for all flesh had corrupted his way upon the earth.

¹³ And God said unto Noah, The end of all flesh is come before me; for the earth is filled with violence through them; and behold, I will destroy them with the earth.

¹⁴ Make thee an ark of gopher wood; rooms shalt thou make in the ark, and shalt pitch it within and without with pitch.

¹⁵ And this is the fashion which thou shalt make it of: The length of the ark shall be three hundred cubits, the breadth of it fifty cubits, and the height of it thirty cubits.

¹⁶ A window shalt thou make to the ark, and in a cubit shalt thou finish it above; and the door of the ark shalt thou set in the side thereof; with lower, second, and third stories shalt thou make it.

¹⁷ And, behold, I, even I, do bring a flood of waters upon the earth, to destroy all flesh, wherein is the breath of life, from under heaven; and everything that is in the earth shall die.

¹⁸ But with thee will I establish my covenant; and thou shalt come into the ark, thou, and thy sons, and thy wife, and thy sons' wives with thee.

¹⁹ And of every living thing of all flesh, two of every sort shalt thou bring into the ark, to keep them alive with thee; they shall be male and female.

[20] Of fowls after their kind, and of cattle after their kind, of every creeping thing of the earth after his kind, two of every sort shall come unto thee, to keep them alive.

[21] And take thou unto thee of all food that is eaten, and thou shalt gather it to thee; and it shall be for food for thee, and for them.

[22] Thus did Noah; according to all that God commanded him, so did he." Genesis 6

A new era was initiated, but because of human continual disobedience, Satan's relentless efforts to corrupt the world persisted. Nevertheless, he knew that a savior would come to defeat him. That savior did arrive—YAH in human form. The Word of Elohim descended to Earth and triumphed over Satan on the cross. Yahushua, the blameless son of Yahushua, dwelled among us, revealing YAH's boundless love for humanity. Yahushua preached about repentance and redemption. The unyielding spirit of death continues to claim lives under both YAH and Satan's influence, ultimately fulfilling YAH's plan for humanity's redemption.

Regardless of belief, every individual is born and dies at appointed times. However, each person has a unique purpose ordained by YAH. It is the believer's responsibility to seek Yahuah to discover their divine purpose for their existence, and the sooner they do, the sooner they can lead a more fulfilling life.

[1] "To everything there is a season, and a time to every purpose under the heaven:

² A time to be born, and a time to die; a time to plant, and a time to pluck up that which is planted;

³ A time to kill, and a time to heal; a time to break down, and a time to build up;

⁴ A time to weep, and a time to laugh; a time to mourn, and a time to dance;

⁵ A time to cast away stones, and a time to gather stones together; a time to embrace, and a time to refrain from embracing;

⁶ A time to get, and a time to lose; a time to keep, and a time to cast away;

⁷ A time to rend, and a time to sew; a time to keep silence, and a time to speak;

⁸ A time to love, and a time to hate; a time of war, and a time of peace.

⁹ What profit hath he that worketh in that wherein he laboureth? Ecclesiastes 3:1-8

When individuals are yet to discover their purpose or are on the verge of achieving their goals, Satan attempts to intervene. However, those who embrace their faith and actively seek guidance from the Creator ultimately strip Satan of his control over their lives. Trusting, accepting, and following YAH's will is crucial. By aligning with YAH's plan, individuals become impervious to the devil's harm. Even in the face of adversity, YAH, in His infinite wisdom, ensures that situations work out for the individuals' benefit as well as for others.

YAH's benevolence and supremacy always prevail. Amid the anguish of losing a loved one, many have found solace, salvation, inner peace, and fortitude through their encounter with Yahushua.

"As for you, you meant evil against me, but God meant it for good, to bring it about that many people should be kept alive as they are today." Genesis 50:20

"The thief cometh not, but for to steal, and to kill, and to destroy: I am come that they might have life, and that they might have it more abundantly." John 10:10

It's crucial to remember that individuals who have turned away from Yahushua often battle with persistent feelings of guilt, shame, and pain, making it difficult to find solace. Many may resort to temporary solutions such as drugs, alcohol, or other vices to cope. Regrettably, some individuals find themselves trapped in a destructive cycle, unable to escape the anguish and suffering resulting from circumstances beyond their control.

"There is no peace, saith Yahuah, to the wicked. "There is no peace," says Elohim, "for the wicked." Isaiah 48:22

It seemed as if Satan was winning when Yahuah sent His son, born of a woman named Yahushua, into the world. Again, Satan struck, but this time, he did not win. He tried to kill Yahushua when He was born, using King Herod's jealousy to carry out his mission.

[1] "Now when Jesus was born in Bethlehem of Judaea in the days of Herod the king, behold, there came wise men from the east to Jerusalem,

² Saying, Where is he that is born King of the Jews? for we have seen his star in the east and are come to worship him.

³ When Herod the king had heard these things, he was troubled, and all Jerusalem with him.

⁴ And when he had gathered all the chief priests and scribes of the people together, he demanded of them where Christ should be born.

⁵ And they said unto him, In Bethlehem of Judaea: for thus it is written by the prophet,

⁶ And thou Bethlehem, in the land of Juda, art not the least among the princes of Juda: for out of thee shall come a Governor, that shall rule my people Israel. ⁷ Then Herod, when he had privily called the wise men, enquired of them diligently what time the star appeared. ⁸ And he sent them to Bethlehem, and said, Go and search diligently for the young child; and when ye have found him, bring me word again, that I may come and worship him also. ⁹ When they had heard the king, they departed; and, lo, the star, which they saw in the east, went before them, till it came and stood over where the young child was.

¹⁰ When they saw the star, they rejoiced with exceeding great joy. ¹¹ And when they were come into the house, they saw the young child with Mary his mother, and fell down, and worshipped him: and when they had opened their treasures, they presented unto him gifts: gold, frankincense, and myrrh.

¹² And being warned of God in a dream that they should not return to Herod, they departed into their own country another way.

¹³ And when they were departed, behold, the angel of the Lord appeareth to Joseph in a dream, saying, Arise, and take the young child and his mother, and flee into Egypt, and be thou there until I bring thee word: for Herod will seek the young child to destroy him.

¹⁴ When he arose, he took the young child and his mother by night, and departed into Egypt:

¹⁵ And was there until the death of Herod: that it might be fulfilled which was spoken of the Lord by the prophet, saying, Out of Egypt have I called my son.

¹⁶ Then Herod, when he saw that he was mocked of the wise men, was exceeding wroth, and sent forth, and slew all the children that were in Bethlehem, and in all the coasts thereof, from two years old and under, according to the time which he had diligently inquired of the wise men.

¹⁷ Then was fulfilled that which was spoken by Jeremiah the prophet, saying,

¹⁸ In Rama was there a voice heard, lamentation, and weeping, and great mourning, Rachel weeping for her children, and would not be comforted, because they are not.

¹⁹ But when Herod was dead, behold, an angel of the Lord appeareth in a dream to Joseph in Egypt,

[20] Saying, Arise, and take the young child and his mother, and go into the land of Israel: for they are dead which sought the young child's life.

[22] And he arose, and took the young child and his mother, and came into the land of Israel.

[23] But when he heard that Archelaus did reign in Judaea in the room of his father Herod, he was afraid to go thither: not withstanding, being warned of God in a dream, he turned aside into the parts of Galilee:

[24] And he came and dwelt in a city called Nazareth: that it might be fulfilled which was spoken by the prophets, He shall be called a Nazarene." Matthew 2

But even though Satan failed at destroying Yahushua when He was a baby, he did not give up. However, when he saw John the Baptist baptizing Yahushua and Yahuah, who announce this is my beloved Son of whom I am well please.

[16] "When He had been baptized, Jesus came up immediately from the water; and behold, the heavens were opened to Him, and He saw the Spirit of God descending like a dove and alighting upon Him.

[17] And suddenly a voice came from heaven, saying, "This is My beloved Son, in whom I am well pleased." Matthew 3:13-17

When Yahushua was led into the wilderness to be tempted, Satan saw an opportunity to attack and derail YAH's plan for His Son. Satan employed the same tactics he used on Adam and Eve and continues to use on many people today. Every believer needs to be aware of these tactics.

¹ "Then Jesus was led by the Spirit into the wilderness to be tempted[a] by the devil.

² After fasting forty days and forty nights, he was hungry.

³ The tempter came to him and said, "If you are the Son of God, tell these stones to become bread."

⁴ Jesus answered, "It is written: 'Man shall not live on bread alone, but on every word that comes from the mouth of God.'"

⁵ Then the devil took him to the holy city and had him stand on the highest point of the temple.

⁶ "If you are the Son of God," he said, "throw yourself down. For it is written: He will command his angels concerning you, and they will lift you up in their hands, so that you will not strike your foot against a stone."

⁷ Jesus answered him, "It is also written: 'Do not put the Lord your

God to the test.'"

⁸ Again, the devil took him to a very high mountain and showed him all the kingdoms of the world and their splendor.

⁹ "All this I will give you," he said, "if you will bow down and worship me."

¹⁰ Jesus said to him, "Away from me, Satan! For it is written:
'Worship the Lord your God and serve him only.'"

[11] Satan has again been defeated, and Yahushua has emerged triumphant over him. Despite Satan's ongoing attempts to thwart Yahushua's purpose, just as he continues to try with believers today, we can take solace in the fact that Yahushua overcame Satan with the Word, and we, too, can conquer him when we are filled with the living Word. HalleluYah!

It's a fact: Satan has never, in any way, defeated YAH, the Hebrew name for God. Thanks to this monumental victory, Yahushua, the Hebrew name for Jesus, has conquered Satan. By accepting YAH's plan of salvation through His son Yahushua, we also have the assurance of eternal life. This promise brings profound comfort and security to our souls. In addition to defeating Satan, Yahushua will also bind him for a thousand years and reign on Earth with His people. The prospect of Yahushua's future reign fills us with hope and anticipation for the glorious days., Then the devil left him, and angels came and attended him. I want to emphasize the everlasting triumph of Yahushua over Satan. Despite Satan's relentless attempts to thwart Yahushua's mission, he has been defeated time and time again. It is important to remember that just as Yahushua overcame Satan with the power of the Word, we, too, can achieve victory when we are grounded in the living Word. This truth gives us hope and assurance, knowing that Satan has never triumphed over YAH in any way. Furthermore, by embracing Yahushua's plan of salvation, we are promised eternal life with YAH. This assurance brings solace and security to our souls. Moreover, the prospect of Yahushua's thousand-year reign on Earth fills us with hope and anticipation for the glorious days to come.

¹ Then I saw an angel coming down from heaven, having the key to the bottomless pit and a great chain in his hand.

² He laid hold of the dragon, that serpent of old, who is the Devil and Satan, and bound him for a thousand years;

³ and he cast him into the bottomless pit, and shut him up, and set a seal on him, so that he should deceive the nations no more till the thousand years were finished. But after these things he must be released for a little while.

⁴ And I saw thrones, and they sat on them, and judgment was committed to them. Then I saw the souls of those who had been beheaded for their witness to Jesus and for the word of God, who had not worshiped the beast or his image, and had not received his mark on their foreheads or on their hands. And they lived and reigned with Christ for a thousand years.

⁵ But the rest of the dead did not live again until the thousand years were finished. This is the first resurrection.

⁶ Blessed and holy is he who has part in the first resurrection. Over such the second death has no power, but they shall be priests of God and of Christ and shall reign with Him a thousand years. 7 Now when the thousand years have expired, Satan will be released from his prison 8 and will go out to deceive the nations which are in the four corners of the earth, Gog and Magog, to gather them together to battle, whose number is as the sand of the sea. 9 They went up on the breadth of the earth and surrounded the camp of the saints and the beloved city. And fire came down from God out of heaven and devoured them.

¹⁰   The devil, who deceived them, was cast into the lake of fire and brimstone where] the beast and the false prophet are. And they will be tormented day and night forever and ever.

¹¹   Then I saw a great white throne and Him who sat on it, from whose face the earth and the heaven fled away. And there was found no place for them.

¹²   And I saw the dead, small and great, standing before God, and books were opened. And another book was opened, which is the Book of Life. And the dead were judged according to their works, by the things which were written in the books.

¹³   The sea gave up the dead who were in it, and Death and Hades delivered up the dead who were in them. And they were judged, each one according to his works.

¹⁴   Then Death and Hades were cast into the lake of fire. This is the second [death.

¹⁵   And anyone not found written in the Book of Life was cast into the lake of fire." Revelation 20

As believer in Yahushua we have a glorious home to look forward to a remarkable unimaginable life that awaits us as well as life and life more abundantly while we are still living on this Earth.

¹ Then the angel showed me the river of the water of life, as clear as crystal, flowing from the throne of God and of the Lamb.

² Down the middle of the great street of the city. On each side of the river stood the tree of life, bearing twelve crops of fruit,

yielding its fruit every month. And the leaves of the tree are for the healing of the nations.

³ No longer will there be any curse. The throne of God and of the Lamb will be in the city, and his servants will serve him.

⁴ They will see his face, and his name will be on their foreheads.

⁵ There will be no more night. They will not need the light of a lamp or the light of the sun, for the Lord God will give them light. And they will reign for ever and ever.

⁶ The angel said to me, "These words are trustworthy and true. The Lord, the God who inspires the prophets, sent his angel to show his servants the things that must soon take place."

⁷ "Look, I am coming soon! Blessed is the one who keeps the words of the prophecy written in this scroll."

⁸ I, John, am the one who heard and saw these things. And when I had heard and seen them, I fell down to worship at the feet of the angel who had been showing them to me.

⁹ But he said to me, "Don't do that! I am a fellow servant with you and with your fellow prophets and with all who keep the words of this scroll. Worship God!"

¹⁰ Then he told me, "Do not seal up the words of the prophecy of this scroll because the time is near.

¹¹ Let the one who does wrong continue to do wrong; let the vile person continue to be vile; let the one who does right continue to do right; and let the holy person continue to be holy."

¹² "Look, I am coming soon! My reward is with me, and I will give to each person according to what they have done.

¹³ I am the Alpha and the Omega, the First and the Last, the Beginning and the End.

¹⁴ "Blessed are those who wash their robes, that they may have the right to the tree of life and may go through the gates into the city. ¹⁵ Outside are the dogs, those who practice magic arts, the sexually immoral, the murderers, the idolaters and everyone who loves and practices falsehood.

¹⁶ "I, Jesus, have sent my angel to give you[a] this testimony for the churches. I am the Root and the Offspring of David, and the bright Morning Star."

¹⁷ The Spirit and the bride say, "Come!" And let the one who hears say, "Come!" Let the one who is thirsty come; and let the one who wishes take the free gift of the water of life.

¹⁸ I warn everyone who hears the words of the prophecy of this scroll: If anyone adds anything to them, God will add to that person the plagues described in this scroll.

¹⁹ And if anyone takes words away from this scroll of prophecy, God will take away from that person any share in the tree of life and in the Holy City, which are described in this scroll.

²⁰ He who testifies to these things says, "Yes, I am coming soon." Amen. Come, Lord Jesus.

²¹ The grace of the Lord Jesus be with God's people. Amen.
Revelation 21-22 1

"Therefore we must give [the more earnest heed to the things we have heard, lest we drift away.

² For if the word spoken through angels proved steadfast, and every transgression and disobedience received a just reward,

³ How shall we escape if we neglect so great a salvation, which at the first began to be spoken by the Lord, and was confirmed to us by those who heard Him,

⁴ God also bearing witness both with signs and wonders, with various miracles, and gifts of the Holy Spirit, according to His own will?

⁵ For He has not put the world to come, of which we speak, in subjection to angels.

⁶ But one testified in a certain place, saying: "What is man that You are mindful of him, Or the son of man that You take care of him?

⁷ You have made him a little lower than the angels; You have crowned him with glory and honor, [And set him over the works of Your hands.

⁸ You have put all things in subjection under his feet." For in that He put all in subjection under him, He left nothing that is not put under him. But now we do not yet see all things put under him.

⁹ But we see Jesus, who was made a little lower than the angels, for the suffering of death crowned with glory and

honor, that He, by the grace of God, might taste death for everyone.

¹⁰ For it was fitting for Him, for whom are all things and by whom are all things, in bringing many sons to glory, to make the captain of their salvation perfect through sufferings.

¹¹ For both He who sanctifies and those who are being sanctified are all of one, for which reason He is not ashamed to call them brethren,

¹² Saying: "I will declare Your name to My brethren; In the midst of the assembly I will sing praise to You."

¹³ And again:" I will put My trust in Him. "And again:" Here am I and the children whom God has given Me."

¹⁴ Inasmuch then as the children have partaken of flesh and blood, He Himself likewise shared in the same, that through death He might destroy him who had the power of death, that is, the devil, ¹⁵ And release those who through fear of death all their lifetime subject to bondage.

¹⁶ For indeed He does not give aid to angels, but He does give aid to the seed of Abraham.

¹⁷ Therefore, in all things He had to be made like His brethren, that He might be a merciful and faithful High Priest in things pertaining to God, to make propitiation for the sins of the people.

¹⁸ For in that He Himself has suffered, being tempted, He is able to aid those who are tempted. My dear friends, it's

completely natural to feel afraid and burdened by the passing of a loved one or to be apprehensive about one's mortality. However, please take comfort in knowing that they are now in a place free from pain, worry, and sickness. And as far as fearing one's death, the scriptures tell us not to fear nor be afraid.

[1] "Let not your heart be troubled; you believe in God, believe also in Me.

[2] In My Father's house are many mansions; if it were not so, I would have told you. I go to prepare a place for you.

[3] And if I go and prepare a place for you, I will come again and receive you to Myself; that where I am, there you may be also. John 14:1-3

While it's okay to grieve, remember that they are in a place more amazing than we can imagine, eagerly awaiting the time we will join them in the Holy City. Let go of any guilt or regrets, as they are not angry and need nothing now.

[9] But as it is written: "Eye has not seen, nor ear heard, Nor have entered into the heart of man The things which God has prepared for those who love Him." 1 Corinthians 2:9

Let me encourage you to embrace the incredible plan of salvation through Yahushua and strive to be willing and obedient to YAH so that you will live forever in Heavenly Bliss when your time comes.

Let us love and support those who remain on Earth and share the hope of the fantastic home that awaits all believers.

CHAPTER 22

PAIN IS GAIN

Pain can lead to personal growth. However, humans would prefer to avoid it; we do not wish to endure its feelings and consequences. Nevertheless, pain is an unavoidable part of life and can enter a person's life at any moment, affecting them mentally, physically, emotionally, spiritually, and even financially.

Let us begin with physical pain. It can arise from harm to the body, often resulting from neglect or mistreatment. Unfortunately, this is common, as it is one of the tools the enemy uses to depress, oppress, isolate, and sometimes segregate individuals from thoroughly enjoying their lives. "I came that you might have life more abundantly." John 10:10

The enemy often exploits practices that harm the body by enticing individuals to seek pleasure in ways that ultimately lead to harm. This may include consuming harmful foods, abusing alcohol, or taking both prescription illicit drugs and illicit sex to alleviate pain temporarily. While these actions may provide immediate relief, they can lead to more severe issues later.

Mental pain is another tactic that the enemy employs. It can cause individuals to overthink, overreact, and worry about situations beyond their control, which may lead to insomnia, loss of appetite, or overeating. Sometimes, people seek temporary relief through unhealthy sexual encounters, which is also fleeting.

Emotional pain manifests as defeat, anger, hopelessness, regret, and fear. It is usually a result of unforgiveness toward oneself or others who have caused them pain. This suffering can destabilize one's mind, actions, and decisions, leading to impulsive behaviors without careful thought. Financial pain, resulting from the inability to afford essentials for sustaining life, has been a driving force behind many suicides and crimes. It can foster dissatisfaction, low self-esteem, and unworthiness, often influenced by society's perceptions of the less fortunate.

Spiritual pain may be the most profound of all. It can create feelings of fear, hatred, unforgiveness, jealousy, envy, loneliness, sadness, and loss. This type of pain can leave individuals unable to regain their path without assistance from others or something more extraordinary.

How can I say that pain is gain? In the situations mentioned, pain serves as an indicator that something is wrong. It is only when we face the issue or acknowledge that there is a problem that we can begin to benefit from the pain. Often, people try to mask their issues through various means instead of confronting them directly and taking the necessary steps to improve their situation.

This process requires brutal honesty, which starts with admitting the truth to oneself. It is not easy and requires conscious effort.

Unfortunately, many individuals fall prey to the adversary, who exploits this aspect of human nature. He uses pain to kill, steal, and destroy lives.

The first enemy to confront in the face of pain is Satan. People must realize that he is a common enemy to humanity, whose primary goal is to separate them from the one who can help—YAH.

"For God so loved the world that He gave His only begotten Son, that whoever believes in Him should not perish but have everlasting life." John 3:16

"The thief does not come except to steal, kill, and destroy. I have come that they may have life and have it abundantly." John 10:10

The longer a person waits to accept this truth, the deeper they feel pain. Pain alerts us that something is wrong and needs correction. In this sense, pain can become a friend, and Yahushua is a friend who sticks closer than any family member.

"A man who has friends must himself be friendly, but there is a friend who sticks closer than a brother." Proverbs 18:24

Yahushua loves us unconditionally, regardless of our circumstances. His words comfort a weary soul, even when they may intensify our pain. Many people suppress their pain, not realizing it hasn't disappeared but is merely hidden, often re-emerging at inconvenient times, especially under the enemy's influence. Phrases like "That doesn't matter to me" or "I don't care" are common ways people bury their pain instead of addressing it. This approach may work for some time, but our minds, bodies, and spirits can only endure so much before they react.

This is when many turn to temporary pleasures to numb their pain, only to find it adversely affecting their mental, spiritual, and physical well-being. Knowing and having a relationship with our Creator is incredibly helpful. Yahushua is a healer who eagerly waits to mend any hurting soul.

3 "Who forgiveth all thine iniquities; who healeth all thy diseases;

4 Who redeemeth thy life from destruction; who crowneth thee with lovingkindness and tender mercies.

5 Who satisfieth thy mouth with good things; so that thy youth is renewed like the eagle's." Psalm 103:3-5

I encourage you to examine your thoughts on life—past, present, and future. If you find areas of hurt, anger, unforgiveness, bitterness, envy, or jealousy, decide today to begin your healing journey. This process doesn't have to happen all at once; take it bit by bit. As you start this journey, more will be revealed as you remember and feel what you previously avoided.

As a believer, know that Yahushua is ready to assist you. While some revelations may bring tears and deep pain—feelings you may have avoided—remember that overcoming them is possible. It's time to forgive, be forgiven, release your burdens, and walk in a newness of life. Be assured that Yahushua has been with you since you first believed.

YAH will be with you; he will never leave or forsake you. Do not be afraid; do not be discouraged.

"If you have not yet accepted Him into your life, I urge you to do so today and allow Him to transform your pain into gain without harming you."

"For I know the thoughts that I think toward you, says the Lord, thoughts of peace and not of evil, to give you a future and a hope." Jeremiah 29:11 New King James Version

CHAPTER 23

A SPIRITUAL ENCOUNTER/OUT OF THE DARKNESS COMES THE LIGHT

Before I close my book, I want to share a spiritual encounter I experienced in East Palo Alto, California, in 1988. I must warn you that the story contains graphic content and is deeply emotional, faith-based, and supernaturally oriented.

At that time, East Palo Alto had become a war zone. Gunshots were frequently heard at night, and sirens blared all day and night. The city had gained a notorious reputation as the "Murder Capitol of the World," mainly due to the influx of crack cocaine on its streets. Drug-related crimes, including shootings and drug overdoses, have become a common occurrence.

As a result, the once close-knit community had fallen into chaos. The older residents had moved away, leaving the streets in the hands of drug dealers. Frequent funerals plagued the city, and many individuals and families had become involved in the drug trade. The situation was dire, and the authorities seemed unable to bring about any significant change.

Despite the dangerous circumstances, I continued my work, selling life insurance. However, it had become increasingly risky, and the once beloved neighborhood had transformed into a nightmarish place. Due to the escalating danger, I faced the dilemma of continuing as an insurance agent. Nevertheless, amidst the chaos, I still felt blessed and appreciated by the community, which had once been full of love and respect.

One day, after a 12-hour workday, I stopped by Chummy Chan Chicken to buy dinner for my children and me. As I returned home, my daughter Yvette eagerly grabbed the food from my hands and ran inside. Amidst the chaos of the neighborhood, moments like these brought some sense of normalcy and happiness to our lives. I had just finished eating, getting ready to check my schedule for the next day, when Faye came running up to the house, banging on the front screen door, shouting, "Your brother is dead, your brother's dead." she repeated herself as I stared in unbelief. Faye, peeping in, saw me as I curled up on the couch, shaking like a tree leaf;' She opened the screen door and came in. I heard her call out to me, but I could not answer her.

Faye, too, has passed since that day. They say that they found her body on the tracks; I digress; let me stay on track. Faye, too, was killed, and nobody knew who did it. She is gone today; however, she did not leave here before she brought me back to sanity that day—R. I. P.

Everybody in the house ran outdoors. I fell back on the couch in total shock and disbelief, trying to understand what I had just heard. "What kind of joke is this?" I said angrily; panic and fear gripped my heart simultaneously as it began to race, skipping beats!

"What are you talking about?" I shouted back, dropping the blue debit binder on the floor in my lap as I stood up! Is this some joke?" "No," Faye said. "Your brother has been shot." He was shot and thrown out of a car on Stephen Street, which was one block down from our home.

"The ambulance got him, and he is on the way to the hospital, another one of the neighbors hollered. Reporters had already pronounced him dead; they said, "he is dead." I went into shock at that moment, and my mind snapped. I could not talk, think, or move. I sat on the couch and curled my legs up on the sofa, Indian style, stunned, in disbelief, and shaking all over.

I must have sat there for about 15 minutes that way. I could hear people frantic in the street, which only heightened my fear of what I had just heard. This was too much for me. The neighbors were outside talking about what had happened. I could listen to them but could not move; my family was all outside, and I just sat there with my eyes wide open, not seeing. I thought to myself, how can all this be happening? I hung my head in disbelief!

My nerves were doing their own thing; every little sound was magnified, like a big boom. I jumped and flinched at the slightest noise. I could not help myself. I wanted to go outside to see if this news was accurate about my brother being shot. Even though I had three brothers instantly, I knew which one it was. It was my brother Reginald. I wanted to hide and escape the pain I was feeling inside, but I could not move. It felt like I was losing my mind; I could not think straight; none of this made any sense. Could this be true, I thought, as I sat there staring into space and shaking.

"They shot my friend," she said. Faye was a drug addict, and the Town's prostitute. This once beautiful young lady in her mid-twenties, a victim of drug abuse, now looking so haggard and worn with the smell of old, stale alcohol on her body, she had a heart of gold. She had become a victim of the drug epidemic that plagued our city.

She went on with such deep love and compassion for my brother. "I loved Abba Dab," she said. "That's what we call him on the streets." "He was my partner," she said with such admiration. "I did not care if he could talk; I loved him, and he loved me; he always had my back," she said. As Faye talked about my brother, tears ran down my face, and my blank eyes began to focus as I listened to her, becoming aware of what she was saying. I could tell she was hurt by what had happened to Reginald and angry with whoever did this. "I will kill them," she said. "Whenever I find out who killed Abba Dab, I'm going to kill them." It was as if she were expressing precisely what I was feeling, what I could not say.

I began to cry hard, bitter tears as I came back to myself; the pain was overwhelming, and the hot tears poured down my face like a faucet. "I've got to call the hospital and see what's going on with my brother," I said frantically. "Okay, you do that," Faye said, hanging her head down before she left. "I love you." Those were the last words I heard her say; shortly after that, she, too, was shot and killed. I stood there in disbelief once again, still trying to gather my emotions from the loss of my brother.

"I've got to call and tell Dad," I thought. At that moment, I was glad momma was at rest; this bad news would have killed her for sure to learn what had happened to her son. I picked up the phone to call Dad and paused. I do not know if I had asked God, but strength came, and I began to settle down. I found myself asking the Father to please help my family and me. It hurts me deeply even now, knowing what happened to my brother. But I am strengthened by the power of Yahuah to continue telling his story. I called my Dad.

Gave Dad the News

Dad, I got some bad news. "What is it, child?" Dad said, sensing it was something terrible from the sound of my voice. "What is it?" he said again. I did not want to tell him Dad but persisted, somewhat irritated now with my hesitation. I finally just blurted it out, "Reginald has been shot, and they said he is dead!" Daddy went silent, and I knew he was in shock. "I know, Dad, I know, I know, I know, I know, I know, I kept repeating until Dad answered, what? Somebody shot him; I went on and threw him out of the car down the street from us. Daddy, please come down here." I will be leaving tomorrow, Dad said. "Tomorrow, I will be there," he repeated to me.

How are you doing my Dad asked me. Alright, I said, trying to be strong and not worry him, but I was terrified. "Try to get some sleep. Call me if any new news comes in," Dad said. "Okay, Dad," I replied. My heart just sunk into my chest. The pain overwhelmed me as I felt the pain in my daddy's heart. Yet I felt relief knowing he was coming to be with us. I love my daddy; he is a remarkable man. I knew he was being strong for me.

"I love you, Dad," I said before I hung up, and he said, "I love you too, baby. Stay strong; I will be there tomorrow."

I held onto the phone until it began to buzz very loudly. I realized that I was holding on to the phone like I was holding on to my Dad.

I had not hung up. The thought that Dad would arrive in California from Texas tomorrow comforted me. I sat staring at the phone before putting it back on the hook. I called the hospital, and they told me my brother was there; he had been shot in the head, but he was still alive. "Oh, thank you, God," I said. I called Dad back and told him, "he is still alive, Dad! He has been shot in the head; he is still alive. "Okay, I will be there tomorrow; get some rest," Dad said. "Okay, Dad," I said, hanging up the phone.

Dad's Arrival

My Dad came in on the 1 O'clock flight the next day. It was so good to see him. He looked old and tired, and I knew he had had a rough night. I ran up to him, and he held me, saying, 'It will be alright, holding me in his arms. Reginald has been shot in the head, I blurted out." I could not hold it in any longer as the tears flowed down my face. "I know," Dad said. I have spoken with the hospital. "Let us get my luggage: Dad said. Watching the rack go around made me feel dizzy, "you alright?" Dad asked. "Yes, Dad," I said, trying to regain my composure and be strong, not knowing he was trying to be strong for me.

"Let's go and see him." I want to see my son," Dad said, picking up his suitcase. "Take me to the hospital."

When we arrived at the hospital, we went to admissions, and they told us to go to the patient information desk. Dad stepped up to the counter at the patient information desk at Stanford Hospital and said, "Reginald McCollough, my son, was brought in last night from a gunshot wound." The lady at the information desk sympathetically said to Dad," Yes, Sir, I am sorry to hear that," looking at her registrar on the computer.

He is in the 3rd West, room 310, Bed A. Dad nodded his head, and we walked away. The attendant at the information desk said we could take the elevator down the hall to the left, pointing to the elevators up the hall a short distance away. People who were getting off the elevator moved out of our path. It was as if they knew we were facing something devastating. "Thank you," Dad said, nodding as we walked into the elevators.

"Are you alright?" Dad asked me again to step back so others could get on. "Yes, Sir," I said. My stomach was flipping, and my nerves were all over the place. My mind was playing tricks on me, not knowing what I was about to see. I mustered up all the strength I could and followed Dad. "Come on," Dad said as we got into the elevators. I must have hesitated, but Dad urged me onward. The elevator door opened, we stepped in, and Dad pressed the elevator button on the third floor. Within minutes, the door opened again.

Dad had the strength I know now could have only come from Yahuah, bless His name. When we got off the elevator, Dad seemed to be in his world, lost in his thoughts, as we arrived at the nursing station to ask about Reginald. "I want to see my son, Reginald McCollough, Dad said with deep concern.

The nurse turned her head so as not to look into Dad's piercing eyes. "He is right this way, Sir. The Doctor will be in to speak with you." She led us into Reginald's room. There he lay on the hospital bed, a sheet that seemed primarily white, with a bluish tint, covering him up to his waist. His chest was bare and connected to wires. His head was bandaged just below His eyes. The curtain was half pulled around his bed. I can feel the tears wailing up in my eyes that I must hold back if I am to tell my brother's story. He was hooked to monitors for his breathing, blood pressure, and heart rate. The machine monitor hung up high to the left of his bed. It seems like I died a thousand times when I saw him lying there motionless. I wanted to scream, yell, howler, fight, and cry; the sorrows filled my heart. I did nothing except just stand there and stare in shock like I had when I first got the news that night that he had been shot.

"Diane," "Diane, stay with me," Dad said. I was shaking my head from side to side in disbelief, trying to hold back the tears. "Stay with me," Dad said. I nodded up and down this time to say yes and that I understood.

Dad stepped up to Reginald's bed, and I managed to get to the other side of my brother's bed. Dad was holding Reginald's hand. "Do you want chairs," the nurse who had followed us into the room asked us. "I am fine," Dad said, staring down at his son lying there. How about you, Ms. she asked. "Yes," I said, feeling my legs would not hold me up. She left the room and returned shortly with a chair, and right on time, I think another second, I would have probably fainted. I plumbed down onto the chair, weeping. Doctor Jones walked in as I was trying to regain my composure. "I am sorry about your son," the Doctor said to Dad, nodding as he glanced at me. "How is he?" Dad asked. "Sir, the back of His head has been removed by the bullet wound; he is brain dead. He is on life support; without it, he will die."

The tears flowed down my face; I could not hold them back. Dad looked over to comfort me, "Diane, are you okay?" I nodded my head up and down slowly, trying to stop crying. I knew he needed comfort now. Dad stood there staring in disbelief at Reginald.

My heart was hurting so badly, and the pain was so deep it felt like it was suffocating me. My brother Reginald's heart was hooked up to the heart monitor. It was beating hard, fast, and strong, the echo of the heart monitor ringing throughout the tiny room. "There is nothing more we can do for him, Sir," he has a strong heart. You might consider donating it to save someone else's life," Dr. Jones said. The look he got from Dad and I made him quickly change the subject. Dr. Jones patted Dad on the shoulder, saying, "You all talk about it and let us know." Giving Dad one last pat on his shoulder Dr. Jones walked away.

Power of Prayer and Belief

I sat there staring at my brother, innately placing my hand on his chest to comfort him somehow, not knowing that the Holy Spirit was guiding me. Desperate, I dropped my head on my brother's side and began to pray. "Father, help my brother," I said. What happened next totally surprised me. YAH took me by the Holy Spirit to a grayish, dim, lit room where Reginald's spirit body was. I saw him pacing up and down the floor. He appeared to be confused, distorted, worried, and very afraid.

He was pacing the floor when he looked up and saw me there. "Diane," Reginald, a deaf person, said to me in sign language and verbally. He was now able to talk in the spirit world. I am so afraid." "I am getting ready to die. I have done so much wrong;

I do not want to go to hell." I was so happy to see him; he was alive, strong, healthy, and could talk!

I wanted to embrace him, but he stepped back. I am getting ready to die, he said. "What am I going to do? I do not want to go to hell." "You do not have to go to hell I told him. Jesus died for your sins; He will forgive you if you ask him to," I said, frantic now!

I could see his desperation and the urgency of the matter. "Just repeat after me," I said, I will lead you through the sinners' prayer; repeat after me, I told him. "Father, forgive me of my sins; I am sorry for all my wrongs against you and others. I added, "Save my soul in Jesus' name," he repeated. "It's done, now you won't go to hell," I told him. Reginald looked so relieved. I immediately returned to my body and realized I had been in the spirit world. I rose in amazement at what had just happened to me. Reginald's heartbeat had slowed to an average pace, and I immediately noticed that. I shared with my Father, amazed by what had happened to my brother and me. "Praise God," Dad said, more like to console me. He knew I was hurting badly, and he did not want me to make myself sick. I kissed my brother, and so did Dad, and we left. Dad was silent, but I chattered all the way home about what had happened. Dad would nod his head every once in a while as I told him the story. "We will come back tomorrow," Dad said. He did not say another word the rest of the way home. However, I pondered the miracle I had just experienced in my heart, and my love for Yahuah deepened. YAH must have been driving for me because we were pulling into the driveway before I realized we were home. The following day, bright and early, Dad was already up and dressed.

"Diane, get ready so we can return to the hospital." We arrived about 9 am that morning and went straight to my brother's room. There he lay, and the pain gripped my heart again as I took my place around my brother's bed. The chair was still there, and I sat down. Immediately, I noticed my brother's heart was racing and beating fast again. I sat in the chair and placed my head on his side and my hand upon his heart, asking God to take me where he was, and again, He did.

Immediately, I was in the dimly lit room again; Reginald was pacing the floor, seemingly more upset than before, "what's wrong"? I asked as he looked up and saw me, "What's wrong?" Again, he expressed deep concerns about his dying and going to hell. I could see he was being tormented, and I began to minister to him, telling him the devil was a liar and he could not believe anything the devil said.

I told him he could trust Almighty God because he did not lie and had to believe this. I told him to be strong and think he was. He exhaled in blessed assurance that what I was telling him was the truth, and again, I was back in my physical body in the hospital room by his bedside.

Dad was standing there in deep pain with stress written all over his face about what had happened to his brain-dead son. Dad was not sure I was going to pull out of this. Dad quickly tried to change his expression when I rose, but it was too late. I saw the fear in his eyes. Dad, it happened again; I explained, "What happened seemed to have made him feel better, just because I was feeling better.

"Good," Dad said. "Let us go." We kissed my brother, and we left. The next morning, Dad was up again. "Are you going with me? "Yes, sir, I am going," I said, grabbing my purse. Come on, are you ready? "I am ready."

"Let us go. We can pick something up on the way if you are hungry, "Dad said. I could tell Dad was feeling better and pleased that I was going. Neither of us was hungry, so we went straight to Stanford Hospital ICU.

When we arrived at the hospital, I tried to reassure Dad that Reginald was all right. Good," Dad said; I could tell he was in deep thought. We went directly to my brother's room. This time, the nurse stopped us. Dr. Jones wants to speak with you before you leave, Mr. McCollough. Nodding his head, Dad and I proceeded to Reginald's room, taking our places by his bedside.

My brother's heart was racing fiercely; you could see it pounding from his chest. I knew he was afraid. I asked Yahuah to allow me to go to where my brother was, placing my hand again on his chest and my head on his side, and He permitted me.

When Reginald realized I was there, he said there is no hope for me; I have done too much." I knew Satan, or his demons, had once again come and stolen the Word planted in his heart. I became angry with righteous anger, and I began to rebuke the devil and his demons and command them to leave Reginald's side. I commanded them to go and to go now in Jesus' name. I did not know Him as Yahushua at that time. When I did this, something unique happened in the room. It was no longer a gloomy gray color; it was now filled with light that grew brighter and brighter! I told my brother to thank God for saving him, and He would give him strength.

Reginald began to honor, worship, and praise the Almighty God. His spirit lit up, and his radiance was the most beautiful light and yellow light combined I had ever seen. He knew he was saved. He knew it, and so did I.

Again, I was back in my physical body. I jumped up, rejoicing, and began to share this wonderful experience with Dad. Oh yes, Reginald's heartbeat was steady and perfectly strong. Dad could tell something spiritual was happening because after each encounter I had with my brother he noticed the changes on the heart monitor. The heartbeats from his chest were calm, and Dad believed! "He is all right now, Dad. I saw his body glow in a brilliant radiance light, and he was full of joy," I proclaimed with great joy and relief. As we left that day, the nurse informed us that Doctor Jones wanted to speak with us. "This way, "she said, leading us into a conference room. Several other doctors were standing, and they motioned for us to come in and sit down. When we took our seats, they sat down. Mr. McCollough, it is time for you to decide concerning your son...

"We can no longer keep him here at Stanford due to his condition. He can be transported to a nursing home and kept alive by machine. He will not recover from this gunshot wound. The only other option is we can disconnect him from life support, and he will expire." We would like you to discuss it with the family and decide tomorrow.

Do you have any questions, Mr. McCollough?

"No," Dad replied. "How about you, Ms. Brown?" the Doctor said in a professional yet compassionate voice. I shook my head from side to side, unable to speak from the moment reality hit home, trying to hide what I felt—a mixture of joy and sorrow. "No, we understand," Dad said, leaving the room. Can we get you all? Something the Dad Doctor said, giving Dad a reassuring hand on his shoulder, stepping back as Dad and I were leaving the room. No, Dad said, shaking his hand before we left. I followed him, but I looked back at my brother lying there in bed.

His heart was beating, studied, and calm. I smiled and caught up with Dad. I could tell the short-lived joy Dad had just experienced was gone and replaced with agony. "It is okay, Dad, he is ready; I saw him light up, I saw the room light up; Reginald is ready, Dad, to go to Heaven now."

Dad was comforted by this as we walked away from the hospital that day to get into my car. I went on and on about what I had experienced concerning Reginald, and Daddy believed me. That evening, for the first time since Dad had arrived four days prior from Houston, Texas, we had an appetite. "Are you hungry: I asked Dad?"

"I think I can eat a bite Dad said.

"Me too," I replied, "I will fix your favorite."

"I fixed him chicken and dumplings, one of his favorite dishes, with cornbread, and we ate and were filled. After dinner that night, Dad and I retreated to the living room. Dad sat down in the armchair. He looked controlled and confident. At least, that was what he wanted me to think. I sat on the brown sofa across from him; it was a little worn but comfortable. I rested my head on one of the soft cushions and listened intently as I waited for my Father to speak about whether to have Reginald taken off the ventilator.

For the most part, the decision was left up to Dad. I could tell Dad was careful with his words, not wanting to excite or cause me a setback. It was then I spoke up, assuring him of the glorious Light of the Almighty God had transformed Reginald. He was in His hand now, and he was ready to go. That night, my Dad and I had to face the single most challenging decision that he or I had ever had to deal with and agreed not to keep him alive on a breathing machine that night, and tomorrow, we would tell the doctor to disconnect him. It was a sign of relief for us both, but I was encouraged because of what YAH had let me experience, knowing that my brother was in His Hands and that even though his body had expired, his soul would live on. And if it were the will of the Heavenly Father, He would let him live, I concluded. That night was the first time I rested in four days, and I even slept some.

The next morning, I could tell Dad felt better, too. After a quick breakfast, oatmeal raisins, and a toast, I gobbled the orange juice with anticipation and some anxiety. I held my own as we walked out to my Honda and opened the door for Dad. He got in, and I reassured him that everything was going to be alright. "Common on, let go," he said, and I backed up and drove off to Stanford Hospital. Doctor Jon s was waiting for us. He was sitting at the nursing station, standing up and speaking to Dad as he saw us approaching." Good morning, Mr. McCollough. He nodded toward me as well

"Good morning," he said.

"We will need to speak after your visit today." Dad nodded in agreement as we walked on to my brother's room.

When we arrived in my brother's room, I first noticed his heartbeat, which was beating steadily and calmly. I knew he was fine. "See his heart rate, Dad. He is all right. He is ready." I said my goodbye to Reginald. When I finished, Dad said his goodbyes to Reginald. "Let's go and speak with the doctor," Dad said. I look back at my brother lying on the bed; this time, I felt only peace from him. When we arrived at the conference room, six doctors and a nurse asked us to come in and sit down as they stood up to greet us. Have you made your decision, Mr. McCollough? Dr. Jones asked.

"I have." Dad said we want him disconnected from the ventilator machine." The doctors commended us for making the decision not to keep Reginald on the ventilator machines with no hope of getting better. Dad, neither did I respond to the Doctor's words. One of the other Doctors said, We will give you time with him while we prepare to carry out the order. You will need to sign some papers, Mr. McCollough, to permit us to stop treatment Dr. Jones said. The nurse, who was standing by, handed Dad some paperwork for him to sign. Dad signed the permission papers, and I signed them, too, as a witness. We returned to room 310, Bed A, and took our places around Reginald's bed.

A thousand memories of my brother and our good times went through my mind. Dad and I did not say much to each other; instead, we spoke to Reginald, bidding him farewell into the Heavenly Father's care. In about thirty-five minutes, a team of people came into the room. I realized now that they were there more for moral support than anything else. Dad was standing on

Reginald's left side, and I was on my brother's right. We both held one of his hands. Someone said, "Are you ready?"

Dad nodded his head.

"You have to give your permission verbally, Sir."

The tech said, "Yes or no."

"Yes," Dad said. An attendant turned off the breathing machine, and the humming sound slowly faded and abruptly stopped, as did Reginald's heartbeat.

My brother flat-lined, and the hand of Reginald, I was holding, he pulled it in and straightened it to give me a victory sign, signifying I am out of here! It is medically impossible for those who have lost the motor skills in their head to move their limbs. But Yahuah allowed Reginald to give us that final victory sign he so often did when he had won a great battle. HalleluYah! Believers in the Most High God, who I have come to know as Elohim, who is Yahuah, and His son Yahushua, the Messiah, Savior of the world, that many times in life, one may fall prey to the spirit of worry, depression, grief, and torment.

However, I want to remind you not to become a victim of these things. That will not change anything; they will only make matters worse. However, if you trust Yahuah's love for you, have faith in His Word, and allow Him to guide you, He will strengthen you and enable you to endure and overcome any obstacles.

All the days of our life are recorded in YAH's book, and nothing is a surprise or hidden from His eyes. He is the answer to any situation and has the power to solve any problem.

He can see just as well at night as during the day. Let His Holy Spirit lead and guide you. Let His love abide in your heart; it will prevail over evil and render you victorious.

To thy self, be true, and keep your faith anchored in Yahuah and His only begotten son Yahushua, because then and only then will you be able to move forward and progress in life. No matter how complex or challenging things may be, that will pass, too.

Come Home to the Heavenly Father, He is Waiting on You.

In a world full of people with so many things to do, but with whom may be the question?

Many things can go wrong, sometimes due to no reason of your own. The only thing that is moving about is your mind, which seems to roam and roam.

I do not want to take any chances that you set all along. Many times, you try, and things go wrong for no reason of your own, and you may find yourself feeling all alone.

With an ache so deep within your soul, longing be to free as the wind, the leaves on the trees it blows. Wishing it were that simple, wanting it to blow your troubles away and bring in the joy of a brand-new day.

Feeling lonely is true. You want to share, but you do not dare think that no one really cares. The pain is that there is no listening ear, no warmth, no smile, no one to help, not a man, woman, or child.

Fear within your soul is great; there must be someone who does, and you wait as the days roll on. That's the time to know that you are not alone.

Remember, the prodigal son in the bible came home. He left the pig pen and came back to where he belonged.

Where there was provision, joy, peace, and plenty of love. given to him by his father. Whose heart was touched by YAH above, and when you accept Him, He will touch you. Written by Nona McCollough © 1989

CONCLUSION

In our world, people fall into two distinct categories: those who embrace faith and those who reject it. This decision is crucial for our salvation and should not be taken lightly. To abstain from making a choice is to side with the enemy of humanity inadvertently.

The common enemy of all humankind is Satan and his followers. He harbors an intense hatred for all humans and everything good, a level of bitterness beyond our understanding. Satan's nature is genuinely vile; he revels in horror and is fueled by a thirst for bloodshed.

Satan and his followers, devoid of any moral restraint, are relentless in their pursuit of harm. They aim to sow chaos, poverty, illness, and suffering and to nurture humanity's most destructive traits: hatred, arrogance, resentment, and pride. Their ultimate goal is to leave humanity bereft of hope, love, and forgiveness and to strip individuals of their confidence, courage, strength, and faith in a higher power.

Satan is corrupt, malicious, conniving, and prideful, seeking to lead as many people as possible down the same destructive path as his. But we must resist. We must stand firm, ultimately facing the judgment he awaits when we stand before the Creator on Judgment Day.

By shedding light on the true nature of the adversary—the once-anointed cherub who lost his divine favor—I hope to unveil the sinister plans aimed at undermining people's faith in our Creator.

Satan has an inherent evil within him that is beyond human comprehension without the guidance of the Holy Spirit.

"The coming of the lawless one is according to the working of Satan, with all power, signs, and lying wonders, and with all unrighteous deception among those who perish because they did not receive the love of the truth, that they might be saved." II Thessalonians 2:9-12

The ultimate goal of our enemy since the dawn of humankind has been to deceive and destroy us, turning us away from the loving Creator, Yahuah. But thanks to Yahushua, our Messiah, we are no longer under Satan's control. He now has to submit to the children of Elohim. HalleluYah!

At Calvary, Yahushua turned the tables on Satan, defeating him on our behalf and paying the debt of sin that we could not. This victory is not just a historical event, but a present reality. Now, Satan must obey us in Yahushua's name. He fears that born-again believers will realize this Truth. He is a defeated foe; once you accept and believe this, you will be more than a conqueror.

Accepting Yahushua's plan of salvation is not just about gaining eternal life; it's about receiving power. Once it comes upon you, the Holy Spirit equips you with the wisdom, tools, and strategies to thwart the Devil's plans. This empowerment allows you to reclaim your soul, achieve victory, and let the Truth liberate your spirit.

Yahushua is not just a path to Heaven but the sole path. He is not just a truth but the only Truth. He is not just a giver of life but life itself. YAH - Yahushua is the one genuine Elohim worthy of praise, worship, and to be served. "Yahushua saith unto him, I am the way, the truth, and the life: no man cometh unto the Father but by me." John 14:6

"For thou shalt worship no other El: for Yahuah, Who is jealous of
His Name, is jealous." El. Exodus 34:14

Psalms 103 is a good example of that.

1. Bless Yahuah, O my soul; and all that is within me, bless His holy name.

2. Bless Yahuah, O my soul, and forget not all His benefits:

3. Who forgiveth all thine iniquities, who healeth all thy disease

4. Who redeemeth thy life from destruction, who crowneth thee with loving- kindness and tender mercies:

5. Who satisfieth thy mouth with good things; so that thy youth is renewed like eagles

6. Yahuah executeth righteousness and judgment for all that are oppressed.

7. He made known His ways unto Moses, His acts unto the children of Israel.

8. Yahuah is merciful and gracious, slow to anger, and plenteous in mercy.

9. He will not always chide; neither will He keep His anger forever.

10. He hath not dealt with us after our sins; nor rewarded us according to our iniquities.

11. For as heaven is high above the earth, so great is His mercy toward them that fear Him.

12. As far as the east is from the west, so far hath he removed our transgressions from us.

13. Like a father pitieth them that fear Him.

14. For He knoweth our frame He remembereth that we are dust.

15. As for man, His days are as grass: as a flower of the field, so He flourisheth.

16. For the wind passeth over it, and it is gone; and the place there of shall know it no more.

17. But the mercy of Yahuah is from everlasting to everlasting upon them that fear Him, and His righteousness unto children's children.

18. To such as keep His covenant, and to those that remember His commandments to them.

19. Yahuah hath prepared His throne in heaven; and His kingdom ruleth overall.

20. Bless Yahuah, ye His angels that excel in strength, that do His commandments, hearkening unto the voice of His word.

21. Bless ye Yahuah, all ye His hosts; ye ministers of His, that do His pleasure

22. Bless Yahuah, all His works in all places of His dominion: bless
Yahuah, O my soul."

"When someone who believes finds joy and expresses gratitude to Yahuah, regardless of the challenges they may be facing, He promises to provide support. He may not always remove the difficulties, but He will stand by you, comforting you through His
Spirit."

"Then he answered and spake unto me, saying, this is the word of Yahuah unto Zerubbabel, saying, Not by might, Not by might nor by power, but by My Spirit, saith Yahuah of hosts." Zechariah 4:6

I firmly hope, pray, and believe that this Book has sparked a transformative fire within you, compelling you to engage in deep Bible study. It has instilled in you a sense of hope, inspiration, and motivation, propelling you to make essential changes in your life. The time has come for you to decide to secure your place in Heaven.

As human beings, we possess the power to shape our world. Despite the challenges we face, we have the capacity to unite and prevent significant losses.

The seventh day is a day of rest, as commanded by our Creator, whom we call Yahuah. In these uncertain times, it's crucial to remember that anything is possible with our Creator, Yahuah. He is the source of our strength and guidance. We also have faith in His Son, Yahushua, our Savior, and the bridge between us and Yahuah.

Remember, no matter your situation, Yahuah is always there for you, a constant source of support and guidance. He can help you through even the most challenging times. As believers, we must ensure that those who have never heard the Messiah's proper name learn it.

Amid our struggles, let us not forget the strength we can find in positioning ourselves under the shadow of the Almighty YAH Wings. This is our survival strategy, our shield against dangers. We can achieve this through repentance for breaking Yahuah's commandments and striving to live holy lives.

I realize these ideas may be new to some of you, but I assure you that I am here to help in any way possible. If you ever need someone to talk to or have any questions, please do not hesitate to contact me.

Let us remember that we have the power to shape our world. Despite our challenging times, we must come together to avoid significant losses.

The seventh day, a day of rest, is a commandment from our Creator, YHUH. This day is a time to pause, reflect, and reconnect with our spiritual selves. All is possible with Yahuah through Yahushua. Now that you know how to live a victorious life on this Earth rest assured that you are headed toward substantial changes. These changes include a deeper understanding of our faith, a stronger connection with our Creator, and a renewed sense of purpose.

Move forward confidently. You are at the right place and time to excel in the incredible creation that Yahuah has made you to be. The Holy Spirit has allowed you to grow spiritually enlightened.

This is a challenging task, but it will bring you immense joy if you do it. Of course, you will need direction; this is where the Holy Spirit comes in. The Holy Spirit, acquired through the sacrifice of Yahushua, the Messiah, is the guiding force in our spiritual journey. This process involves acknowledging our wrongdoings, asking for forgiveness, and sincerely committing to change our ways. Only the Truth can do this. Yahushua, the Son of YAH, is the Way to the Truth and Life.

We believers are called to 'fight the good fight of faith.' This means we must be prepared to face the challenges of maintaining our faith. To do this, we must be clothed with the breastplate of the righteousness of our Messiah Yahshua, with His Helmet of Salvation upon our head. This means submitting our minds to His Holy Will for our lives and allowing Him to grant us the grace to accomplish it. I will detail His whole Armor, weapons, spiritual tools, and virtues that will help us in our journey.

Once you are saved and redeemed from the law, Yahuah, mercy is renewed daily. He is so Good. Only the heavenly Father is good. His Holy Spirit is full of Grace and Truth. He will lead and guide you every step of the way. He will protect you and give His angels charge over you if you acknowledge him in all your ways; He will direct your path. Yahuah desires to prosper you and give you a prosperous life. A life filled with love, forgiveness, freedom, faith, hope, health, compassion, mercy, grace, and so much more, eternal. It also includes life with him in Heaven and the new Earth that will one day come.

Dear YAH

YAH, will you let your Holy Spirit be my constant companion?

You have always led and guided me, revealing deep mysteries, giving me wisdom and comfort, and showing me the right way to decide.

Your Holy Words are my soul's need; may I forever take heed.

Yahushua, fill me with your unfailing Love, given to me from above.

Abolish the fear that, for me, has been near for too long.

Forgive me and protect me from all evil and wrong.

Amazing Grace will forever be my song. When my life is over and my day is done, I forget about the wrong that I have done and be free from sin.

Where my new life with you will never end.

Written by Nona Mccollough © 1999.

I trust you have decided to follow YAH and enlist in His Army!

Recite the sinner's Prayer, a prayer of repentance and acceptance of Jesus as your Savior and mean it with all your heart.

I, [Your Name], accept you today as my Elohim (a Hebrew word for God) and Savior. I desire to know you as YAH (a Hebrew name for God)-Yahushua (a Hebrew name for Jesus).

Yahuah, my Elohim, oh how I desire to know you as YAH-Yahushua.

You are perfect in all you do. I believe that you sent your Son Yahushua to the world to pay the sin debt, and I acknowledge that my sins were included.

I confess my sins before you, whose eyes are in every place. I ask for your forgiveness and that you will cleanse me with the precious blood of your Son Yahushua and wash all my sins away. In this act of confession and forgiveness, I feel a weight lifted off my shoulders, a sense of liberation and peace. I accept you, Yahushua, as my Savior, and I ask you to come into my heart now and make me your sheep and be my Shepherd.

Please fill me with your Holy Spirit and make me your bride.

I will serve you all the days of my life, and I ask this in your Son Yahushua's Name.

If you have prayed this Prayer and believe with all your heart, then today you are spiritually born again, and your name has been placed in the Lamb's Book of Life (a metaphorical book in heaven where the names of the redeemed are written) for all eternity.

HalleluYah and so be it unto me.

It would please us greatly if you would join us in the fellowship of walking as our Messiah Yahushua walked, doing things the way He did and as He commanded us to do them. We would be so blessed if you would join us as we sojourn in this walk as Disciples of Yahushua.

But bear in mind it is not I who have called you over and over again, but YHUH who is calling you out from among pagan practices into His "Marvelous Light." May you continue to walk in the liberty and freedom we have today in the blessed USA and the world, which is our Prayer.

We will make a difference as believers together in Yahushua, the Messiah. "Thy Will Be Done YAH." WELCOME TO THE FAMILY OF ELOHIM. AS YOU BECOME WHAT YOU WERE INTENDED TO BE BEFORE THE BEGINNING OF TIME, A SAINT!

I CONFIDENTLY ACCEPT THE SINNER'S PRAYER and declare my belief in YAH-Yahushua as my Savior. I acknowledge that Yahuah sent Yahushua to pay the sin debt for the world, including your and my sins. I confess my sins and ask for forgiveness, trusting in the cleansing power of Yahushua's precious blood. I have invited Yahushua into my heart and am committed to serving him for the rest of my life. I am spiritually born again; my name has been written in the Lamb's Book of Life.

I eagerly embrace the teachings and commandments of our Messiah Yahushua and look forward to journeying together as a disciple united in faith and love for Him. I am confident I have been called into His "Marvelous Light" to walk in liberty and freedom. I enthusiastically welcome myself to the family of Elohim, the Almighty God! HalleluYah!

Date_____

Sign your name_____

Back of book

With the Earth entrusted to the people of Elohim, it is essential to know that we have an adversary bent on usurping our authority. This book, however, is a beacon of hope. It guides those who have strayed, offering them a way back to the right path that leads to eternal life.

Embark on this journey to discover how we, as believers, became the rulers of planet Earth. Learn the art of healing in mind, body, and soul. Uncover the secrets to living a victorious life on Earth. Understand the high cost of an unforgiving lifestyle. Explore the significance of blood sacrifices and why they are no longer needed. Reclaim your soul and become a Saint. Learn how a dying man, the author's brother, escaped Hell. Understand the singular path to Heaven. Unveil the secrets that have been hidden for hundreds or even thousands of years. It's all in the book and so much more.

A Lifetime

Everyone will write their own story, unfolding page after page, line after line, by their choices as they perform age upon age, day after day, with the world as their stage.

It will all be done in one's lifetime with the world's people looking on. Our audience carefully watches as we play each role, exposing our deeds and revealing our souls.

Be counted among the wise; obey YAH and be blessed. His Holy Spirit will show you how.

Your journey may be sweet and bring great love, peace, and joy. If you have faith, act after act; this becomes a fact, day by day, as you are promoted to a higher way.

One day, you will stand before the Judge, the Creator of everything; for sure, you will need the pure blood of the Savior Yahushua shed to save the lost souls and purge sin away to save the lost.

He is the door through which we must enter heaven. Accept him right now; this book will show you how. Allow Him to be your friend. He will make you the pin of a ready writer, author, and finisher of your faith.

Moment by moment, second by second, minute by minute, hour upon hour, let Him shower you with His love and power.

Written by Nona McCollough Lang © 2015.

www.ingramcontent.com/pod-product-compliance
Lightning Source LLC
LaVergne TN
LVHW021220080526
838199LV00084B/4292